Hush Now, Baby

The Help Becomes Famil~

What People are Saying . . .

Hush Now, Baby is not only a portrait of the astonishing strength and beauty of a Southern black woman, but it also brings a focus to the history so many Southerners only dimly grasp: the ongoing evolution of their society. And all this is accomplished within a gripping novel-like family narrative.

Rosa Shand, author of *The Gravity of Light*

Hush Now, Baby is the moving, insightful story of stalwart caregiver Eva and the stability, love and example she brought to the life of her charge, Angela, during a tumultuous time in the American South. This is a tale of transcendence, love, and devotion, of a family and a people tattered with strife. Angela Williams writes with grace and bravery, and with a seasoned storyteller's pacing and command of figurative language. A captivating memoir, *Hush Now, Baby* will leave you loving and admiring Eva, and cheering for her and Angela all the way.

Michel Stone, author of *The Iguana Tree*

Angela's memoir belongs right next to Rick Bragg's *All Over but the Shoutin'* and James McBride's *The Color of Water*. It is truly wonderful on any level you measure it."

Mary B. Johnston, Editor, *Word Works Stories*

Angela's prose plunges us back in time when a generation of white children were raised by the calloused hands of slaves who, despite being freed by Lincoln, remained chained to a stubborn way of life. Instead of killing us in our sleep, they became our guardian angels, for reasons still mysteriously misunderstood.

Ken Burger, author of *Swallow Savannah*

Hush Now, Baby is a moving and unforgettable memoir which explores the complexity of race, family, love, loyalty, self-awareness and forgiveness with rare courage and honesty. This is a book you'll want to give everyone you know!"

Cassandra King, author of *Moonrise*

If you liked The Help, you'll love *Hush Now, Baby.*

You'll not put this aside until you've read it cover to cover. When a rich little white girl, newly born, is placed into the arms of a poor and uneducated black woman, it's a beginning to last a lifetime. Angela Williams is audacious. In this true, brave tale she honors the woman who became, in essence, her mother, while in so doing, she unveils the secrets of her influential white family. All this, with the backdrop of a confused and racially changing south. Just when I thought I understood the South, here came Angie and Eva.

As the cocoon unraveled around Angela, we see her spirit awakening and a deep resolve to speak out for the African-American voices often hushed in the 40s and 50s. Her account of Southern life provides a thought-provoking, realistic view of those turbulent decades. While slowly grasping how injustices permeated Southern culture, she faced her own family's struggles with abuse, alcoholism, and philandering—Eva the steady core through it all.

Angela Williams has an amazing story to tell about her life growing up in South Carolina. Angela (now 73 years old) was raised by an African American woman in her parents household. The story is not about her "black mamie" but a story of the extraordinary bond she shared with a woman that she identifies as her "mother." Angela's, *Hush Now, Baby* has tremendous potential to highlight race relations, the civil rights movement, and southern life from the perspective of a white female growing up in a chaotic period in American history.

Hush Now, Baby

The Help Becomes Family

Angela W. Williams

Texas Review Press
Huntsville, Texas

FIRST EDITION, 2014
Requests for permission to reproduce material from this work should
be sent to:

>Permissions
>Texas Review Press
>English Department
>Sam Houston State University
>Huntsville, TX 77341-2146

Cover Designer: Nancy Parsons

Library of Congress Cataloging-in-Publication Data

Williams, Angela W., 1941- author.

Hush now, baby : the help becomes family / Angela W. Williams. --
First edition.

>pages cm

ISBN 978-1-68003-034-1 (pbk. : alk. paper)

1. Dysfunctional families--South Carolina--Fiction. 2. African
American women household employees--South Carolina--Fiction.
3. Women household employees--South Carolina--Fiction. 4. Women
slaves--South Carolina--Fiction. 5. South Carolina--Social life and
customs--Fiction. I. Title.

PS3623.I556285H87 2015

813'.6--dc23

2015003436

In Memory

Eva Edwards Motte Aiken, whose unconditional love shaped the person I have become,

Roberta S. Chalmers, whose teaching became an inspiration for doing the hard work of introspection,

Richard O. Straub, whose unswerving encouragement brought me professional and personal joy.

Dedicated to

LaClaire and Erick, my precious children—and Bobby, Josh and Gray. May understanding the past enrich your future.

Contents

Prologue

Hush Now, Baby emanates from personal reflections of Eva Aiken's influence on my early life, an exploration of civil rights issues and the subsequent embarrassment that I *knew* so little, *did* so little. As an adult I have felt guilt and rage, rage at myself and my country. The urge to do something, if nothing more than to reach back and touch the Eva wisdom, has plagued me for years. I grew out of an uneasy childhood on the backbone of a black woman who loved me unabashedly. And I'm grateful.

Soon after I was born in 1941, Eva Aiken, a forty-two-year old black woman, joined my traditional Lowcountry South Carolina family. She became the central figure in my life from then until the day I married.

My father was charismatic—a man about town, seasoned in Southern politics, the county clerk of court, a mover and a shaker. My mother was a Southern lady—a beautiful woman, the perfect hostess of lovely parties, president of social clubs—proper, compliant, and hopelessly in love. They traveled extensively, hobnobbed among the elite who lived on surrounding plantations, rode horses, shot quail.

Beneath this idyllic setting, another world churned during the 50s and 60s. Amazingly, I grew up in the South without any idea of the deep racial struggles that were going on right under my nose—in my own house, my own state, and my own country. I lived in bubble-wrap—protected by Eva, my family, and Southern protocol. Eventually everything in my airbrushed world slowly, ruinously, unraveled. All I could do, it seemed, was watch the colorful tapestry of our old life come undone one thread at a time. Amidst all the hush—of alcoholism, abuse, infidelity, prejudice—Eva was there.

Though she never had a child curled under her ribs, from the day I wriggled out of my mother's womb, I was Eva's. When I nestled into her breast, sat on her lap, or felt her hug—at two or twenty-two—I heard Eva's heartbeat, the only thing that remained steady and sure in my life. Eva lived the paradoxes that kept her people (and me) safe and moving forward on tenuous ground: fear and courage, compliance and resistance, flight and fight, distrust and loyalty.

In the microcosm of my world, I watched Eva's wisdom and strength. And I learned. I learned not only how to survive but also how to overcome. But mainly I felt her unconditional love. And even today, when I'm feeling down, I can still hear her say: "Hush now, Baby."

I am still discovering ways that my family enriched my life. We each have our own histories, our own stories. Although Eva took care of all of us— Mother, Daddy, LaClaire, Rusty and me—I thought she was all mine. I do not presume to speak for anyone else. I've tried to see through my eyes only. When I've erred, as I surely have, please forgive me.

I frequently struggled with airing the family linen in telling this story. But I kept coming back to the encouraging words by poet May Sarton:

> I believe one has to stop holding back for fear of alienating some imaginary reader or real relative or friend and come out with personal truth. If we are to understand the human condition, and if we are to accept ourselves in all the complexity, self-doubt, extravagance of feeling, guilt, joy. . . we have to be willing to go naked.

This coming-of-age story is larger than me or my family; it brings to the fore issues long swept under the rug in our society, Southern culture particularly. This re-seeing, this re-weaving, with all its inaccuracies and imaginings, gives tribute to the Evas of our country—the long-delayed mourning and glorying of the host of African-American women whose physical strength and moral courage permeated the lives of Southern families. Many children of the South are a product of those stalwart women who reared us as their own.

Hush Now, Baby is a tribute to Eva—and to all who have their own stories.

—*Angela W. Williams*

Hush Now, Baby

The Help Becomes *Family*

Map
Lower Coastal South Carolina

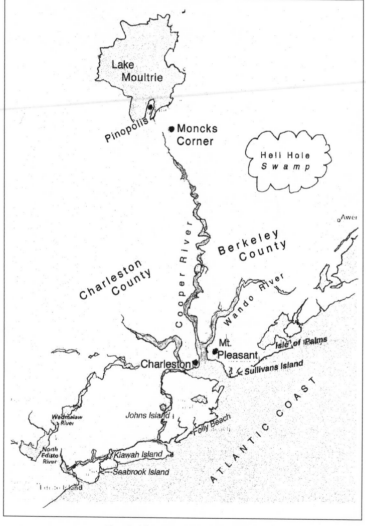

The Setting of *Hush Now, Baby*

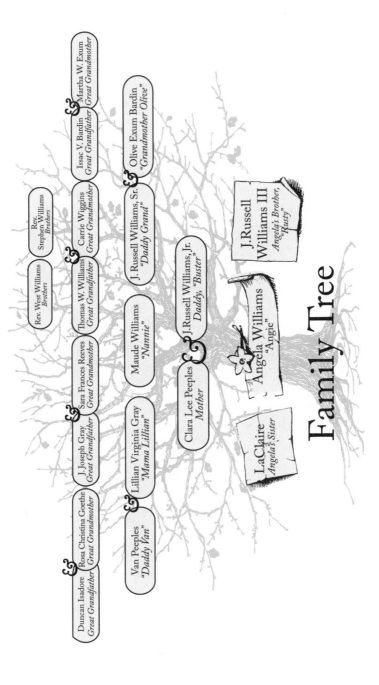

Family Tree

Duncan Isadore
Great Grandfather

Rosa Christina Goethe
Great Grandmother

Rev. West Williams
Brothers

Rev. Stephen Williams
Brothers

Issac V. Bardin
Great Grandfather

Martha W. Exum
Great Grandmother

J. Joseph Gray
Great Grandfather

Sara Frances Reeves
Great Grandmother

Thomas W. Williams
Great Grandfather

Carrie Wiggins
Great Grandmother

Olive Exum Bardin
"Grandmother Olive"

Van Peeples
"Daddy Van"

Lillian Virginia Gray
"Mama Lillian"

Maude Williams
"Nannie"

J. Russell Williams, Sr.
"Daddy Grand"

Clara Lee Peeples
Mother

J. Russell Williams, Jr.
Daddy, "Buster"

LaClaire
Angela's Sister

Angela Williams
"Angie"

J. Russell
Williams III
*Angela's Brother,
"Rusty"*

The Heart of Dixie

Dixie worked for Mama and took care of me
In my eyes she was family
But you know kids are color blind
Jesus said we were all alike
And Daddy said, "Yes, chile, but not quite"
And while I tried to figure who was right
Dixie loved me like one of her own.

The only love I knew that knew no color,
The only love I knew that knew no bounds...
Lived in the heart of Dixie.

Now when I get troubled
And start feeling down,
I can hear ol' Dixie's voice saying,
"Baby, come here and sit down."
I wonder if a love like that can still be found...

The only love I knew that knew no color,
The only love I knew that knew no bounds...
Lived in the heart of Dixie.

Adapted from "The Heart of Dixie" © Tricia Walker

Chapter 1

The Wedding

Nobody has ever measured, not even poets, how much the heart can hold.
　　　　　　　　　　—Zelda Fitzgerald

Sweat dripped down the inside of my legs.

"Take that slip off, Baby," Eva said. "It too hot today." Despite the scooped neck, I sweltered in a long-sleeved satin wedding gown splashed with swirls of pearls. My sister LaClaire had worn it four years earlier, and I was determined to wear it too, slip and all, even though it was 90 degrees outside. I pulled down the underskirt. Mother frowned.

"Young ladies always wear slips," she said as I stepped out of it—ignoring her penchant for decorum.

On this scorching South Carolina summer day smothered in humidity, Eva stood with me outside Trinity Episcopal Church in Pinopolis. It was June 25, 1965. The small white clapboard building with its round columns and green shutters stood nestled under a cathedral of towering long-leaf pines. Just inside the door, a thick rope stretched up to the bell in the steeple that children had rung for decades. A narrow aisle led to the altar framed by windows to the ceiling that gave a view of the surrounding woods.

Trinity Episcopal Church
Pinopolis, South Carolina
courtesy of Robert Cuthbert

Trinity opened its doors in 1873 when the pineland village became a refuge from malaria for wealthy white lowlanders. Anything to escape the dreaded onslaught of mosquitoes in the summer. It's thought that the pine trees deadened the sensory system of the disease-carrying insects. I had dressed in the Parish House made of timbers from the old Black Oak church. The pillars came from Belvedere Plantation in the wake of "the flood" that swallowed up precious land to form Lake Moultrie. Our old homeplace was just up the road half a mile from this church we'd attended all our lives.

On this day, folks gathered for the wedding that turned out to be the talk of the county that summer. They wore their Sunday best: linen suits, flowing knee-covering dresses, pillbox hats that First Lady Jackie Kennedy brought into fashion that year. Men pulled at their collars in the stifling heat. The open windows and cardboard fans with Dial Funeral Home ads on the back brought scant relief to the packed crowd inside.

As tradition dictated, I'd not seen the groom all day. I smiled thinking of our first date. I was in graduate school at Duke, and he attended medical school in Charleston. After many letters crossing the Carolina line, he came for a visit. I opened the door to the clear blue eyes of a black-haired country boy holding a tomato plant. Later that evening we sat on the steps in the dark as he told me about his family, his daddy's farm, his mother's death from cancer. He asked about my family. I spun stories of Eva until the sun peeked through the trees across the way. By morning my throat was dry, his eyes were not.

Eva and I stood on the sandy driveway by the church porch. Shoulders more rounded, chin less high, middle some thicker, Eva at sixty-five on the surface seemed changed. She pulled a hanky from the cuff of her black uniform. Eva made all her uniforms, which she wore every day—a short-or long-sleeved collared dress that buttoned down the front, topped with a full white apron and bib. She always wore a starched white nurse's cap trimmed with rickrack, a carryover from her hospital days, and white lace-up shoes. No smudges on anything. She'd step in her bedroom off the kitchen and flip on a fresh apron as quick as a gnat could scat. On this occasion, she'd added an organdy collar to her uniform. She blotted the perspiration off my forehead with her handkerchief. Through rimless glasses slipping down her chestnut nose, her dark eyes latched onto mine; sweat and tears blended in rivulets down her worn cheeks. Eva's hug looped round me as I pressed into her shoulder. Tears pooled in my eyes for all the years she'd sacrificed for me, my family.

"I gonna miss my Baby," she whispered through a sweet potato smile that had drawn me to her since birth. In the comfort of her presence that day, I felt the fabric of Eva woven into me so tightly that no old pain nor new sorrow could rend it loose.

I was wet out of the womb when I first met Eva. She was a nurse's aid in the Berkeley County Hospital. Dr. Norman Walsh, the local surgeon and family friend, delivered me, as he had my sister two years earlier. Lela Session was the nurse on duty the day LaClaire arrived. Having just finished her nursing degree at Howard University in Washington, DC, in 1939, Session recorded the arrival of my older sister that cold January day when Daddy stole the show:

> Mrs. Williams was doing beautifully in the delivery room. But my oh my, Mr. Williams was a riot in the waiting room. He received more attention than his wife. He made the delivery difficult with his restless, impatient, nervous, panicky disposition that drew everyone into his anxiety. Tears ran down his face as he sat on the edge of his seat and hollered as if he was in labor.

From that day on, Daddy and LaClaire were tight as seeds in a cotton boll. He lost the battle of naming his firstborn after his wife but cleverly switched the "Clara Lee" to "La Claire," getting in the last word, as usual. And, as was his fashion, Buster showed his appreciation to Clara Lee. He presented her with a twelve-piece place setting of silver. The engraved chest plate read: *Mother from LaClaire.*

On *my* birth day, Dr. Walsh handed me to Eva, who cradled me in her strong arms. Eva cooed my cries to silence, wrapped a cotton diaper around my bottom and fed me my first bottle. That's when I became Eva's "Baby."

With me in the crook of her arm, Eva walked out of the delivery room to greet my father. With an uncommon assuredness, she paraded me around the waiting room. What a bright countenance! There's no record of his exuberance, but Daddy knew a good thing when he saw one: Eva Edwards Motte Aiken. And when James Russell Williams, Jr. set his mind to something, people better look out. A few days later, Daddy drove us home in his '41 Packard that smelled of new leather while he hummed to Glenn Miller's "In the Mood" that played softly on the radio. Mother sat

1941 Packard

beside him up front. Settled in the back seat, Eva held me in her lap. He had charmed Eva into walking right out of that hospital and into our brand new house—just three blocks down Main Street—where she stayed for over twenty years.

It was a major move for Buster to relocate from the small village of Pinopolis, not two miles away, to the provincial bustling town of Moncks Corner with a burgeoning population of close to 500 households. The town had recently celebrated the opening of a library within walking distance of our new home.

Any celebration of my arrival in 1941, however, was short-lived. Pearl Harbor was bombed just three months later. More significantly, I was not the boy my parents had hoped for. Daddy told tales of putting a girl behind every azalea bush until he got his boy, and we had a passel of azaleas. So, with some ambivalence, Buster and his young wife Clara Lee arrived at their new home with another baby girl and, thank God, Eva.

Almost twenty years older and wiser than the privileged young couple that hired her, Eva came at a bargain—a few dollars plus room and board. Eva thought *she* was the one who got the bargain—a spanking new house, her own room with an indoor bathroom, heat that poured out of the ceiling, and marvelous machines that washed clothes and dishes! Never mind she had to run a large house, chase a toddler, and tend a newborn baby.

It was Eva who bathed my pudgy limbs in the kitchen sink, who slathered baby oil on my bottom and sprinkled powder in the crevices to absorb the sticky August moisture. Eva who washed my cotton diapers and watched them dance in the breeze like whitecaps on the wire clothesline out back. Eva who placed me naked on a blanket in the yard to soak up "a little of God's sunshine."

I can't remember life without Eva. "Beba" was my first word. "Come to Beba" sang in my young ears. I never heard Eva called "nannie," "maid," "servant," or "help." And I can't remember calling her anything but "Beba" or later "Eva." And she called me "Baby," never "Angela," "Angie" or "Bugs."

She stood about five feet barefooted. Her upright posture and stocky stature conveyed confidence. Skin the color of a Tootsie Roll and teeth

Eva as nurse's aid on the steps of the hospital

white as piano keys. Her sunny disposition and daz-zling smile enchanted babies, children, friends, and townspeople alike. Everyone knew Eva Aiken—a heart as big as Lake Moultrie. She was simply another member of the Williams family.

Eva exuded energy. Whatever Eva did, whether she was riding me on her shoulders, flapping the bed sheets smooth, or jerking shirts off the clothesline to beat the rain. "Got no time to waste, Baby," she'd say. She cooked three meals a day. Washed and ironed every blouse, skirt, dress, and shirt. Kept four tile porches sparkling. Cleaned all seventeen rooms: liv-ing room, dining room, sun parlor, six bedrooms, four baths, laundry and kitchen. Eva took pride in her kitchen. She'd get on her hands and knees to scrub the linoleum until it shone. I forever saw her armed with a broom and dust pan ready to corner the last biscuit crumb or errant pea after mealtime. She loved the fancy Electrolux, a fat tube on runners that she dragged behind her, snuffing up a speck of lint or cigarette ash in the living room. In the bed-rooms, she pulled out chests and beds to chase the smallest dust ball.

"If you gonna do it, do it right, Baby," she'd say.

On top of it all, Eva kept up with three ram-bunctious children. (Rusty arrived two years after me.) I dogged her every footstep, whether traipsing behind the Electrolux or trotting to keep up when she bounded down the long hallways with her clean-ing bucket.

There was always a bubble of joy around her. Hanging around Eva was like seeing the horses on a merry-go-round pump up and down. Something just made you want to jump up on a painted saddle and go round too, ride up and down, up and down, holding on to the pole . . . knowing if you let go, you wouldn't fall off the sturdy back that swirled you round. Watching Eva made me dizzy, giddy—yet I always landed in her lap.

One of my earliest memories of Eva's bustling is a tea party under the oak tree in the side yard. I was three and LaClaire five. Eva set up a small table under the moss-covered limbs that beckoned our little group. We tramped out the back door, down the brick steps, along a rock path, past the playhouse. A scene from *Alice in Wonderland*—Eva marching behind us balancing a tray of sugar cookies, a pitcher of lemonade and a miniature tea set. Through the oak limbs, dapples of sunlight danced on tiptoes at our tea party. My pudgy fingers could barely grasp the delicate handles.

"Don't poke out your pinkie," Eva warned. "Say *'please* pass the cookies' and *'thank you.'* Them words can open many a door. Memba now." Afterward, we trooped back to the kitchen, washed and dried the little cups and saucers and put them away in the China cabinet in the dining room.

Eva took every opportunity to teach us proper table etiquette. At mealtime, we didn't raise a fork before the blessing, and LaClaire, Rusty and I knew to push the soup spoon *away* from us and to fold our napkins to the *left* of our plates before asking to be excused.

"Push in your chair, chile," she'd remind us before leaving the table. We learned that one served food from the left and picked up dishes from the right. We also learned the difference between a cocktail and a salad fork, a fish knife and a butter knife. A quick study under my mother's tutelage, Eva absorbed everything. In a few short years after her arrival, Eva could have been the lady of a big house in downtown Charleston—under different circumstances, of course.

Yet in all Eva's busyness, she occasionally got real still, especially if we were running through the kitchen on the way to the back yard. She put out her hand like a train-guard arm—we'd come to a halt.

"Walk on tippy toe now. Don't want ma cake to fall," she whispered.

"Shh now," as she cracked the oven door to peek at her pumpkin pie.

Sometimes when work was done, Eva slowed down her rapid pace to walk our short legs to the library up the block. Mrs. Julia Kirk, the librarian, always welcomed our little entourage, Eva too, even though blacks weren't allowed in the library. When we read books or listened to Story Hour in the front of the library, the same Lela Session who witnessed LaClaire's birth, labored on her thesis away from prying eyes in a back room. I sometimes glimpsed her when I went to the bathroom. She regularly slipped in the back door to Mrs. Kirk's office to do research for her graduate degree.

Lela, almost twenty years younger than her friend Eva, was fortunate. Her family was able to send her to the Avery Normal Institute in Charleston. Tuition was $3.50 per month, a big expense for her family, so Lela's mother moved to Charleston where she made quilts and took in laundry for soldiers at the Naval Base and cadets at The Citadel for $8 a basket. Lela herself sold boiled peanuts, plums, and blackberries to help with tuition.

Most blacks, however, attended the local public schools. School ended around third grade for Eva when she was big enough to work the family fields. But as adults, Eva and Lela were breaking the color barrier in their individual quiet, determined ways, with the subtle assistance of forward-thinking people like Mrs. Kirk.

Eva never contemplated going in the back door anywhere. She led our parade through the front door of the library and hunkered down on a stool beside us as we pulled book after book off the shelves. Eventually she'd stand up and say, "That's a plenty now. Take your books over yonder. Come on now." We hauled our pile to the desk to stamp in the due date with black-inked rubber numbers. Eva led the group back home, laden with the choices for the week, including Uncle Remus tales, subtle stories of black Uncle Remus making fun of whites' naiveties. When we read these aloud, I wonder if Eva "got it." I surely didn't at the time. I remember her joking once that little black Sambo "sho need a lesson on proper butter making."

As we children grew older, we splashed in puddles with our galoshes or skipped ahead of Eva to the corner. Making sure not to step on a crack or we'd break our mama's back. If we split around a light pole, we said, "bread and butter." She taught us not to walk under ladders or cross a black cat's path— all bad luck. She made me cross my heart to prove I wasn't fibbing. I'm not sure when I learned to cross my fingers behind my back to cancel out crossing my heart, but it came in handy many times. I didn't want to tell an out-and-out story to my Eva, that's for sure.

Often we cut through the privet hedge to the library while Eva crossed the street to pick up a few groceries from the Piggly Wiggly, where Mr. Orvin kept a running tab for the Williamses, adding ten cents for bread or sixty cents for ten pounds of sugar. Then she'd pop her head back in the front door of the library and whisper across the small room, "Yenna come on now," and we'd all head back home.

Eva was a childless widow in her forties when she joined our family. She was the second of six children of Bill and Hattie Edwards, sharecroppers who farmed out on Whitesville Road by the time I knew them. Her daddy, the son of a blacksmith, grew up near Abbeville, South Carolina, one of Jackson and Lianella Edwards' ten children. Daddy Bill, that's what we called Eva's daddy, and his wife Hattie then lived for a time in adjacent Dorchester County where Eva was born. By the 1930 census, the family was living on Moss Grove Plantation on the edge of Moncks Corner, which the Williams family later owned. Interestingly, they were listed as "mullato" in the census, not "black."

In their later years, Daddy Bill and Miss Hattie lived in a neat clapboard house down a long dirt road on the Pinopolis side of town. Plopped right in the middle of a cotton field that stretched out on all sides, the house looked like it was riding on a fluffy white cloud. A big catalpa tree grew in their front yard, and there's nothing quite as fascinating to young children as watching those catalpa worms emerge out of their green wrapping. The fat, black, juicy caterpillars were treasured because of their status as prime fish bait. Cut in half, turned inside out, they lured many an unsuspecting fish. Daddy Bill loved to show us his catalpa worms.

"Daddy Bill" Edwards, Eva's Father

Brown as a toasted pecan, Daddy Bill stood slim and straight as a hickory stick. His dark pupils floated on moist, yellowed balls. He often pulled a white handkerchief from his overalls pocket to dab at his damp eyes. The hair of his head was like pure wool, the first black person I'd ever seen with white hair. It was screwed tight just like the lambs in the Jesus picture at Sunday School. Daddy Bill smiled soft like Jesus too. Only he was black. And we all knew that Jesus was a white man.

Daddy Bill was a regular sight striding square-shouldered behind his mule Agnes. Agnes, whose docile and angelic face reflected her master's. Together they plowed the sandy soil that cotton favors. You'd hear in the distance an occasional slap of the reins on the mule's back, a "gee" or "haw" to keep her going left or right as he laid by his crops. When the weeds took over, he grabbed his hoe and chopped away.

"Pray for a good harvest but don't never stop hoein'," he said.

Riding down Main Street sitting high on the buggy seat, Daddy Bill doffed his hat and bent his chin at passersby—young and old, black and white. The black and the young he looked in the eye. The others, his eyes slid across their faces as he held a half-smile.

I missed Daddy Bill when he died. Born before the Civil War, he lived to be 105. What I wouldn't give to have talked to him about his long life through turbulent times. He was buried right there at Rock Hill Baptist Church, where he carried his family Sunday upon Sunday.

Miss Hattie, now, she was a sweeper. Meat falling away from her bones, her fragile frame belied her energy. All the time sweeping her porch or sweeping the dirt in the front yard. Perhaps a hold-over from the days of being "dirt poor," when many lived in shacks with dirt floors in need of regular sweeping. When any-one walked by or pulled up to the house, she put both hands on top of the handle to ground her broom and leaned forward.

"Well, ain't you a sight for sore eyes!" she'd say with vigor.

The Edwards family poured into Rock Hill Baptist Church on the outskirts of Moncks Corner every time the doors opened. Eva's primary education came from the church—spiritual, academic, social and political. I remember Eva's cousin Marie

"Miss Hattie" Edwards, Eva's mother

Motte telling me, "Eva was always a good, happy girl. The Edwards and them was strict. They would lay that religion down." Though exposed to little formal schooling, Eva knew her Bible up one side and down the other.

"All you needs to know be right chere, Baby," she said, thumping her Bible with two fingers. Preachers delivered passionate sermons that left indelible marks on Eva. Ministers lifted up Biblical principles of peril and promise, leading their people through the desert as Moses did—keep the faith, call on God for strength, forgive your enemies.

Eva knew about turning the other cheek and longing for heaven, not gold. She could put everything she owned in a cardboard suitcase. When I was a teen-ager, I learned that she was paid five dollars a week.

"Why in tarnation don't you ask for more?" I asked Eva.

"My reward be in Gloryland, Baby. Your daddy don't let me want for nothin'. Now hush yoursef." Eva kept the reins tight on her feelings about anything except her love and devotion to us. Towards the end,

I'd see her eyes water, her cheeks quiver, her lips purse, but she always remained calm, controlled . . . and forgiving.

Miss Hattie and Daddy Bill also gave Eva "fireside training," they called it, teachable moments while cooking, canning, gardening, and sewing. "Do right," "keep your eyes to de ground," and "speak when de speak," they said. When young Eva asked why she couldn't drink "white" water at the fountain in town, her parents said, "Mind, chile. That's de way it be. Don't be making no trouble." Eva learned her lessons well.

By the time she was a middle-aged adult and part of our family, she'd long since chunked the "eyes down" part and taken up the "look em in the eye" mantra of the newer generation. But as a child, Eva followed the spoken and unspoken dictums of the segregated South.

Young Eva learned to count with chicken eggs and corn kernels and how to make do with dresses her mother sewed from printed feed sacks Daddy Bill picked up from my grandfather's farm supply store. In winter, Miss Hattie starched Eva's dresses stiff to keep out the cold because her daughter had no coat.

Eva worked the fields when cotton was king in the South. Her calloused fingers testified to the years of plucking stubborn cotton from prickly bolls. Each morning before first light, Miss Hattie stirred up grits, eggs, sausage and biscuits spread with her scuppernong jelly. From sunup to sundown, Eva, her brothers Julian, Louis and Alvin (called J. B.), her sister Alice, and her parents (Hattie carrying baby Frank strapped to her breast) worked the rows, then dragged the stuffed crocus sacks to Daddy Bill's wagon. During breaks, they'd stretch their spines, bending backwards with hands behind their hips, wipe their brows with a sleeve, and drink tepid water from a nearby bucket.

At day's end, Daddy Bill's overflowing wagon waddled its way through town to my family's ginning house. Throughout the South in the early 1900s, cotton bound black and white to the soil and each other. It was no less true for the Edwards and Williams families. They depended upon each other. Eva's coming to live with us merely deepened the connection. My granddaddy, "ole man Russell," took care of Berkeley County's farming needs, everything from hog feed to cottonseed and plows. Most could only pay off bills at the end of the cotton season. He was kind and understanding to sharecroppers who fell behind on payments. My daddy inherited this penchant for charity, to his demise.

One day my granddaddy paid Daddy Bill for his ginned cotton, and Eva's Daddy marched with money in hand to Law and Mims Dry Goods across the railroad tracks. Most of the black establishments were "across the tracks." Mr. Mims was wise enough to open his establishment on the cusp so that both whites and blacks patronized his store. Well, Daddy Bill walked straight in the door and proudly bought his Eva a pair of black patent leather shoes for $1.98 and white socks for 25¢. Eva said she never forgot that day and wore the shoes to church every Sunday until her feet hurt so bad she couldn't buckle the straps.

Young Eva

During her late teens, Eva took a bold step; she abandoned the cotton fields to become a maid at the local hospital, about a thirty-minute walk from her house. Inside the spacious hospital out of the sweltering sun, she gave a cheery word to patients as she emptied bedpans and changed the linens. She was proud to earn a scrap of money to take home to her parents.

Before long, a handsome older man named Sam Motte from Eadytown up county married the resourceful young woman. They headed north, Eva armed with a letter from Mrs. Elma Loring, the hospital Superintendent, who wrote, "It is a pleasure to recommend her to anyone in need of a reliable maid who takes interest and pride in her work." After Mr. Motte died, Eva married another older man, a brakeman on the railroad, Sammy Aiken, and they moved to Winston Salem, North Carolina. There she found God's calling—"raising up churren." Eva and Sam later moved back to Moncks Corner when Eva's parents took ill. LaClaire recalls Sam reading her the funny papers on the back steps of the house, but I don't remember him at all. He too was always off on a train somewhere, which is probably why Eva could live with us in our house most of the time. Sam died shortly thereafter. After losing two fine husbands, Eva became the mainstay for both her parents and the Williams family. No easy jobs those, it turned out.

When she and Sam moved back to town, Eva immediately got a job in the hospital where she'd worked as a youth and found herself in the company of doctors and nurses who noted her potential. They took her under wing, encouraged her to take the midwife course, quickly elevating her status from maid to nurse's aide. Tenderhearted, she soothed fevered brows and rubbed aching joints with concern and competence, never dreaming her gift of service would be used in any other setting. Eva was content at the hospital until the day I was born. That's when her joy arrived. That's when she heeded God's call and got busy taking care of LaClaire and me. Two years after me, my brother Rusty. We became Eva's children.

But I thought she was all mine.

Eva dispensed words by the teacup.

"Ain't much need talking bout, Baby," she'd say. But her face spoke. All it took was showing clean hands before supper or being on time for breakfast for her to flash a full-toothed smile. If I mashed a finger in the dresser drawer, she soothed away the pain with a gentle rub and tender eyes.

No softy, she could give a look that disciplined in a heartbeat. Slam the screened door and Eva gave me a quick glance with widened eyes and raised brows that meant business. I'd retrace my steps and gently pull the door to without a sound. If Eva stopped in her tracks, cocked her head to the side and sent a hard look, it meant I'd traipsed across her freshly-mopped floor, an offense that required a prompt "scuse me."

Back in her bedroom behind the kitchen, she often talked to Jesus and sang real soft like. Eva's serene look came when she sang, "Nobody know de trouble I seen, nobody know but Jesus," as she knelt beside the bed with eyes closed. I sneaked to watch her during prayer time. "Just listenin' to the Lawd, Baby," she'd say.

That's the first place I ever heard "Amazing Grace." I later wondered whether she knew the words were written by John Newton, the captain of a slave ship, and the melody was inspired by singing below the deck. Did she know that most of the old spirituals she sang could be played using only the piano's black notes, called "the slave scale"?

When she went home to her family every Sunday to sing in the choir, she wore a felt hat and a dress she'd sewn herself with red and yellow flowers all over it. She carried a black plastic purse with two silver knobs that snapped shut with a click. Near as I could tell, they spent most all day in church singing.

Eva's faith gave her the strength she needed to live in two worlds, to keep her dignity, to tend to her parents. The strength to love me. And my family. I learned that Eva and her people really did need strength and were, in fact, in a heap of trouble as she and I lived in our lily white world in the '50s and '60s. But when I was a little girl, I didn't know this. I just soaked up all Eva had to give. And, glory, did she give.

My clearest memories involve Eva's touch. How many times did she wiggle my toes playing "piggy goes to market" or pinch my fat cheeks saying she's "stealing some sugar"? It was magic. I loved running to Eva, my chubby arms outstretched. Her arms mirroring mine, she lifted, swung, corralled and hugged. When my body plunged into hers, it was like diving into a down pillow. I burrowed my head in her bosom or nestled my nose in her neck where the skin was soft as a lamb's ear. I never felt so safe as buried there, breathing in her musty sweetness.

When summer thunderstorms came in the night, all three of us children ran from the far end of the house to Eva's bedroom behind the kitchen. When we hit the sun parlor, the lightning shot through the ceiling-to-floor windows scaring the pants off us until we clamored into Eva's bed. As the thunder rolled, Eva's arms pulled us in and she crooned, "Hush, now. God jes talking. Gonna be awright."

In later years when family storms in Mother and Daddy's bedroom became even more frightening, Eva was our shelter as she gathered us in, rocking us in her arms, and saying so softly we could barely hear, "Lawdy me. Help us, Jesus." She squeezed us tight.

When our father's anger spilled over, Eva soothed us with those thick hands—dark and rough as a raisin on top, light and smooth as a mango underneath. On the good days, Daddy merely relegated me from the dinner table to the bedroom for breaking an antique vase, running in the house, or refusing to eat Brussels sprouts. It wasn't long before Eva sneaked around back, slipped in the side porch and down the hall to my room with a tray of butterbeans and biscuits. She'd stand there, eyeing me till the last bite, then rub my back till I fell asleep. After Daddy's worst tempests blew over, many a time her warm palm cradled my head into her starched apron.

"Leave it be, chile. You my Baby," she'd say.

Eva turned 66 the year I married. She'd grown weary by then, yet her mood lifted as my wedding date neared. We filled our last days together with quiet smiles and spontaneous hugs. She ironed my blue linen dress for the honeymoon, showed the postman where to put yet another package, and gingerly opened my presents, like the blue box from

Tiffany's that yielded china candlesticks. Her eyes stretched wide as she unwrapped a large, hand-painted Chinese bowl from cousin Lawton Wiggins's antique shop on Church Street in Charleston.

"This the finest mixing bowl I ever seed," she beamed, turning it round and round in gnarled hands.

By then, gray sprigs sneaked beneath the edges of her cap, and she'd begun to rub her arthritic knees. She slit the side of her right shoe "to get some air to de bunion" as her weight increased and her feet spread. She eventually lost all her teeth. She and Mother made many trips to the dental clinic to get her dentures adjusted.

"They ain't never fit right," she said.

Eva and Angie at the wedding

On the day of the wedding, Eva's face glistened with heat and happiness, and she'd worn her white lace-up shoes. But she left her teeth at home. Mother was appalled . . . and let Eva know it in no uncertain terms. The mood dampened.

Eva and I stood outside the church, stepped back, sliding our hands down each other's arms, ending in a doubleclasp. Oh, those warm hands. We gave each other one long look that edged into broad smiles. When was the last time I'd seen this open-faced joy, Eva's square-shouldered pride? What had seeped it out of her during two decades of being with our family? We dropped our hands. Time to go—for both of us.

Mother set up a cane-bottom, ladder-back chair behind the last church pew so Eva could enter and exit undetected. The only blacks who'd ever entered Trinity Church were the cleaning women, and they always used the back door. With a warning look and firm voice, Mother instructed Eva one more time.

"Straighten Angie's train. Then sit in this chair by the door." Without looking Mother in the eye, Eva dipped her chin in a token nod. I should have suspected something right then.

A lemony aroma drifted across the vestibule from the magnolia boughs and honeysuckle vines that decorated the church. The afternoon sun streamed through the arched window behind the altar where the pines of Pinopolis sparkled. The bridesmaids looked crisp in green linen party dresses, the groomsmen handsome in their tuxedos. Mother, Mama Lillian, and Uncle Charlie sat on the front row. My brother Rusty's three-year-old son Brett, the ring bearer, fiddled with the ring pillow; my niece Sharon, the perfect picture of a flower girl in her long white dress and blue sash, stood demurely to the side. Solemn-faced, the groom and the minister faced the entrance.

Scanning the crowd, I saw the back of my daddy's head. He was sober. Still punishing him for not being the father I longed for, I had chosen Rusty to escort me. I hooked arms with him while waiting for the music to begin.

Rusty, LaClaire and I had many memories growing up in this church, not the least of which was getting the church giggles more times than we could count. As if it was yesterday, I could hear the Reverend Loren Mead say, "Would the Williams children please excuse themselves." I smiled at the thought and gazed up into Rusty's handsome, tanned face, a little taken back.

When did my little brother grow up? He's so tall, so mature, I thought. His eyes smiled into mine, and I felt comfort from his strong arm as Eva arranged my train.

The pump organ sounded an opening chord. As we started up the aisle, it wasn't the groom who caught my eye. It was my sister, the matron of honor. LaClaire was gesturing rapidly behind her daisy bouquet. She stabbed her forefinger forward in frantic bursts. Had we started walking too soon? Clearly something was drastically amiss. Did we need to stop? Back up? Her signaling confused me. Poking that finger back and forth, back and forth, she looked so silly!

Rusty and I were half way to the front when I felt as if everything slowed, like a record on the wrong speed. I heard an odd sound. What was it? Was that me? I listened. A nervous laugh burst out of my mouth. Yes, it was me! I jerked my head forward and focused on the altar cross. Trying to reign myself in, I held my breath, tightened my stomach and clenched my teeth.

A loud snort echoed through the church—me again! I felt Rusty's arm shudder. We struggled to stifle our laughter. We both lost control, shaking and giggling toward the altar. The scene played like an old black-and-white Abbott-Costello movie jerking across a screen, the characters careening into each other with dissonant music in the background.

LaClaire eventually replaced her distressed look with a wide smile that sailed over my shoulder. Clustered in the small chancel up front, the bridesmaids and groomsmen threw their heads back with open-mouthed grins. The groom, on the other hand, was tight-lipped, blue eyes marble hard. Then I saw Mother turn her shoulder to watch the procession. A look of horror swept across her face.

Eva had crossed the line—one final time.

Chapter 2

The Watermelon Queen

Oh, she was beautiful in every part!—
The auburn hair that bound the subtle brain;
                              —Edna St. Vincent Millay

How, from where it started, had it come to this? A quarter-century relationship of mutual trust and loyalty between Mother and Eva severed on my wedding day. But like Eva, Mother too once committed a similar impulsive, courageous act that sent her spinning toward an unfamiliar, exciting adventure.

At twenty-two, young Clara Lee wore another man's engagement ring when she and Buster Williams ran off to get married. Her fiancé worked in the financial world of New York, an ideal suitor by all accounts. What a shock to learn his bride-to-be had run away with another man! But the Watermelon Queen of Hampton County couldn't resist the magnetic young bachelor of Berkeley County. One cool fall evening, they held hands in the home of a judge in the small town of Barnwell, only a few miles from Clara Lee's hometown in Estill. She and Buster "just couldn't wait," she confessed. (I think I know what that meant back then.)

Clara Lee was teaching fifth grade in Beaufort, a sleepy coastal town an hour south of Charleston. Buster led a work crew in Luray, a skip and a hop from Estill. He worked for the Civilian Conservation Corps, which President Franklin Roosevelt initiated to get people working during the Depression. They no doubt crossed paths when she spent weekends and holidays in her hometown. Besides, Buster had a reputation for ferreting out attractive girls, no matter the location.

Their hasty marriage upset a number of people

besides Clara Lee's fiancé. Friends had planned parties. Relatives had addressed invitations. Sisters had bought dresses. Clara Lee, the eldest of four children, was the pride of her parents and her community. Her wedding was anticipated as the social event of the season. A pall no doubt fell over the Peeples family at the abrupt, clandestine marriage.

After all, the Peeples clan was held in high regard in Hampton County. Except perhaps for a political argument that put Jessie Willliamson Peeples in his grave in 1853. On his gravestone is written: *Lay me down for Alford Martin has cut and stabbed me to pieces.* These words precipitated the South Carolina legislature to write a law that prohibited murderers' names on tombstones. (Jessie was my grandfather's grandfather.) But I digress.

The Peeples family had been leaders of the agricultural, social and church communities since the Revolutionary War. The Peeples clan probably originated near the town of Pee*b*les in Scotland; say it fast, and it sounds like Peeples.

Rosa Christina Goethe and Isadore Peeples, a Confederate veteran, could boast that eight of their twelve children settled in Hampton County's farming communities. Van Peeples, Clara Lee's father, was the tenth child. They lived in the family farmhouse west of Estill, a small drive-through agricultural town on the way to Savannah, Georgia. Estill itself built up around a railroad track that distributed timber, cotton and truck crops that flourished in the rich earth.

It hugged the outer edge of Hampton County created from the western portion of Charleston County. Known statewide for its pretty girls, sweet watermelon, and Southern hospitality, the county was named for Confederate General Wade Hampton, who later became South Carolina's governor. The black rivers of the Coosawhatchie and Salkehatchie, named by the Native American Indians who first inhabited the regions, were a bonus to the county. Spotting an arrowhead in Van Peeples' fields was not uncommon when they tilled the soil. The Peeples boys grew up with a love for the land and the hunting and fishing it provided.

Education was always a priority. Van attended Morrison Academy near Estill. As an adolescent in the early 1900s, he traveled to Charleston to attend the prestigious Porter Military Academy. He lived with the Reverend and Mrs. Toomer Porter, its founders. Dr. Porter, a former rice planter, entered the ministry and envisioned an institute to educate former soldiers and boys left orphaned or destitute by the Civil War. General Sherman strongly supported Porter's converting a former arsenal into an educational facility. One of only two remaining military buildings in South Carolina built by the Confederate government, St. Luke's Chapel, originally a part of Porter, rests on the campus of Charleston's Medical University of South Carolina. Van's formal schooling continued at Bailey's Military Academy in Edgefield, South Carolina, and Osborne Business School of Augusta, Georgia.

Van Peeples at Porter

But Van Peeples was meant for neither city nor military life. The land called. Young Van put his energy into becoming a successful farmer of about two thousand acres in Hampton County. After he married, he raised his own family right there on the homeplace until he built a house in town in Estill as a gift for his wife Lillian.

With an eye for what the area needed and a desire to give his family the best, Van also ran a mercantile store, as well as a steam-operated cotton gin and a large cattle operation. Van Peeples became a man of considerable influence and means.

He also liked to keep up with the times. Not wanting anybody to outdo him, Van and his friend

George became the first in Estill to buy automobiles. In 1904, they went to Olar, South Carolina, to jump on the horseless carriage bandwagon when vehicles with gasoline engines became popular.

They'd seen a newspaper advertisement with a picture of a sporty car for $600 that read: "It Only Costs 29 Cents a Day to Run this Maxwell 200 Miles a Week." Neither had ever driven a car, so they studied the "How to Drive a Car" chapter in the owner's manual and returned with two brand new motor cars.

1904 Maxwell,
Van's first car

We grandchildren called him "Daddy Van." Eva called him "Mista Van" and declared him "one o' God's fine creations." A handsome man, he stood well over six feet, had wide shoulders, and arms and legs as solid as pine trunks. A gentleman farmer, Van wore a suit, white shirt, tie and hat every day, rain or shine, hot or cold. When he arrived home at dusk for supper, he hooked his hat on the hat rack by the door, revealing a shock of brown hair and a band of white across his broad forehead, with the rest of his face deeply tanned. Because of his olive complexion and high shirt collar, there was nary a trace of a red neck on Van Peeples.

When I was about eleven, Mother showed us a national magazine that featured agricultural enterprises in the South, and lo and behold if Daddy Van and the Peeples farm didn't have a spread. Daddy Van stood tall in the middle of a plowed field wearing his business suit and hat. He was flanked by twenty mule teams and their Negro drivers, each man dressed in his finest. I thought he had to be someone real special to have his picture in a magazine.

All of us revered—and feared—Daddy Van. His seldom-heard voice rumbled deep and firm. We could count on hearing it twice a day, for sure. When he came in from the farm, he'd ask for the paper. He read *The Savannah Morning News* and *The Farmer's Almanac* religiously. And after supper, he'd say, "That's a mighty fine meal, Miss Lillian," dipping his head to my grandmother, his blue eyes softening.

Lillian Gray Peeples

Lillian Virginia Gray, my grandmother, was the epitome of a lady. She was born in the small community of Barton, South Carolina. She too was a tenth child, the baby of her family. The Grays farmed too, so Lillian and Van had much in common. Lillian's grandfather left considerable property when he died—livestock, land and slaves. According to the Last Will and Testament, her father inherited about four hundred acres as well as "four Negroes, Old Jim, Nancy, George and Jim also the increase there of if any." I felt uneasy when I read what the "property" entailed, surprised to learn Mama Lillian's family owned slaves. No one ever mentioned such things in our family.

The Gray family reared a sensitive little girl who became the elegant Lillian. Her body regal, tall and slender. Her smile close-lipped and sweet. When she hugged her mother goodbye to go off to college, tears welled up but didn't spill. She was only sixteen years old when her father Joseph Gray accompanied his baby girl on the train ride from nearby Luray to Columbia, South Carolina. She was to start her freshman year at Columbia College, a women's Christian school. They rode a buggy from the station to the college, where her father situated Lillian in the women's dormitory.

It had been a long day for them both. When her father returned to his hotel for a good night's rest, he lit the gas lanterns in his room, readied for bed, and fell asleep reading the local paper. During the night, the lanterns' flames flickered. Joseph Gray did not wake the next morning, his life snuffed out by asphyxiation.

I can't imagine young Lillian's hearing the news. The next day she boarded yet another train to accompany her father's casket back home. The young Lillian kept her poise and returned to school immediately after the funeral.

Reserved in demeanor, Lillian nevertheless radiated an assuredness that rarely wavered. This and her loveliness attracted young Van Peeples, who married her as soon as she finished college. Lillian and the prize of the Peeples family began married life joining his mother on the old farm place.

Babies started coming. Seven years and three children later, Van built a stately two-story brick home in downtown Estill, a present to his wife. And in this house, they functioned as a team, mutual affection and admiration evident. He set the rules. She carried them out. He ran the farm. She ran the house.

If anyone deserved the venerable name of "grandmother," it was Lillian Peeples. I can see Mama Lillian now, slim as a pencil in her ankle-length gray skirt and a long-sleeved, high-necked white silk blouse edged with lace at her neck and wrists. She wore only two pieces of jewelry: her father's gold pocket watch hung from a thick chain around her neck, and a diamond in a white-gold filigree setting ringed one of her fingers. No ear adornments

We grandchildren called her "Mama." At the age of two, I was whisked away to Estill because I caught the mumps—a dangerous situation because Mother was pregnant with Rusty. I became the darling of the Estill household full of cookies and coddles.

When Mother came to take me home, she called, "Come to Mama!" I turned and ran away . . . grabbing "Mama" Lillian's leg. Perhaps because I was the most loquacious of all the grandchildren, "Mama" stuck.

How we loved visiting Mama Lillian's house in Estill. I'd wake in the big bed upstairs, smiling as light streaming in the window warmed my lids open. I stretched lazily looking forward to a joyful day. I'd hear the click of Mama Lillian's heels on the polished stairs. Otherwise, she moved silently, smoothly throughout the house, gliding like a swan across the surface of her life, certainly "paddling like hell underneath," as the saying goes, to keep her large household running. The stately Lillian descended each morning ready for the day, hair coiffured, a touch of powder on her nose, a hint of color on her lips. And fully dressed in her classic, understated style. She wore muted, solid colors, never a primary color or a print—and always stockings and heels, never bare legs or flats.

The Peeples' house was the finest in town. The property covered almost an entire block, plenty of space for grandchildren to roam. The bays of the brick garage to the right of the house sheltered two matching black Cadillacs. Mama Lillian's Caddy knew the road to Savannah by heart; it was the nearest town for serious shopping. She was a shopper, a shopper with discriminating taste in everything from Oriental rugs to birthday presents. I always opened her gift last because I knew it would top the others.

In the sprawling backyard, we chased chickens, ducks, dogs, and spotted guineas that ran loose. Beyond the backyard stretched a fenced vegetable garden lined with rows of corn, tomatoes and beans. On the dirt alleyway beside the main house, Van built a small brick duplex for Ma Mary Riley, his elderly nurse from childhood, and Janie Graham, the cook.

"Great lawdamercy!" Eva cried out when she first saw the Estill house—tall white columns in front of a two-story brick structure. A foyer as big as our dining room at home and high-ceilinged rooms created a striking first impression. Two sets of stairs, one from the foyer and one from the kitchen, converged at a landing with a glass door before going up another half flight to the second floor.

"Ain't they got steps aplenty," Eva said, her chin pointing toward the steep stairs. Quite a contrast from the modern low-slung house we lived in. She had a fit keeping us children from sliding down the slick banisters.

But it wasn't the stairs we careened down that intrigued me the most. It was the Estill dining room. To my eyes, the long room seemed right out of a medieval castle. The massive German table stretched the length of the room,

Daddy Van and Clara Lee

a heavy matching sideboard to one side, a china cabinet on another wall, and a large fireplace at the far end flanked by floor-to-ceiling windows. Over the mantel hung a gold-framed picture of cows grazing by a stream under bended branches, in paints of soft blue-green tones. On the side wall, I never tired of looking at the mauve tapestry that hung above the sideboard, a bucolic scene of a large draft horse with tufted hooves eating from an overflowing grain sack.

For a long time, I couldn't pull out the chunky dining room chairs, so Eva had to give me a boost until I learned to step on the bottom rung to climb up to the seat, feet dangling a foot from the floor. I felt like a princess, albeit a mute one. In the Peeples' household, especially at the dining table, children were seen and not heard. They spoke when spoken to. As a rule, Daddy Van didn't converse with children. But we'd get an occasional smile, a pat on the head, or a thump on the rump as we passed. Daddy Van sat at the head, his back to the fireplace. He'd look down the expanse of family making sure no fork nor goblet lifted before his short, spontaneous blessing for good health, good food, and "a little rain for the corn, please, Lord."

A stack of pink-flowered Haviland china plates rested on the table. Mama Lillian set her own table with a white cloth, linen napkins, silver goblets and sterling flatware—a pattern my mother followed in our own house, where Eva did the setting. Eight, ten, twelve adults and children ate falling-apart roast beef, Janie's crisp fried chicken piled on an oval platter (children got drumsticks only), steaming white rice served from a china bowl with a spoon notch in the lid, thick brown gravy lippin' over the

Janie Graham in Estill

gravy boat, fresh string beans swimming in fat-back liquor, a succotash of okra, tomatoes, corn and butterbeans, and Mama Lillian's watermelon pickles. After all had helped their plates, Janie walked in with a basket of biscuits.

Ah, Janie. Janie Graham was said to be a housewarming gift that a friend bequeathed Van with a warning, "She's mean as a snake." Far from ebullient, Janie nevertheless was a loyal member of the Estill household, along with Ma Mary Riley, the cleaning woman, and Leroy Brown, the yard man and farm hand whose father was a slave to Van's father. Word was that my great-great grandfather Duncan Peeples had been good to the slaves who worked "the Peeples place," as folks called the farm and surroundings. Like many blacks after the emancipation, the Browns chose to remain with their white family into following generations.

But back to Janie. Inside the Peeples' house, Janie was their Eva. Well, not quite. Janie and Eva were as different as a crabapple and a peach—one hard and piquant to the taste, the other soft and sweet on the tongue. Janie, wiry; Eva, thick. Janie stood even shorter than Eva, just up to her shoulder. Janie's skin, black walnut; Eva's, warm chestnut. Janie was sharp around the edges: boney fingers, pointy elbows and knobby knees. Eva, rounded at the corners.

Janie dressed in a makeshift uniform that included a bibbed white apron dotted with spills and spots. Her white cap sat askew. She wore tennis shoes with holes and white socks rolled down to her scrawny ankles. Janie's brow scrunched in a perpetual frown and a low grumble trailed her stirrings. She reminded me of Grumpy in Snow White. Eva's impeccable dress and sunny countenance annoyed Janie no end.

Eva's honing in on Janie's territory didn't help their tenuous relationship. I often wondered how the two fared sharing Janie's house out back or on family vacations to Bluffton on the May River with both Eva and Janie in tow. My earliest memory of Bluffton was when cousin Van, about twelve years old, lost the motor off the boat on the bottom of the river. Neither Eva nor Janie could save him from Daddy Van's wrath.

I believe the battle of the biscuits finally pushed Eva and Janie over the edge of civility. Eva's job was to tend the children. Period. Keep us from running in the house, remind us to flush the toilets, take us outside when we got noisy, as well as bathe and tuck us in at night. In Estill, every day before dawn cracked, even on Sundays, Janie was inside Miss Lillian's kitchen rustling up breakfast.

"Dis yere's my kitchen," she mumbled when Eva entered her space.

Well, one day Eva overstepped her bounds. Why? Because I begged for Eva's biscuits. Eva felt compelled to oblige. Tension mounted as Janie banged pans, shuffled her feet, and escalated her grumbling while Eva quietly rummaged through Janie's pantry, cabinets and drawers to find what she needed.

"Go right on 'bout your bid'ness 'n lemme tend to mine," Eva said quietly. Eva was clearly more polished, more accomplished, and certainly more social than the homespun Janie. She fit right in in the big house in Estill, and nothing was going to deter Eva from stirring up her signature biscuits.

Next thing you know, Eva was serving us her biscuits in the big dining room, face beaming. So began the competition: Eva's fat, fluffy biscuits versus Janie's small, buttery biscuits. Daddy Van was partial to Janie's biscuits, Mama Lillian usually abstained, most of the children liked Eva's bigger biscuits better. I ate both with equal relish—far too many according to my mother.

Things were never the same in Estill after Eva made her biscuits in Janie's kitchen. When we children got big enough to fend for ourselves, Eva stayed home in Moncks Corner when we visited Estill. A surefire relief for Janie.

As we got older, we ate quickly and scampered up the back steps to the big bedrooms on the second floor, where LaClaire, Rusty, cousin Van and I played Parcheesi or checkers. Sundays were sacred: no movies, no cards. Sometimes on Sundays we sneaked upstairs to play Canasta or battle, praying Daddy Van wouldn't catch us. I learned other things upstairs too—sex things. Expressions like "tough titty" if you said something cousin Van didn't like. "Little Van" they called him. As we got older, we sometimes sprawled out on Van's bed to hear tales of his sneaking out at night in Mama's Cadillac to romance his girlfriend Christine. One night I was totally bumfuzzled when he talked about boys "coming." I asked LaClaire.

"You're too young to understand," she said dismissively. But I filed it away. Because we spent so much time in Estill, vacations and summers, when we became teenagers, it was natural that Van's friends became the boys we first dated. LaClaire ended up marrying her Charlie, and I'll always remember my first kiss from brown-eyed Bro Wiggins. Oh, and Van married his Christine. We learned a lot in Estill.

Years before we grandchildren came on the scene, the Peeples' house rang with foot races up the stairs from Van and Lillian's four children. My mother was the firstborn. A serious girl she was, and from her first shy smile, Clara Lee captured her daddy's heart. Firstborns seem to do that. Rudolph, my uncle Rudy, arrived a couple of years later, the prized son to carry on the family lineage. Proud as a peacock, Van passed out fine cigars across Hampton County.

Virginia, "Ginger," came shortly thereafter. Her sunny side showed immediately. Sara, the welcomed late child, was born to Lillian and Van a decade after Ginger's arrival. The whole family fell in love with this beaming baby with the big blue eyes.

The Peeples children grew up in a household very similar to Eva's—lots of unspoken love and no monkey business. Perhaps that explains why Mother felt so comfortable leaving much of our child-rearing to Eva. Like the Edwards, when the church door opened, the Peeples family flocked in. It helped that Lawtonville Baptist Church was just across the side yard. And as in Eva's family, Sunday School training wasn't lost on my mother, who often won the sword drills for finding Bible verses the quickest.

Van and Lillian practiced diehard Southern Baptist rules: no drinking, no smoking, no dancing, and no games on Sundays. Swearing was unheard of—literally. Women didn't wear pants. Everyone in the household was expected to be responsible, do his or her best, and not complain. Living was serious business.

And no one crossed Daddy Van. At home he captained a fair but firm ship. Once when my mother was in high school, she returned home a few minutes after curfew. She felt nervous. So did her date. He'd heard of Mr. Van's strict regulations. The car pulled up to the front walk. No front porch light burned. But in the shadows they made out a figure—Van Peeples, clad in his one-piece long johns, standing like a statue on the top step of the porch. He held a 12-gauge shotgun in his hand pointed directly at the beau.

A beau who never came calling again. But others kept calling. Clara Lee had blossomed into an intelligent, lovely young woman. She'd inherited her father's olive complexion and her mother's quiet demeanor, height five-feet-seven inches, high cheek-bones, and a bonus blessing—two deep dimples.

Clara Lee Peeples

Young Clara Lee adored her father, respected her mother, and exhibited exemplary behavior by keeping the house and church rules as well as excelling in academics, sports, and music. They trained her from birth to be well-spoken, well-groomed, and well-disciplined. She earned the reputation of being an all around "good girl." The school principal wrote on her college recommendation:

Well prepared for strong college courses
Intellectually above average
Thoroughly conscientious and diligent
Conduct and character above reproach

High endorsement for the small-town girl.

Clara Lee's breaks from the serious and sometimes somber life at home and church included summer vacations with family and friends in Bluffton on the May River and at Tybee Beach near Savannah. A yellowed postcard shows the family in their old-timey bathing suits posing for the camera. Mother also worked some summers as a Red Cross Lifesaver Instructor, as her mother Lillian had in her youth. (My sister LaClaire carried on that tradition.) All told, Clara Lee Peeples was quite an accomplished young woman in her corner of the world.

Southern towns are known for festivals celebrating everything from peaches and azaleas to grits and chitlins. Sally, South Carolina, is home of the Chitlin Strut. "Chitlins" are intestines, usually from pigs, for those who might wonder. In college I was the only person in class who knew what Thomas Hardy was referring to in *Tess of the D'urbervilles*, when the father of a poor family says, "Tell 'em at home that I should like for supper . . . lamb's fry if they can get it; and if they can't, black-pot; and if they can't get that, well, chitterlings will do."

A notch or two up from the chitlins, Clara Lee reigned as the Watermelon Festival Queen of Hampton County in her teens. She traveled around the state riding on crepe-paper-flowered floats or on the back of convertible sports cars, her dress spread wide. She waved and smiled to the crowds and danced the nights away with young men eager to win her heart . . . which she saved for my daddy.

The Van Peeples family expected my mother to make an imprint on a larger stage—to become a concert pianist. Music was always a part of the Peeples' family life. It centered around three groups. Lawtonville Baptist Church was the hub of social and musical events in the community, and Clara Lee played piano for many cantatas and concerts. Then there was the Social Dozen, a gathering of elite ladies who brought their handiwork and sewing to enjoy sipping afternoon tea and occasional musical programs. And finally, the Estill Music and Study Club, another women's group, lent an air of sophistication for those who appreciated good literature and classical music.

Did Clara Lee have a proclivity for music, or was she merely drawn to the music that surrounded her? Her diligence cannot be questioned. Most of her growing-up years, my mother rose hours earlier than the rest of the household to practice scales, Chopin, Beethoven and Brahms. Her broad hands spanned beyond an octave; her fingers flew up and down the keyboard. Her father rewarded her perseverance with a grand piano, which they placed in the corner of the large living room that stretched the breadth of the house. Clara Lee frequently gave recitals at home and elsewhere, followed by teas attended by Hampton County music aficionados.

For her efforts, she earned a full music scholarship to Converse College in upstate South Carolina.

Converse was well known as an institution with a reputation for its outstanding music department. At seventeen Clara Lee boarded the train in downtown Estill for Spartanburg, a wooden trunk her only company.

"You make us proud now" was her father's sendoff at the station. She prayed she'd meet his expectations.

Converse College, famous for sending students

Clara Lee at Converse College

to the best music conservatories in the world, seemed the perfect place for Clara Lee to pursue her dream. Begun in 1889, Converse was a finishing school for refined (and refining) young women. Clara Lee herself could have taught the required classes in etiquette and dress. Wear hat, gloves and stockings when leaving campus; keep distance between you and your date when in cars; no hand-holding or public displays of affection—dictums echoing those she grew up with. So the academic and social transition was easy. The school of music, however, presented a challenge.

Her freshman year, she added a strict practice regimen to her academic and social activities. Keeping her scholarship was paramount. And she did . . . until the day her fingers touched the ivory keys for the last time.

That day came after her sophomore piano recital. For two years she had strained under the demanding tutelage of the music department head. She conquered every piece he put before her. She woke with trepidation the day of her recital but afterward felt she had played her best. Anxiously she awaited her professor's critique. From under bushy gray brows, the maestro's eyes locked onto hers.

"Miss Peeples, you have mastered the piano. Your Chopin was technically flawless," a compliment that brought a flutter to her chest. After a pause, his voice flattened, crushing her with these words: "Unfortunately, my dear, you have no ear for music—and that is vital for a career in music."

Clara Lee never touched a keyboard nor sang a note from that day forward. Stoic as stone that fateful day, young Clara Lee spoke not a word, shed not a tear. She changed her major from music to math and chemistry, a fortuitous decision, given how those skills helped her in later years.

Despite Clara Lee's huge disappointment, her college days were largely happy ones. People were drawn to the pretty girl with a ready, dimpled smile. When the sun grazed her brownish short hair, red streaks glimmered. Nearly a dozen organizations occupied her time—from her role as president of the YWCA and vice-president of the International Relations Club to her memberships in the Carlisle Literary Society and the swim team. She also assisted in the chemistry laboratory; she actually knew the components of 5-10-10 fertilizer that she sold years later. Clearly a popular student at Converse College, this gregarious image of my mother in college remained an enigma to me.

She did keep one habit she picked up in college: smoking.

"Everyone did back then," she said. It would come back to plague her.

Growing up, she watched the father she adored create thick, round puffs of smoke from his cigar while sitting in his leather chair after supper. The sweet, sharp tobacco smell wafted toward her as she played the piano for him. His smoking, however, didn't give license to his children to smoke. Certainly not women! Until the day her daddy died, Clara Lee never smoked in his presence. Ladies should be ladies, and she was—until October 4, 1935, the day she eloped with Buster Williams.

Clara Lee's breach of protocol was minor compared to the blows the family experienced that would have rocked the stability of those with less fortitude. But Van Peeples had not built his house of straw or sticks. The big bad wolf could not blow down Daddy Van's house of bricks, though he tried several times.

The first strike came early. My uncle Rudy, the Peeples' heir apparent, was just nine years old. From servants to sisters, the household fawned over little Rudy. Everyone said he was a miniature of his father—handsome, sturdy, quiet, and inquisitive.

One day Rudy was playing with Bubba Shoe Riley, Ma Mary's son who lived behind the house. They rooted out some 22-gauge shells from Daddy Van's gun closet in the hall and went outside to figure a way to make the shells pop. I can envision Rudy's small fingers beating a brass shell on the concrete bench on the front porch. Nothing happened. Ingenious little fellows, they moved to the yard where Rudy placed a shell on a brick. He smashed the shell with another brick—POW! The shell's casing shattered as the boys fell backwards. Rudy felt a searing pain in his eye and cried out.

Rudy, Ginger and Clara Lee Peeples

The ride to a Savannah hospital an hour away must have seemed endless to Mama Lillian, her son not making a sound in Ma Mary's arms in the back seat of the car. After a grueling operation, the doctors declared too much damage had been done. Only weeks away from his tenth birthday, the explosion left Rudy without a left eye.

Uncle Rudy wore a glass eye for the rest of his life. Although it moved in sync, it never quite matched the right one. In an oval-framed picture of the three Peeples' children, Rudy in his sailor suit stands on a wicker chair beside his sister Ginger; big sister Clara Lee stands beside the chair. Rudy's head is turned slightly so that a shadow is cast over his bad eye.

This shadow followed Uncle Rudy thereafter. His affinity for alcohol began early—before he had a chance to measure up to his father's expectations. A disciplined man of faith, Van Peeples believed the solution simple.

"Just turn your back on the demon drink," he instructed Rudy. But sons cannot be saved by fathers' admonitions.

Uncle Rudy was the only uncle I've ever had. He seemed a clone of Daddy Van, except softer in body and manner. I loved it when he bent way down to encircle me with one of his warm hugs. He visited us in Moncks Corner when his Merchant Marine ship sailed into Charleston Harbor. I didn't realize that he spent the bulk of his time sleeping off a hangover in our guest room. Eva often came to Rudy's temporary aid.

*Uncle Rudy
as a Merchant Marine*

"This Miss Clara Lee boy," Eva said, and did what she did best . . . started cooking. Rudy awoke from his heavy or fitful sleeps to the smell of percolating coffee and frying salmon cakes. He'd amble into the kitchen and wrap a thick arm around Eva and muster a sweet, sad smile for us both.

"Mista Rudy, God de

onliest one can help you lick that drink," Eva'd say.

"I know. I know," he'd whisper, looking at the floor.

I was in college when Mother called to tell me that Uncle Rudy had died—run over by a train. On purpose? Who knows. Inebriated? Most certainly. No matter, the passing of this promising Peeples son scorched the heart of those of us who loved a dear man that alcohol grabbed by the throat and wouldn't let go.

And years later, had Daddy Van known my daddy smuggled Jim Beam into his suitcase on our Estill visits, he'd have thrown him over the upstairs banister. I pictured the scene in my head many times. One day I spied the bottle and spilled the beans to Eva that Daddy was packing alcohol. Back then, I had a terrible tendency to tattle. "*Tattletale, go to jail. Hang your britches on a nail.*" LaClaire and Rusty often taunted me with that ditty. Eva's dark eyes bored into mine.

"You best tend yo' own red wagon, missy," she said. It was never a good sign when Eva called me "missy." Even in Estill, Eva never let up.

Aunt Ginger visited us lots too. Eva perked up during those visits and fixed fried chicken and banana pudding "to put some meat on dem skinny bones," she'd joke. I perched on the kitchen stool wrapped in the bubble of their banter as Ginger flicked her fingers through my flaxen curls. Eva liked to wind my hair tightly around her sausage fingers making ringlets that covered my head and bounced prettily when I skipped.

Aunt Ginger added zest to the Peeples family. Outgoing, adventuresome, fun loving—the opposite of her older, quieter sister Clara Lee. How she loved to dance. *The State* listed Virginia Peeples among those who made their debuts at the Assembly Ball hosted by "that notable organization of Columbia society matrons" and marked by "brilliance and distinctive dignity" at the Jefferson Hotel. I'm sure she had no trouble filling her dance card while she jitterbugged to Buster Span and his orchestra that evening.

Aunt Ginger was a flirt too. She'd cut those

sparkly eyes to any man around, whether her brother-in-law Buster or some dashing pilot she had in tow after she became an airline "stewardess," as they were called then. One day she met and fell in love with Guy Seashole, an exuberant, wealthy widower and Florida hunting buddy of her daddy. Guy was 68, Ginger 32. Uncle Guy and Daddy Van, contemporaries, were fast friends and killed many a deer together.

The couple was blessed with a young son named Sammy. They lived a charmed life on the St. John's River in Jacksonville, Florida. When my parents deemed me old

Virginia "Ginger" Peeples Seashole

enough, I took my first train ride. Daddy had the train stop at the Moncks Corner depot, and I rode it by myself all the way to Jacksonville, Florida. The highlight—traipsing up and down the aisle to the water-jug cooler where I filled countless pointy paper cups with water. No surprise I had to ask the conductor where the bathroom was. The plan was for me to babysit young Sammy. I stayed a couple of weeks in their huge glass house overlooking the river, Aunt Ginger spoiling me along with Sammy. She never let either one of us out of her sight.

I lost a treasured possession on the train ride home: my first big-girl purse. Mother let me pick out a small, black velvet, conical-shaped pocketbook topped with a red flower. It closed with a sturdy snap, not little balls that clicked, like Eva's. A change slot for pennies, nickels, dimes and quarters attached to the underside of the round top. Inside I had a few coins, a pack of Juicy Fruit gum and a letter that

Mother had written to me while I was in Jacksonville.

"Where yo new purse, Baby?" Eva asked as she helped me unpack.

Where was it??? I'd left it on the train! Eva brushed my tears away. I pouted for days, but as luck would have it, a lady found it on the train's seat and noted the letter's salutation and the postal mark. A week later I received a package from Washington, DC, addressed to BUGS, Moncks Corner, S.C.

No one called me "Angela," most called me "Angie," but "Bugs" was my nickname in the family. My two big front teeth sported a gap I could put my finger through, just like Bugs Bunny in Saturday cartoons. Guess the postmaster knew everything. Only in a small town!

Some years after my train trip, Uncle Guy died suddenly of a heart attack. Aunt Ginger's world buckled. She lost both her love and her lavish lifestyle. She turned to the bottle . . . and my mother. I noticed that Ginger's silver, china and antique vases quietly appeared in the cabinets and tables in our house. When Ginger was struggling to make ends meet, Mother bought her household items to tide her over. Striving to find her equilibrium, she finally hit bottom, living in a car with barely enough money for bread and booze. Sweet Ginger eventually died of sclerosis of the liver. My grandparents buried their second child in the Peeples' plot, another victim of the demon drink.

Sara Peeples

Arriving a full ten years after Ginger, my aunt Sara's birth was a happy surprise for the Peeples household. Clara Lee, however, found it a bit embarrassing to tell her college friends that her mother was prenant because such subjects were taboo. Hair of spun gold and a sunny smile, Sara brought delight to the entire family. She grew into the clichéd gorgeous Southern blonde. Along with her sisters, Sara inherited the Peeples' high cheekbones (striking), nose (prominent) and deep dimples (irresistible). She became a beauty queen at the University of South Carolina, with an attraction to strapping football players.

After college, Sara married and had a baby named Stevie. While in a Denver hospital giving birth to Stevie, Sara was diagnosed with a brain tumor. Mama Lillian flew to Denver for the operation. The doctors removed the malignant tumor. Unfortunately they also disturbed a portion of the brain that controlled emotional stability. What a solemn day when doctors gave my grandmother the sad prognosis that Sara, barely in her twenties, wouldn't be capable of rearing the child she'd just birthed. And the father was long gone—or so we thought.

The next day, my mother, the ever-responsible daughter and sister, flew to Denver to pick up little cousin Stevie, only a few weeks old. That's how Stevie became my baby. But that comes later.

The stigma of mental health issues haunted our family, both sides, for years. "She's resting on Bull Street," Mother explained when I asked where Aunt Sara was during one of her long absences. I didn't realize until I was older that "Bull Street" was a euphemism for South Carolina's state mental institution located on Bull Street in Columbia. "Asylum" remains embossed on the outside of the building. Sara died many years later, well cared for in a nursing home near my sister, who met all her needs . . . just as Mother, Sara's big sister, would have it. No one probed the elephant.

Amazingly, the tragedies that plagued my mother's family never overshadowed the outright joy of going to Estill. Christmas holidays, summer vacations, birthday celebrations. In the early days, we piled into Daddy's latest Oldsmobile and hunkered down for the two-hour drive, sometimes waving to the families picking cotton in the fields we passed. Mother and Daddy up front, Eva in the back with Rusty tucked under one arm, LaClaire under another, and me in her lap.

We drove to Estill on Christmas Day after opening Santa's presents.

"We're going to Estill! We're going to Estill!" I chanted, skipping down the hall to pack my pj's and new bride doll. It was to Estill we went every summer for weeks at a time. We sang "Jesus Loves Me" at Bible School across the street. We swam at Davis Swimming Pool until our finger tips folded like prunes. And it was in Estill that Mama Lillian made caramel cakes like heavenly manna, which she always declared "not up to usual." In Estill LaClaire met the shy boy she'd eventually marry, and I got my first kiss in the backseat of a 1954 Ford. A halo surrounded most of my memories of Estill, even after Daddy Van died.

"Has you heard from Mista Van lately?" Eva asked one morning when she took a breakfast tray to Mother.

"No. Why?" Mother said.

"You might wana get in tetch with Miss Lillian," Eva said as she looked down at the carpet. By this time, we knew about Eva's premonitions. We didn't take them lightly. She'd wake up on a blue-sky morning and declare, "Hit be raining by noon." She dreamed the cotton gin caught fire, and the next night it did. And she predicted people were "going to cross over," and they died. Sure enough, my grandfather Daddy Van had suffered the last of his three heart attacks just hours before Eva warned us.

Young and old clustered around the Peeples fenced plot at Lawtonville Cemetery near the Peeples old homeplace. Even the oak trees surrounding the graveyard mourned, their mossy shawls hanging heavy. Van Peeples' funeral was a sad day for hundreds who knew him in his prime, watched him build a thriving farming business, witnessed his devotion to his wife and his church, and marveled at his strength of spirit in spite of the troubles that battered each of his children—Rudy, Ginger, Sara, and eventually my mother Clara Lee.

I stood in the shade looking at the freshly

turned dirt that would cover Daddy Van's casket. I smelled the musky earth, thinking how many years he worked it, how much he loved it. A sliver of light glanced off a shiny oak leaf, and I smiled inside. I remembered the drives to my grandparents. Leaning forward to the front seat, asking, "Are we there yet?" at Summerville, at Walterboro, at Snyder's Crossing, at Varnville. Finally we'd arrive in Estill to see Mama Lillian and Daddy Van standing on the porch with welcoming smiles.

But there were few smiles this day. Under the shadow of the old tree, Mama Lillian held onto her daughter Clara Lee's arm as she would for the remainder of her life, the strength transferred. She fingered a lace handkerchief, occasionally dabbing an eye. Her straight shoulders started to curve that day, the day she buried her life's mate, the Peeples' patriarch.

Clara Lee's loss, however, was indiscernible, unfathomable. She and her father shared an understood love, no less ardent than a voiced one. She stared dry-eyed as the minister tossed soil on the grave, stood erect as her mother's arm pressed into her side. Did she suspect that from this day forward, she, the eldest child of Van Peeples, would become the ballast for her mother . . . her siblings . . . their children . . . her own children?

My mother's rock was buried that day. Only the women were left, the Peeples women—and Eva.

Where is Eva? I wondered, returning from my reverie. When Eva's parents, Aunt Hattie and Daddy Bill, died, her people invited us to the funeral and treated us like family. *Had we not asked Eva to come? She's family! Why isn't she here?*

Eva loved her Mister Van as much as any of the people at the gravesite. And wasn't she the first to know he'd "gone home to Jesus"? Yes, I mourned that day for my grandfather. But I also mourned something larger, something I couldn't then name— the invisible divide between Eva's world and mine.

Chapter 3

The Catch of the Lowcountry

While one is still grandiose and naïve, a young man lives inside, shiny-faced, expectant, hopeful, dandified, a prince.
—Robert Bly

Clara Lee would continue to plumb the Peeples' courage, as she had since the day her heart ran away with that dashing Berkeley County boy who became my daddy. Who was this valiant young man who swept my mother off her feet on the brink of marrying another? A man who would exhilarate and exasperate her for decades to come. She'd never even met his family until the day after they said their "I do's" in front of a justice of the peace in the small South Carolina town of Barnwell, known back then for quickie marriages. Undaunted, the newly married couple rode a romantic high as they crossed two county lines in my daddy's new Oldsmobile coupe to face the Williams family.

Buster Williams's homeplace of Pinopolis, far more intriguing than Clara Lee's peaceful Estill in Hampton County, lay smack in the middle of Berkeley County where bootlegging and assassinations wrapped around its history. A rough and tumble place in the 1900s, Berkeley County was where folks carried a gun and didn't worry about the law. Local politicians went itching for a fight. Stories abound of Hell Hole Swamp dotted with stills that supplied liquor to Chicago and New York during Prohibition. Shootings weren't uncommon.

As they breezed through Moncks Corner, did Buster tell his new bride about the big shootout during Prohibition? Probably, because my daddy loved to tell a tale.

When Daddy was a boy, *The State*, Columbia's newspaper, aptly labeled the county "bloody Berkeley." Senator E. J. Dennis of Pinopolis, a family friend, was assassinated on Main Street walking to the post office in broad daylight. The Dennises lived across the dirt road from the Williams family in Pinopolis. The Senator's son, Rembert, was Daddy's childhood friend and later godfather to my brother Rusty.

The elder Senator Dennis, born and bred a hard-shelled Baptist, was hell-bent on wiping out the county's lucrative illegal whiskey industry. Most prominent folks turned a blind eye to Prohibition. The locals joked that it was a battle between the Baptists and the Whiskeypalians. In a letter from the South Carolina Penitentiary to Senator Dennis's widow, the assassin claimed he was bribed with a car, money—and liquor. Moonshine, no doubt.

The hired shooter also named county leaders, my godfather Dr. Kershaw Fishburne among them, as conspirators in the assassination plot. When the dust settled, Mrs. Dennis, a stalwart Christian woman, visited and took food to her husband's killer. That's what good Christian women did in the South.

Corn liquor flowed freely in the county before, during and after Prohibition. Years later Eva was holding my hand walking down that same Main Street when she made one of her spiritual pronouncements. It was the day of Glenny McKnight's funeral, a man notorious for his underground "white lightnin" or "moonshine" operation. When his hearse passed through town, the sky turned black, so dark that the street lights came on. Eva clicked her tongue to her teeth, "tch, tch," and shook her head.

"God done spoke. Mista' Glenny ain't gonna get tru the pearly gates," she said.

Eva knew these things. Seemed a shame to me. I loved the shine of the moon. Eva didn't explain. The man I knew owned Green Gables Grocery. When asked to pick up a loaf of bread, I biked to

Mr. McKnight's store so I'd pass the house of a boy I was sweet on. Why in the world did everybody have a conniption fit over the word "moonshine"? But I didn't know much back then.

On that ride with his bride, did Buster weave a snapshot history of the provincial town of Monck's Corner? If so, he might have told her that it grew up around a vital Indian crossroad of the Cherokee Path at the headwaters of commercial navigation on the Cooper River near the port at Charles Towne. (The original spelling for the community settled in 1670 was Charles Towne, later changed to Charleston.) In 1753 an astute English businessman, Thomas Monck, bought considerable property at this juncture and opened a store . . . on a corner. At this time commerce came more easily over water than through the rough overland terrain to Charles Towne.

After her husband Thomas died, Mary Monck kept the first store in this hamlet—probably one of the first female proprietors in the Lowcountry. Later, Charleston stores like Dumas opened branches to sell hunting paraphernalia. Several taverns operated there as well. Planters traveled to Colonial Monck's Corner, then merely called "the Corner," to sell crops, attend to business, and dine at taverns on their way home.

So, how did my father end up in Berkeley County, where the family broke from a long tradition of being preachers? Best I can tell, my great-grandfather Thomas Williams lived in the village of Mt. Pleasant across the Cooper River from Charleston. Originally, Berkeley County's seat of justice was in Mt. Pleasant, and Thomas served as clerk of court. However, when the first Cooper River Bridge was built to connect Charleston to Mt. Pleasant, Mt. Pleasant became part of Charleston County. Moncks Corner then became the seat of Berkeley County. These changes altered the location of my great-grandfather's career. This, in turn, influenced his son as well as my father. Thomas moved his family to the hinterlands in order to continue serving as Berkeley County clerk of court.

Situated under a large stand of virgin yellow and long-leaf pines thirty miles from Charleston, Pinopolis was settled in the early 1800s by families trying to escape the dreaded malaria fever that haunted plantations in hot summers. In 1834 it had only two permanent families. Locals built a post office in 1894 that still stands today. At the end of the 18th century, the county itself had about 103,000 slaves to some 30,000 whites. The slaves were largely responsible for producing the lucrative crops of indigo, then later rice and cotton—the cotton that produced the livelihood of the Williams family for over three generations, a tradition that began with Thomas Williams's decision to keep his job. By the time my daddy was born in 1909, about thirty white families and a handful of blacks called Pinopolis home.

Many prominent Berkeley County people lived a couple of miles up the road from Moncks Corner (apostrophe dropped) in this tiny village of Pinopolis. And that's where Thomas Williams, his wife Carrie and their two teenagers settled—back into the very land of his ancestors who left Europe to find religious freedom in America.

Thumbing back through time, I've learned that the Williams men originated from sturdy English stock with more than a dollop of Christian zeal, a dash of leadership and a pinch of rebellion. My daddy developed two of those traits in spades. Who'd have believed my daddy's family was churning out preachers from way back?

"I knowed Mista Busta come from good stock," Eva said when she heard about the passel of preachers. "Knowed it when I set my eyes on that boy." Though I tried, I myself never saw the religious connection. When I was growing up, the only spiritual bent I noticed was C-and-E religion—my father's Christmas-Easter church attendance. Eva's the one who donned her Sunday best and headed for church every Sunday. Way back in the family, though, it was a different story.

Daddy's great-grandfather was the Reverend West Williams, a Methodist minister and a Confederate veteran. He and his brother Stephen became Circuit Riders, ordained itinerant ministers as well as prominent planters. Because Circuit Riders remained in one location for no more than two years, and the church promised only $100 a year, many left their itinerant ministry and worked in local churches or supplied nearby churches when a shortage of ministers occurred during the Civil War. My great-great-grandfather West Williams, for instance, began preaching in the upstate on the Reedy River. But when appointed to Charleston, he decided to settle down at Spring Hill, a hamlet northwest of Pinopolis. He preached there for about fifty years. His portrait shows a handsome, square-faced, serious man.

The Reverend West Williams Methodist preacher and prominent planter

The Williams brothers, West and Stephen, both in the thick of church and political life, were respected for their largess as well as their leadership. In the mid-1800s Reverend Stephen Williams built a fine new house in Sand Ridge in upper Berkeley County to get away from "swamp fever" (malaria). It had already killed his wife and all seven of his children. A small group worshipped for a time under a bramble bush at the top of a knoll when Stephen challenged the congregation to build a church at Spring Hill. This spot was so tucked away in Berkeley County that when Mother died over a century later, half of the funeral guests got lost driving to the cemetery. West Williams was treasurer of the building committee and his brother Stephen was the largest contributor for the Spring Hill Methodist Church.

Among the more recent graves is Daddy's—and later Mother's, at his feet.

So when looking for a spot to settle in Pinopolis, it seems appropriate that Thomas, my daddy's grandfather, put down roots within spitting distance of the Methodist Church in the village. In fact, everybody in the county, black and white, attended church—not only to worship but also to socialize, gather news, and politick.

When Eva and I talked about church-going (her to the Baptist, my grandparents to the Methodist, Daddy to the Episcopal), she made things clear. "Jes keep the Sabbath holy, Baby. Don't matter where it be." When I got old enough to notice, I asked Eva why blacks and whites went to different churches. "It always be that way. Ain't no nevermind, chile," she whispered, not eager to elaborate.

But I learned it wasn't always that way. As a teenager, I often attended St. Philip's and St. Michael's in downtown Charleston. I did know then that the balconies we rushed to sit in were designed for black worshippers. I also knew that the view was worse up there. When did worshipping in the same building cease? I wonder whether Eva knew about Henry McNeal Turner, a black man born in upstate South Carolina. Two lawyers in Abbeville took the bright boy under wing, securing him a solid education. Turner had an actual dream in which blacks had their own freestanding church. When his vision became a reality, it caused an uproar among whites and blacks following the Civil War when tension was already high. Eventually Turner became bishop of the African-Methodist Episcopal Church and preached, "God is a Negro."

Most congregations made no fuss when blacks broke away from side entrances and galleries of the white churches to form their own churches. Members of Spring Hill Methodist (where West and his brother Stephen preached) actually provided the land, a church and a parsonage for Ebenezer Christian Methodist Church—the first black church in the area. The Methodist families like the Williamses in

England had left their home countries to cross the Atlantic seeking freedom, and they could readily identify with the plight of blacks and their thirst for sovereignty.

I doubt my daddy knew much about black history back then; it certainly wasn't taught in schools. But he was aware that blacks comprised a good percentage of the population in rural Berkeley County where he grew up. Even so, it wasn't proper newlywed conversation, and not as titillating as the tales of his boyhood.

Yet those blacks who settled in the Lowcountry were by no means all slaves. Negroes were freed as a reward for public service or by individual owners out of love and affection. Many worked and saved to buy their own land—just as Eva's parents did. Records bear out that South Carolina was unusual; blacks and whites respected each other from the earliest days—which would prove a blessing as our country struggled during the Civil Rights era. And a blessing to our family, which included a descendant of freed slaves, Eva Edwards Motte Aiken. "Ain't it something? A white man's religion set us free," Eva spoke to the air one day. I had not an inkling what she meant at the time.

Unlike Daddy Van's and Mama Lillian's families, there's no official record of the Williamses owning slaves. Eva's family lived and worked on Moss Grove Plantation, but it seems they were sharecropping as free persons. Many blacks worked for white families through the years and apparently were well taken care of. Often the loyalty was reciprocated.

An example close to home was the time the Hartwell Raiders, who ransacked the Lowcountry during the Civil War, approached Moss Grove Plantation—the very land Eva's family lived on and land my grandfather and father would hold years later. With the owner away fighting with the Confederates, Henry Brown, the black overseer, hid all the livestock in the swamp. He told the Raiders that he was a free Negro and owned the place. The band of Northern soldiers and freed blacks from the

Sea Islands believed the lie. They bothered nothing at Moss Grove.

The Raiders also hit another plantation. LeRoy Neal, a white manager who worked for Maria Porcher, hid her French china piece by piece at the bottom of a mosquito-infested pond to save the valuables from the Raiders, who burned and looted anything in their path. When they stood LeRoy up behind the smoke house to shoot him, a black man named John Grant ran out to stand in front of him saying, "If you kill Massa Roy, you have to kill me too." They shot neither.

Eva knew far more history about the struggle between blacks and whites than my father. Far more than she let on, according to her relative Samuel Taylor, a Berkeley County man who became a prominent Civil Rights activist—under wraps in South Carolina and out front in New Jersey. But Eva never talked to me about such things.

Did Eva know that the tenuous relationship of state to national government had its genesis in South Carolina—with men like my daddy's great-grandfather, the Rev. West Williams? As a member of a States Rights (anti-tariff) Committee, West backed Charleston's John C. Calhoun's contention that states could nullify federal laws that went beyond the Constitution. He also served as a member of the Resolution Committee, which eventually led to South Carolina's being the first state to secede from the Union. Six states followed South Carolina's lead and seceded from the United States. Anti-secessionist James Petrigrew in 1860 assessed his home state as "too small to be a republic and too large to be an asylum."

This secession resulted in The War, also referred to as the Civil War, the War Between the States, the War of Secession, the War of Northern Aggression, or "the late unpleasantness," as Lowlanders and some texts refer to the conflict. In a final display of leadership, West Williams served as a commander in the Confederate Army from 1862 to 1865. If you drive around the South, you see so many Confederate monuments, you'd think the South won the war. I'd give my eyeteeth to know whether my great-great-grandfather believed the breech was over state's rights . . . or slavery. Or both.

But Thomas Williams, West's son, was *not* a preacher. He married his sweetheart Carrie Mellard Wiggins and settled in Mt. Pleasant, a small village situated in Berkeley County at the time. When he agreed to serve as clerk of court, he had no idea the county seat would change to Moncks Corner and precipitate a move.

Thomas was forty-three when he and Carrie moved to settle in Pinopolis with their two teenage children—Russell (sixteen) and Maude (fifteen), my grandfather and great aunt. Thomas, prominent in the public affairs of Berkeley County, served thirty-six years as clerk of court, a position both his son and grandson Buster would hold in subsequent years.

Buster and Grandparents

Did Buster ever show Clara Lee the somber picture of him sitting between his two austere grandparents, Thomas and Carrie, on the tall steps of the house that Thomas built in the mid-1800s? What a splendid structure three generations of Williamses called home.

When my mother first glimpsed Daddy's home, did she have any idea that she'd be living there with his family for six years, long after their first child was born? Did she see the house the way I did years later during our regular Sunday visits? Looming large, the wooden structure seemed to grow out of the ground with brick-pillared trunks. Broad porches with high rails wrapped arms around the two stories. Smoke belched out of four chimneys in winter. The kitchen off to the side of the back porch. Inside, the wide hallway lined with stuffed animals—squirrels, owls, deer heads—staring. Lots of deer heads. Lots of eyes staring. Bright yellow canaries chirping from cages in the corners. High-ceilinged bedrooms upstairs with huge poster beds.

A children's paradise beckoned outside the Williams house in Pinopolis. Huge holly trees lined the property to ward off witches and winds. A nymph spitting water in a reflection pool with goldfish to feed, magnolias with drooping limbs to climb, and a tent of juicy brownish-green scuppernongs to gobble. A pointy-roofed cottage near the grape arbor housed hundreds of canaries. When I cracked the door, I was assaulted by twittering sounds and caustic smells.

However, alluring aromas of burning wood and smoked sausage came from the servant's quarters. Jacob Bash's unpainted two-room home was a perfect replica of an old slave cabin. A stone's throw from the main house, the tiny house looked like a dollhouse to me. The only light came

Jacob Bash's Cabin

from four openings bracketed by wooden shutters poised to close in bad weather. A fireplace, table and rocking chair occupied one room. A rope bed and bench in the other. A kerosene lamp darkened with soot perched on a pine shelf. Newspapers covered the wall planks to keep the cold from seeping through the cracks. No bathroom or kitchen.

Jacob's skin shone like licorice. He and his older brother Jim had been the Williamses' domos since they were teenagers. I never knew Jim. Rumor had it that Jacob had a family on highway 17A and played a mean game of poker. Jacob was "well-spoken with an air of elegance about him," according to Bea Dennis, a neighbor, who noted it was unusual to have a man servant. Village folks enjoyed seeing Jacob stride through the village in a starched white uniform and cap; it meant my great aunt Maude was sending cakes or cookies to someone who was sick, had a baby or a birthday. Newlyweds like Anne and Kershaw Fishburne looked forward to Jacob's arrival in a cotton coat and white gloves holding a silver tray with one of Maude's bountiful suppers.

Jacob Bash

A favorite old family picture shows Jacob at day's end sitting in an Adirondack chair, his legs casually crossed, white cap on his head, full apron over his dark pants and tattered shirt, and a shiny-faced smile inviting you to join him for a little mischief.

Jacob was the second black person I came to love, but nobody topped my Eva. Jacob beamed when he saw my chubby legs struggling up the tall back steps of the Pinopolis house every Sunday. He lifted me high and set me down in front of a thick pine shelf on the porch. With ceremony, he handed my sister and me a wooden mallet and a canvas sack with a chunk of ice. The ice truck delivered huge ice blocks covered with thick canvas. Jacob stored the blocks in a wooden ice box and chiseled it off in hunks for such occasions. Jacob stood to the side, thick arms folded, grinning like a Cheshire while we bashed and banged the bag to crush the ice small enough to fill the sweet-tea glasses for dinner. At Sunday dinners in Pinopolis, I liked placing the iced tea spoon on the little glass coaster with a notch for the neck of the spoon. No dripping spoon on my aunt Maude's table cloth!

Was Eva a tad jealous of our Sundays in Pinopolis, and my allegiance to Jacob for just one day? When she headed to her church, and we went to Pinopolis, she sometimes joked with me. "Now don't you let Mista Jacob steal none o' my sugar," she'd say. She needn't have worried. Eva was the only one I let nuzzle my neck to steal sugar.

Long before I was born (or Daddy, for that matter), the Pinopolis house bustled with Williamses— Thomas, Carrie and their teenagers, Russell and Maude. Thomas had in his employ a cook, a chamber maid, a laborer, and a janitor. The house brimmed with Southern hospitality and Lowcountry food. By the time Russell and Maude were in their twenties, the family had six servants to help with daily living and with relatives who visited often.

Carrie's brother, J.B. Lawton Wiggins, visited the Williams family frequently. He greatly influenced my grandfather Russell to break with the family's Methodist tradition. Wiggins, a graduate of the University of the South, the prestigious Episcopal college for young men in Tennessee, became a Greek professor at twenty. By age thirty-two, he had become chancellor of the University of the South, or Sewanee, as it's called.

Wiggins was an important force in Southern education at the close of the 19th century when Reconstruction focused on technical and vocational schools. He believed strongly that the original vision for universities that provided a liberal arts and classics curriculum served all students best, regardless of their prospective professions. His strategy was rewarded in 1908 when the Association of Southern Universities and Colleges voted to make his curriculum compulsory for all its members.

Russell admired his uncle and relished his stays with Pinopolis relatives. It was no surprise that Russell chose Sewanee when he became college age. My grandfather loved the rugged Tennessee mountains and the proximity to his favorite uncle. He became a strong student as well as the manager of the football team. During that time, Russell grew to six-feet-two inches and was good-looking as all getout. Later he added a bowler hat and a cigar for panache.

It came as a big surprise, however, when he eschewed his Methodist heritage and turned Episcopalian while at Sewanee. Fortuitously, young Russell stayed connected to his lively Methodist cousins who lived at The Rocks Plantation in Eutawville. Half-day carriage rides between the two families were not uncommon. On one such weekend, the dashing Russell met a raven-haired beauty at a holiday dance hosted by his cousin who attended Converse College.

When the hand-written invitation to his cousin's party arrived, my grandfather Russell had recently graduated from Sewanee. He no doubt brightened because he enjoyed the rollicking weekends of dancing, eating, drinking, and hunting—hunting in particular, for game and girls. Plantation parties brought in men on horseback and women in carriages from far corners of the state. They sojourned for days, enjoying the festivities, which included accomplished riding and shooting from the ladies as well as the gentlemen; feasting on game and specialty pastries; and dancing, which lasted long into the night until all were exhausted, but not too tired to stroll through the Connors' garden.

Olive Bardin

From the moment he laid eyes on Olive Bardin, the keen, brown-eyed beauty from Charleston, my grandfather was infatuated. I fantasized what it must have been like that first weekend. Their dancing, a sight to see. Less than five feet, Olive barely reached the chest of the tall young man dressed in tails who gazed down at her with a smitten smile. After the dance, they strolled arm-in-arm through the rose garden with a white moon shining above. On the daily outings, did Olive, an accomplished equestrian, outride Russell on the hunts? Did he outshoot her on those fox chases?

A sparkling outsider like Olive turned many an eye. In her senior picture at Converse College, Olive wore a cap and tassel and a black robe draped around her high-collared dress, luxuriant black hair piled high upon her head. A quotation under the picture belies her serious look:

> Heart on her lips and soul within her eyes,
> Soft as her clime, and sunny as her skies.

A text continues, attesting that Olive is "pretty to look at, and her company is a pleasure at all times. Her hearty laugh reveals an inner nature as jolly." No hint of Olive's dark, enigmatic side. She's also pictured with the Golf Club and the Tennis Club, the most petite in both groups. The first three years she studied the traditional English, history, Bible, math, and French courses, in addition to piano and art—the latter ultimately becoming her passion and her undoing. Her senior term she delved deeper, taking courses in French history, physics and philosophy. A classic education with depth.

Did my granddaddy learn anything that weekend about his sweetheart's family? Could he imagine that Olive would one day entice him to try city life in Birmingham among her relatives? Did my grandfather have an inkling that most Bardins immigrating to the new country originated as Bardinsteins, possibly members of the Jewish bourgeoisie in the Ukraine? Did he know anything at all about her family?

Olive's parents, Isaac V. Bardin and Martha Washington Exum, grew up on neighboring farms in rural Williamsburg County, South Carolina. In time the friends married, Martha sixteen years younger than Isaac, the age difference not uncommon at the time.

My grandmother Olive was the baby, the last

of the Bardins' eight children. Isaac moved his family to Charleston and became a prosperous cotton broker, first as Bardin & Pittman, then Bardin & Murdoch, at the corner of Brown's Wharf and 7 Prioleau Street. The family of ten lived in a sprawling Greek Revival brick house that still stands at 214 Calhoun Street on the Charleston peninsular.

There's a bit of intrigue in the family about the time Olive was a teenager. According to Thomas Stoney's history, during the ownership by the Bardin family, the Calhoun Street house was connected with the unsolved 1899 slaying of Thomas Pinckney, Jr., a young attorney. Pinckney was found across the street in the graveyard of Bethel Methodist Church, having been shot twice in the back. He died two days later without naming his killer. He was said to have been "visiting a Miss Bardin on the night of the shooting." Closed hearings were held, no charges were filed, and the details of the case were never made public. Could the feisty Olive have been involved? Was she sent out of town temporally to stay with the family of her uncle Culpepper Exum in Birmingham? Hmm.

It's likely that the Bardin and Williams families came to know each other since both became traders in the cotton business. Olive's father died in Charleston, and her mother continued to reside downtown before moving to live with another daughter in West Virginia.

Did Olive ever talk about her parents or tell her son Buster of her own childhood? Did she take him to see his Bardin grandparents' impressive stone-cross grave markings in Charleston's Magnolia Cemetery overlooking the Cooper River? Isaac Bardin died ten years before his grandson, my daddy, was born. His grandmother Martha only two months before his birth. Sadly, my father never met his maternal grandparents.

After a fairy-tale courtship, the magical, mysterious Olive Exum Bardin pledged her troth to the respectable, promising James Russell Williams. Both attractive, well-educated and fun-loving, the couple seemed a match made in heaven. It wasn't.

My grandmother's presence in Pinopolis elicited some jealousy because of her beauty and no little envy because of her audacity to defy tradition. Villagers said, "She did exactly as she pleased." An avid horsewoman, Olive was the first to respond to the horn echoing through the pines signaling fox hunters to gather at the Fishburne's place. A legend persists about this wisp of a woman galloping on her black stallion down the Pinopolis road, her flowing black hair the only covering of her bare torso.

When the newness of marital passion wore off, the high-spirited, sophisticated young woman felt constrained by the bucolic life in rugged Berkeley County. Still spinning from Olive's charm, in an effort to please, my young grandfather consented to move to Birmingham where Olive's uncle Culpepper Exum was mayor. Records show that Russell was associated with the Jemison Real Estate and Insurance Company. My daddy, James Russell Williams, Jr., (Buster) was born there in 1909. Russell was twenty-six, Olive, twenty-three.

But like my other grandfather Van Peeples, city life couldn't hold Russell Williams. The Lowcountry land beaconed. When my daddy turned three years old, they moved back to Pinopolis where his father became a successful cotton factor for a number of years, being associated with William Ravenel and Company of Charleston. His mother Olive didn't stay long. She was none too pleased with the slow pace and isolation of rural life, and possibly Russell's long hours working, hunting or gambling with his friends.

When Russell and Olive moved back to Berkeley Country with their toddler son, Olive's city-girl spirit couldn't be corralled in the Pinopolis village. My grandfather never knew quite what to do with his feisty wife who did not fit into the life-

Trinity Episcopal Rectory
Home for a time.

style of tending children, growing flowers, and cooking for church picnics . . . or into a household where his sister Maude ruled the roost.

Some effort must have been made to give Olive much-needed space because for a short while he rented the Episcopal parsonage only a football-field's length from his parents' home. Daddy once showed us where he carved his initials JRW into the doorframe.

When Eva worried about our falling out of the unscreened windows in the Pinopolis house, Daddy regaled us with a funny story of the time when he was a toddler living in that tall rectory. One moonlit night he left his upstairs bedroom walking in his sleep. A white moon glowed through a nearby window, and he mistook it for the porcelain chamber pot. He pulled down the back flap of his one-piece sleeper, placed his small behind on the window sill and fell two stories down into the dirt yard—landing on his pet pig Easter. "Not a hair on my chinny-chin-chin was hurt," he laughed.

Olive, however, found neither humor nor satisfaction in the new residence. Thus began grandmother Olive's peripatetic life. Russell and his little son Buster shuffled back to the comfort of the Williams family home, complete with two doting grandparents, Aunt Maude, Jacob and other servants.

My grandfather was a visionary. He saw a desperate need for a farm supply business in the largely agricultural county. At the time, Berkeley County was one big cotton field. He launched Williams Farm Supply and became a respected cotton broker, landowner and farmer, a multi-facited businessman as well as clerk of court after his father Thomas died.

The burgeoning Williams Farm Supply took up about a block of property in the center of Moncks Corner. Strategically located, it nosed up to the railroad tracks so that tons of bulk feed, seed and fertilizer could be delivered easily by train. In addition, thousands of cotton bales were shipped in boxcars to mills along the Eastern seaboard.

By the time I saw Williams Farm Supply, what

we called "the warehouse," the large wooden building sported huge red-and-white squares advertising Purina Feed. It had an office up front and a long warehouse out back filled with stacks of feed, seed, and fertilizer. Hundreds of chirping pullets spilled feed as they welcomed customers with eager children in tow who wanted biddies to raise or dye at Easter. Two loading docks, one beside the rails and another out front, provided easy access for loading and unloading supplies. An egg room and bathroom were off to the side.

A multipurpose shed was a short walk across the yard, its holdings changing from season to season, year to year, depending upon farmers' needs. Full of plows and tractors at one time, pig-fattening stalls and cucumber grading machines at another. Trucks—everything from two-ton fertilizer trucks to delivery pick-up trucks—parked under this shed too.

A glass-topped gas pump stood locked alongside the shed. My grandfather gave the pump key to his faithful drivers. One day Jim, one of the elder drivers, came to turn in his key. "What's the problem, Jim? Your folks putting the squeeze on you to lift gas outta my pump?" my grandfather asked. "Mista Russell, suh, to tell de trut, that thing been pickin' at *me*," Jim said as he handed in his key, for fear he'd succumb to temptation.

We spent hours playing and working at Williams Farm Supply. The tin building that housed the cotton gin towered over the back part of the property. After Daddy took over the business and we were big enough not to be supervised constantly, we'd beg Eva to let us "go to the gin," two long blocks from our house. She reluctantly agreed every single time.

"Ya'll be careful, now, yere me?" Eva called as we ran through the woods. She knew the dangers that lurked among the huge machines, the gin fires that set off the water tower siren day and night. But off we'd go. After the cotton was ginned in the gin house, an expanse of cotton bales was laid out behind the gin before they were put on the box cars to take to the mills. We jumped from bale to bale playing a giant form of hopscotch on the crocus and metal-bound bales that spread out like checkers on a broad board. No doubt Daddy played these games before us when he tagged along with his father as he built Williams Farm Supply into the most successful, lucrative business in Berkeley County.

But back to the story of my granddaddy Russell. He delighted in his return from the city of Birmingham to the Lowcountry, back among family, old friends, and familiar hunting grounds. He must have figured that there was no taming Olive, no place to hold her—so he chose to put down roots in Pinopolis where he and, he hoped, his son would thrive. As a bachelor of sorts, he and Buster lived in the family house with his spinster sister, Maude.

Berkeley County teemed with strong-minded, high-spirited men like my grandfather who were polished in the parlor and wily in the woods. One of Russell's hunting buddies was Dr. Kershaw Fishburne, who became my godfather. Everyone in the county called him "Doc." Russell and Doc were fast friends; they lived down the dirt road from each other in Pinopolis. Their lives intersected often, including weekly poker games. As early as 1904, two of the first six telephones in the country went to Pinopolis, to my grandfather's and Doc's houses.

Hunting, however, was their favorite pastime. Every winter Russell, Doc and other ardent outdoorsmen trooped through the swamps to Hagan Plantation to camp, hunt, gamble, and drink for several days.

Hagan rests on the eastern bank of the Cooper River in the middle of the dense forest of Hell Hole Swamp. Berkeley County native Francis Marion was named "the Swamp Fox" for the sly ways his troops hid in these very swamps to ambush the British during the Revolutionary War. (Buster surely told Clara Lee about one of his heroes.) On the back road to Charleston, some thirty miles from Pinopolis, my grandfather's hunting party traveling along the

Williams Farm Supply
Moncks Corner, South Carolina

muddy winter roads to the rough camp, was a sight to see: men in buggies laden with provisions, others on horseback, hounds trotting alongside. They were accompanied by Doc's man Peter—cook, hostler, and general handyman.

Russell and his hunting dogs

On this cold December evening, Russell was bringing up the rear when his galloping buggy jumped the muddy path and crashed into the forest, catapulting him into a tree. Doc rode back to the scene to see Russell writhing in pain on the side of the road. He declared Russell's leg broken. The consensus was to take him to the hospital in Charleston down the Cooper River by boat, a trip that would take at least two days because they first had to travel along nearly impassable roads to find a boat.

Meanwhile, Peter rode on horseback to the nearest country store to buy their full supply of Perry Davis Pain Killer, a patent medicine popular with the black population. Russell needed the elixir to abate the pain of the jolting, snail's-pace buggy ride to the hunters' cabin and for the long wait for a boat to arrive to take him to Charleston for treatment.

Once safely at Hagan, Peter created a bed of straw and blankets for Russell. After supper that night and the two evenings that followed, the hunters played poker until dawn—lying on the floor beside Russell, who refused to be left out of the gambling. While the others pursued their game, Peter tended Russell, with the considerable aid of Perry Davis.

Finally on the third day, a motorboat chugged up the river. Doc and a couple of mud and blood-splattered hunters loaded their injured friend on an improvised stretcher and put him in the boat.

They arrived at Riverside Hospital in Charleston, where the motley group was greeted with looks askance until Doc boomed, "Stop gawking. I'm Doc Fishburne. Get me somebody who can fix this god-damn leg!" They treated my granddaddy's leg as best they could, given the wound was three days old. His leg eventually healed, but he walked with a decided limp after that. Doc claimed the limp came from his overactive patient's not giving the leg a chance to heal properly. His friend Russell claimed it came from a rogue doctor on the scene. For years, the two friends shifted the blame.

My grandfather's toughness matched his robust spirit. A few years after the hunting accident, he wrecked his car and broke his jaw. Doc almost had a fight with him before Russell consented to go to a Charleston surgeon to have it set. When the time came to have the wiring removed, he asked Doc to do it. Doc, refusing, insisted that the surgeon needed to do it, but Russell argued that the trip to Charleston was too far and waiting to see the doctor would take too long. Besides, it was the height of the busy cotton season. He didn't have time!

Half an hour after this heated conversation, Doc saw his friend walking out of Berkeley Motor Company garage. Russell wore a huge grin, waggling his jaw at Doc and saying with a jaunty air, "You doctors take yourselves too seriously. Earnest Wyndham did the job for me with a pair of pliers, and my jaw feels fine."

My grandfather's passion for the land often got him involved with politics. Political intrigue not only affected prohibition issues in the Lowcountry but also surrounded the decision to inundate thousands of acres of fertile plantation country. The proposed creation of Lakes Moultrie and Marion as part of a hydroelectrical plant proved controversial. It pit-ted family against family. This project would join the Santee and Cooper Rivers to provide power for the expansion of industry and the Naval Base in Charleston, but many folks were none too pleased. They agreed with Eva that the land should not be "gobbled up by the gob'mint." At the time, money was not the commodity by which people's worth was measured in the South—it was land. Eva knew this as surely as my grandfather and my father did.

Russell and Buster joined others who lobbied fiercely against the new lakes. Unsettled by the prospect of the lake's inundating precious Lowcountry landmarks, my grandfather turned his contained fury into saving Hanover Plantation. He headed a syndicate which had bought the house and land in 1920. He used the modest house as a hunting lodge and the land for raising timber and growing cotton.

When Russell purchased Hanover, a unique cypress house built in 1714, it was falling into disrepair. The massive chimneys were made of multicolored bricks made on site; the mortar contained shell fragments and marl, also found on the property. A stucco band at the top of one chimney bore the words "Peu à Peu" taken from an old French proverb: "Little by little the bird builds its nest." This indicated the thrift and hard work of the French Huguenot family who built the house "little by little."

As the lake project loomed, Russell partnered with R. L. Montague of Charleston to save his treasured Hanover Plantation. It required considerable political influence and a great deal of maneuvering by my grandfather and like-minded friends. The Department of the Interior labeled Hanover as "the only house in the proposed region of inundation of national importance."

Hanover Plantation

President Roosevelt became interested in the hubbub going on in the SC

Lowcountry over his pet Public Works Project. As a last-ditch effort to save Hanover, the men offered to donate the historical treasure to a land-grant school. Clemson College, the nearest, was a logical choice. But during the Depression, funds were low for everyone, including state institutions.

The very week after Eva and I moved into our new house in Moncks Corner, my grandfather learned that a grant of $1,270 had been awarded by the Public Service Authority to save Hanover house, perhaps a soothing-of-feathers gesture from the group that flooded the Lowcountry?

The move began. Each board of Hanover was numbered as Clemson College staff and workmen from the Works Progress Administration dismantled the house piece by piece. It was placed on a long-bed truck from Williams Farm Supply and hauled upstate in 1941. In 1944 Hanover House was renovated and became a museum on the campus of Clemson College (now University), thanks to my granddaddy's zeal. Though he couldn't save the land, my grandfather Russell did save his beloved Hanover house, a symbol of his passion for the land it had rested on.

Lake Moultrie alone swallowed up approximately thirty-five plantations, over sixty thousand acres of forest, hunting grounds, farmland, and swamps by the early 1940s. Only two plantation houses survived—Woodlawn and Hanover. The tiny village of Pinopolis miraculously remained a pinkie finger jutting into Lake Moultrie. Politics?

A Berkeley County boy and family friend, U.S. Senator L. Mendel Rivers, headed the powerful House Armed Services Committee and for years brought many projects to the area. The joke in Washington was that if Rivers brought in one more project, the Lowcountry would slide into the Atlantic Ocean. Some say Mendel Rivers "looked after his friends," small comfort to my granddaddy who woke each morning to a field of stumps rearing ugly heads out of the water abutting his homeplace.

Russell Williams never ate a fish that came out of the new lake.

Though Eva's family did not live in the flooded basin that the lake covered, I imagine they knew some of the folks in the black settlements scattered across the area. These vibrant settlements laced among white plantations remained a forgotten society until seventy years later when Pinopolis natives Richard Porcher and Norman Walsh explored their history in *Lost Heritage*. Each settlement had its own identity with churches and schools, functioning autonomously by fishing, hunting, and farming small plots for domestic food or to sell to nearby plantations where many worked.

"The land produced all our needs," said William Canty, a descendant of these self-sufficient communities. The lake swallowed their gardens and hunting grounds, schools and churches. No welfare, social security, or food stamps back then. I can only imagine the shock of readjustment. Santee-Cooper offered assistance for relocation to the white plantation owners, none for the displaced black families.

Well before the formation of Lake Moultrie, Russell was active in civic and political affairs. An important business venture established in the early 1920s greatly impacted the infrastructure of the growing town of Moncks Corner as well as the county. My grandfather and his cohorts, including his buddy Doc Fishburne, created Berkeley Barrel and Basket Company, which manufactured 450,000 barrels and 650,00 hampers at its peak. Russell was its president. Later the Board of Directors drastically amended the original purpose to manufacture and control the following: electricity, waterworks, sewage, telephone and . . . ice plants! As one researcher said, "Talk about wanting to corner the market of an up-and-coming cash cow . . . " Russell and Doc also helped launch the Moncks Corner Pharmacy and Motor Company. These vibrant young men plunged headlong into shaping their vision for Berkeley County.

In 1922, South Carolina Governor Richard I. Manning appointed Russell to fill out the unexpired term of his father Thomas, who died while holding the clerk of court position. Russell also served on the governor's staff. He was on the original board of trustees of the Berkeley County Hospital, the Berkeley High School Board, and the Santee Bridge Commission. Most everyone called my granddaddy "Mr. Russell." We called him Daddy Grand. To us he was indeed grand, a combination of Paul Bunyan and Santa Claus. I smile when I think of the immense man who always stooped down to look me in the eye and muss my hair. Eva attributed my fondness for ice cream to his visits.

"Reg'lar as a clock, Mista Russell would drop by the house with a paper cup of chocolate ice cream," she said. I'd lift my arms to him, he'd swing me up from my playpen, and feed me with a little wooden spoon that scratched my tongue. I recall his sure hold and eyes soft as marshmallows. I remember Mother's telling me how fond she was of him and that in the early years of her marriage, "Mr. Russell was my best friend," she said. I adored him too. He died when I was six years old.

Despite the tenderness Russell felt for his young son, by the time Buster entered sixth grade he was sent away to boarding school, a common enough occurrence in those days. His parents were estranged. Olive no longer lived in Pinopolis. Buster's "home address" at boarding school was in New York City! Olive's Converse College alumni records show multiple address changes. Charleston, Pinopolis, and *four* different New York City locations: Washington Square, 26 E. 10th Street, The Cambridge on 68th Street, and West End Avenue. She listed her occupation as "creative artist." By 1953, grandmother Olive had sent Converse a Moncks Corner address and a note written to the office, "I wonder why I never receive news of Converse?"

In the spring of 1961, Converse wrote a personal letter inviting her to their class of 1906 reunion. She responded in her scrawled hand on a note card with Trinity Church in Pinopolis on the front.

*This is our little Episcopal Church—my son &
family are members. My membership is still at
Grace Church in Charleston—I am going to Lake
Waccamaw, N.C., on a visit. If you acknowledge this
soon, write there.*

> *Sincerely,*
> *Olive Williams*

To an earlier query for someone who will always
know her address, she wrote in the blank space, "the
First National Bank of Birmingham," clearly some
connection with her uncle Culpepper Exum who
served with that bank. Perhaps she enjoyed a trust
fund that allowed her to live an independent life. The
majority of the lady's life for her middle twenty years
remains obscure.

One thing we do know: My grandmother Olive
loved New York. I picture her swooping through the
etched-glass doors of the Algonquin Hotel, heels
clicking on the black and white tiles, throwing off
her fur coat as she bursts into the oak-paneled room
to join the actors, authors, and journalists like
Dorothy Parker and Robert Sherwood at the Round
Table.

Young Buster vacationing in Colorado

What a tantalizing city to broaden her son Buster's cultural education during his school holidays. A far cry from the wilds of the Berkeley County woods, the pair traipsing through the Metropolitan Museum and taking in Carnegie Hall performances. What a sight they must have been, dressed to the nines strolling down Fifth Avenue or eating lunch at the Plaza. Did mother and son discover themselves kindred spirits during those dizzying days that took them from New York City to Colorado? A postcard documents that Buster's mother exposed her son to broadening experiences. The little fellow is the only child riding a cable car up Echo Mountain in Colorado. What a thrill for an eight-year-old boy!

But an accident turned her world upside down, and sent her back to a place she tried to escape. Toward the end of Olive's wanderings, she lived in Colorado Springs. She resided in the Broadmoor Hotel, where in the early 1950s she was attacked, robbed and nearly strangled to death. This assault prompted a move back to the Lowcountry, where she lived in the Charleston Hotel on King Street and sometimes let an apartment on Legare Street downtown.

My sister LaClaire remembers spending the night with Grandmother Olive in the Charleston Hotel. "She constantly had her head over a pot of steaming water. She had a persistent, hacking cough. I thought she was sick, but she said it was from being choked in Colorado. It wasn't a fun time," LaClaire said.

A snapshot shows LaClaire and Grandmother Olive walking down King Street on one of those overnights. Both faces appear grim: LaClaire look-

LaClaire and Grandmother Olive

ing straight ahead. Grandmother, carrying an umbrella and handbag, holds her head erect, her lips pursed. She wears a hat, heels and a long coat with fur around the collar and down the front. Both look closed. Tight. It didn't look like fun to me either.

By the time Grandmother Olive moved back to stay, her husband Russell had been dead several years. Buster bought his mother a small stucco house in Moncks Corner on California Avenue, only two blocks from our home. My great aunt Maude did not invite Olive to Pinopolis. Olive never appeared at family functions. Her only interest—art. She painted incessantly.

Her first project was to paint a wide band of vivid red and yellow flowers in thick oils directly onto the stucco all the way around the bottom of her new white house. The flowers stuck out in bas-relief. They looked eerie.

"Well, now ain't yo' grandma got a gift. Dem some purty flowers," Eva said when she and I saw my grandmother smearing paint hither and yon. She was serious. I was aghast! What would people think?

My initial memory of Grandmother begins with her return to town after her Colorado trauma. I was twelve years old, and she scared the bejesus out of me! The image is vivid and the foil of my earlier imaginings of her as a dazzling beauty. I gawked at the woman before me—clothes in disarray, cheeks carved with folds deep as a peach pit, blackheads around a pinched nose, and an off-putting smell. A gnome-witch.

Olive Exum Bardin Williams

I stumbled across a stunning portrait of my grandmother Olive buried among family photographs. She wears a white lace dress. Two black braids fall to her lap. A ring circled in diamonds glitters on her little finger. On her face, a hint of a smile—a smile I never saw.

I retrieved that picture of beautiful young Olive,

showed it to Eva and asked whether she knew her back then. She simply glanced at it and spoke to the air.

"Ain't time a killer?"

I learned a disconcerting truth that day—the power of beauty has a used-by date.

Eva was adamant about my making regular visits to "go see Miss Olive." I dreaded the short walk and begged to duck the duty. "She yo' flesh 'n blood, missy. Now git," she said. Eva was big on family. And if she gave an order, I could talk every-which-a-way but she wouldn't budge. Sometimes her firm look would follow me until I turned the doorknob to leave our house. When I was particularly ornery, she'd walk me to the door, push it open with her wide palm, and pull me from under her arm, guiding me out the door with a pat on the rear.

When I finally entered Grandmother's house, an acrid smell of turpentine and tobacco filled my nose. Once I said "hello," she'd look up—cigarette dangling from puckered lips, eyes squinting from the smoke. Her dark hair streaked with gray was twisted up in a knot, errant strands hanging down. I stood frozen. I could muster no words, no smile. My feet rooted to the doorway.

Her piercing dark eyes bore into mine, but I steeled myself, calling on my secret power to keep her at bay with my own stare, to keep her from coming close, to keep her from touching me. The small wrinkled hands that held a long paintbrush were stained with cigarette and oil paints, her nails long and uneven. I was terrified those creased lips would kiss me or those stained hands would draw me in for a hug. They never did. We had no conversations that I can recall, but my entrance triggered a barrage of husky accusations against my mother, Daddy's friends, and the U.S. government.

From the moment I walked through her door, I was planning my exit. Eventually I screwed up the will to back out of the door, sprinting home to the kitchen, to Eva's apron.

"Now that a good girl, that my Baby," she said when she stooped to squeeze me to her chest. "Miss

Olive gots her own burden, Baby, memba that."

As a child, how could I understand the plight of a city girl driven by love to a pine village in a remote rural county where her *joie de vivre* was frowned upon and her artistic bent unappreciated? I wish I'd known Olive in her heyday, dancing on tiptoe at The Rocks, twirling Daddy Grand to distraction. I'd liked to have appreciated the full portrait of a fascinating, spirited woman whose blood flows through my veins.

With his mother Olive in and mostly out of Buster's early life, many thought Aunt Maude was his mother. Maude worshiped her older brother Russell and his baby Buster. When his three children came along, Daddy's Aunt Maude happily took on the role of surrogate grandmother. We called her "Nannie."

Aunt Maude
"Nannie"

"Miss Maude," as every one else in the county called her, was an imposing woman. Tall like her brother, she stood over six feet. Her wide face white as a communion wafer, long gray plaits twisted around her head, laughing eyes undimmed by rimless glasses, and a smile as bright as headlights on high beam. She never met a stranger. She could talk to a post. The world's caretaker, she visited the sick, baked for newcomers, arranged church homecoming dinners. And spoiled my daddy and later his children with kitchen goodies.

An entrepreneur as well, on weekdays she folded her large frame into a black Austin coup and drove from Pinopolis to Moncks Corner to her Tea Room. The little house with green cedar-shake siding and a small front stoop was strategically located across from the grammar school yard. Before the school lunchroom was built, the children who could afford it ate lunch at "Miss Maude's Tea Room." She served homemade vegetable soup along with crustless egg-and-olive sandwiches. Cheese straws and cinnamon stickies were her specialties . . . and my favorites.

The Tea Room was a child's dream—jars of Mary Janes that stuck in my back teeth, boxes of Cracker Jacks with pink plastic rings inside, baskets of Toll House cookies hot from the oven, and bright red candied apples on sticks, upside down on a tray. Plus, a change drawer that opened with a "ching."

Nannie's Tea Room

After school on hot days I'd run across the street, bolt through the door, and grab a teeth-cracking-cold orange Tru-Ade. Never had to pay. Other children envied that, I suppose. And they might have envied my having Eva always waiting for me on the stoop of the Tea Room.

"Eva, go around back and help yourself to some refreshments," Nannie said. Once.

"Thank you, Miss Maude. I jes fine," Eva answered, nipping further invitations in the bud. "I ain't going round back fo' nobody," she added under her breath. And she never did. She always waited out front for our walks back home.

Nannie liked giving orders—to Jacob, to Tea Room help, to rowdy children, to church committees, and to our family. She reminded us every single solitary Sunday to eat each morsel on the plate, feed the canaries, reline the cages with old newspapers. All with her blinding smile. Nannie relished reigning as the matriarch of the Williams family. We relished her vigor and her food. Everyone seemed to jig to Maude's music.

Except Eva.

Maude never transitioned well from being the main cog in young Buster's world to being one spoke in the wheel of his new family—a wheel that turned with ease, with Eva at the center. That was when

Eva and I entered the family portrait, the year we all moved to a new house in town. Before Eva, Maude had enjoyed her brother Russell, her darling Buster, his quiet wife Clara Lee, and their first-born little LaClaire all to herself in the Pinopolis home. So when Eva became the center of the Moncks Corner house, Maude's role shifted. Surely it stung to have Eva become the major player in her nephew's family. The dance of power between Eva and Maude lasted for twenty-four years, the pace ever increasing.

Nothing if not resilient, Maude had already survived an earlier threat to her position when her brother Russell brought his bride Olive into the Pinopolis home. When Russell and Maude's parents died, both siblings inherited the property and continued living together. Maude ran the house and met her brother's every need. Enter, new wife Olive. Russell brought his bride to the home in Pinopolis expecting a smooth conversion, which didn't happen.

Maude's personality was as strong as her body was tall. Petite Olive was surely put off by Maude's six-foot frame and overbearing ways—always with her wide, patronizing smile. Maude's sharing her home with "the other woman" during Russell and Olive's early marriage no doubt exacerbated the strain on the triangled relationship. Who indeed was the woman of the house? Maude certainly didn't intend to abdicate. Never did.

So the couple left for those few short years. A respite of sorts, for all, I imagine. Then they returned from Birmingham with an adorable toddler. Maude's attention easily transferred from Russell to Buster, whom she fattened up in no time. Just as my grandfather Russell became the man Maude never married, my father Buster was the child Maude never bore.

Even with Russell's and Olive's and Maude's influence, or perhaps because of it, my father's home environment was not an emotionally stable one. Olive and Russell argued over many things, even who had the best family background, for goodness sakes. She told everyone she wanted to leave "the godforsaken swamp." What's more, Aunt Maude and Olive competed for young Buster's love and attention. And his mother didn't cook sweets.

Buster was a lively, handsome boy with thick brown hair spilling over his forehead and ears. He looked like Buster Brown in the shoe ad, thus his nickname. Bea Dennis, Buster's neighbor and childhood friend, reported emphatically, "Miss Olive and Miss Maude spoiled your daddy rotten."

As a child, he was wooed with everything from his Aunt Maude's sweets to his mother's ponies. As a teenager, he was showered with everything from guns to cars. As an adult, he was gifted with land and political clout.

But it was Buster's outgoing personality and enthusiasm for life, not his family connections, that made him socially popular. Small for his age, Buster took after his mother in stature. Nonetheless, he excelled at sports—everything from swimming and riding to shooting and fishing. Indoors, he charmed by spinning stories and swinging girls

Young Buster Williams

around the dance floor. By the time he was a young man, Buster Williams was the catch of the Lowcountry.

Buster learned early how to win the women in his world—an engaging smile, a ready compliment, and impeccable manners. Bea, Buster's childhood sweetheart, fell in love with the charming man who drove up to her house and teased her into taking rousing rides in his convertible or startled her with verbal repartee that pinked her cheeks. She called him "a smart aleck," quick with a quip. Yes, Buster turned into quite a lady's man—and then some.

He probably picked up some of his banter as a way of gaining attention in new surroundings at a young age. At eleven years old, Buster was sent off to boarding school at Asheville School for Boys in

North Carolina. After that, he attended high school at Staunton Military Academy in Virginia.

He embraced the new environments with enthusiasm, even joining Staunton's football team. Given his small stature, football could have been daunting to a less passionate fellow. Other activities, however, enticed him more, especially ones that dealt with language, like the Woodrow Wilson Literary Society and the Blackfriars, the drama club. He was both yearbook business manager and editor of the Blue and Gold. With his excellent writing skills, he worked on the Cadet Handbook committee. And he was chosen a delegate to the national YMCA Convention.

Buster at Staunton Military Academy

Buster's leadership and political skills budded early. His penchant for neatness and organization helped him respond well to the military regimen and academic rigor. He rapidly moved from "rat" to sergeant. His quick wit and winning ways made him popular with his classmates. His intellectual curiosity and diligence made him stand out with his teachers.

Buster's homecomings from Staunton were spectacles. His father arranged for the Atlantic Coast Line passenger train to stop just for him at the Moncks Corner depot within hollering distance of Williams Farm Supply.

"And your daddy would walk off the train like he was President Roosevelt," his friend Bea told me. Being sweet on him, she often met him at the station.

After Staunton, Buster entered the University of North Carolina at Chapel Hill in 1929. He joined Beta Theta Pi fraternity, which encouraged his affinity for parties and pretty women. For initiation, his head was shaved. His straight Buster-brown hair came back in thick waves of molasses falling across his forehead. His warm, chocolate eyes held fast to those he looked upon, giving them his full attention. He worked as a reporter for *The Daily Tar Heel* newspaper, which fed his proclivity for being in the thick of things. Buster also made life-long attachments to men who would become the siblings he never had. Charlie Gold, our "Uncle Charlie," was one of them. They graduated with the class of 1933.

And in 1933, FDR, a man who couldn't walk led a crippled country. When the Great Depression hit, life changed for everyone. Buster became an inspector with the U.S. Department of Agriculture and later a forester and crew leader for the Civilian Conversation Corps (CCC). He put thirty dollars a month in his pocket.

The job was made for a natural-born leader and land-lover like Buster Williams. The CCC brought an avalanche of President Roosevelt's New Deal assistance to South Carolina when jobs were scarce as sugar coupons. Intensive cotton farming and logging had left much of the state's land devastated by deforestation, fires and erosion. Buster's crew and others restored hundreds of miles of terraces, planted more than fifty-six million tree seedlings and built seventeen state parks. At one point he worked in Luray near Estill while Mother taught in Beaufort down the coast. Buster always could spot a pretty girl.

After introducing Clara Lee to his family, Buster had to face reality. Being newly married during the Depression was tough on two people used to having everything. In 1936, after only a year in Spartanburg selling fertilizer, Buster returned to Moncks Corner with Clara Lee to join his father as a cotton broker, ginner and farm supply merchant. For ten years, Buster and his father made up for those long years of separation from the time he was a callow student at Asheville School.

My mother Clara Lee and my father Buster both came from good, hard-working folks with big hearts and more manners and education than most. They seemed suited for each other. Mother's large, solid family that bore tragedy head on was attractive to Daddy, whose small family was alternately indulgent and unpredictable. He admired the quiet dignity Miss Lillian had passed along to her daughter, so unlike his capricious mother. And Van, his father-in-law, surely reminded him of his own father Russell—dependable, successful, larger than life.

Mother was used to the buttoned-up life of the Baptist Peeples, so she felt comfortable with the Williamses' Methodist values, yet she was intrigued by Daddy's sophistication and happy-go-lucky style. She was accustomed to strong male leadership and immediately cottoned to her father-in-law Russell. Also, the couple's tastes matched because both the Peeples and Williams taught them to appreciate the finer things in life.

In personality, they complemented each other: Buster the extrovert, Clara Lee the introvert. Buster the pheasant, Clara Lee the dove. Buster the comet in the sky, Clara Lee the salt of the earth. In the end it was my father's exuberance and affection that drew my mother like a monarch to milkweed.

Like both their parents, during the early years of Buster and Clara Lee's marriage, they also lived with family. Unlike Olive and Russell, Clara Lee and Buster's romance transcended mundane domestic affairs.

And this passion carried over into a home of their own when Eva and I joined the household. "Those were the happiest years of our marriage, the happiest of my life," Mother said. And Eva's entrance helped make it so.

Chapter 4

Flying High

Before this longing,
I lived serene as a fish . . .
But now—
The wild stream, the sea itself cannot contain me.
—Theodore Roethke

"I gonna work for Mista Russell's boy now," Eva told Daddy Bill and Miss Hattie. Eva Aiken had captured the attention of the brightest young couple in the county. The two seemed the perfect match—the beauty queen daughter of a prominent Hampton County gentleman farmer, and a handsome prince of the largest farmer's merchant in Berkeley County. Their courtship and sudden marriage set the Lowcountry abuzz.

After a short detour in Spartanburg, where Buster worked selling fertilizer, it didn't take long to be lured back to the Lowcountry. He wanted to help his father with the farm supply business since the Depression was hitting the area hard. And, no doubt Buster longed to keep his bride "in the manner to which she'd been accustomed." The newlyweds moved into the Williamses' grand Pinopolis house. It seemed an ideal homestead for a couple still riding the magic carpet of love in the middle of the Depression. Plenty of room for everybody: Russell, Olive (on rare visits), Maude, Clara Lee and Buster, and after four years their first baby, LaClaire. A young maid named Minnie cleaned and tended LaClaire, and Jacob Bash cooked and lived nearby.

Every day the couple drove into Moncks Corner just two miles from Pinopolis. Buster joined his dad at Williams Farm Supply in the center of town. Clara

Lee taught fifth grade at Berkeley Grammar School on Main Street and gained a reputation for being the most demanding teacher on the staff. Superintendent Bonner also declared her the prettiest. Maude ran her Tea Room across from the school. Meanwhile, Olive was traveling to heaven-knows-where. Life seemed sweet. Buster was the focus of an adoring household of women, and his father had high hopes for his only son—his namesake.

LaClaire and her nurse Minnie in Pinopolis

Buster became his father's apprentice learning the farm supply business. He took pleasure in greeting customers, calling out their feed, seed, and salt blocks orders to the warehouse workers whom he enjoyed bantering with. During lulls, he walked the grounds in his suit, surveyed tractors in the shed, made sure trucks were gassed up and ready to deliver fertilizer to nearby plantations. He especially enjoyed the bustle around the gin house during ginning season when hundreds of farmers like Daddy Bill lined up their wagons spilling over with cotton. August through November was the time of year that they "settled up wid Cap'n Buster" and his father.

Daddy Bill and other farmers put their feed, seed, and fertilizer on the tab until the cotton came in. Farmers signed a promissory "Note and Mortgage of Personal Property and of Crops to J. Russell Williams." Stacks of these official blue documents filled the large iron safe in the back of the office. Cash, fertilizer, seeds and supplies were advanced "with eight per cent interest." According to the note, "if the amount advanced should exceed the amount agreed upon," the farmer must sell for "ONE DOLLAR all crops now growing and which shall be made, planted and grown." In these lending matters, Mister Russell and Captain Buster, however, tended toward leniency. Daddy Bill signed his X on many a promissory note that Buster ignored during a poor growing season, always looking out for Eva's family . . . and others. Countless others.

Buster's favorite activity during ginning season was talking to Harry Hutchinson. The black gin manager was a core employee of Williams Farm Supply once the gin was built. Mister Russell relied on Harry to run the ginning operation, start to finish, from supervising the workers to repairing the machines. Harry had watched Buster grow from a tot into "a fine young buck," he said. Harry loved Buster like a son. A rare ease flowed between the two men: one young, white and school educated; the other older, black with trade expertise.

When the newly-married boy returned home to work in the business, Harry took pride in teaching Buster the workings of the gin. Buster respected Harry's knowledge and was curious about all aspects of the ginning process. Serious in his role as mentor, Harry pointed out the safety precautions and the shut-down process when the cotton clogged a machine or fire smoldered in a corner. He taught Buster about the complex ginning process—the suction tube carrying the cotton to a fierce machine that separated boll from seed, and pressing machines that molded the bales, which workers wrapped in burlap and belted with metal straps. Hard, heavy work.

From early on, Harry cautioned Buster to be careful when walking near the row of cylinders with thousands of metal teeth that stripped the seeds from the cotton tuffs. (This was before metal shields covered the cylinders.) A few months before his first daughter LaClaire arrived in 1939, Buster was doing his daily walk-through of the gin in his brown herringbone suit. On this cool winter day, he and Harry talked to each other over the clatter of the steel-toothed cylinders that scraped the seeds from the fluffy bolls.

As they walked the narrow aisle beside the machines, a point of steel snagged the edge of Buster's pants. The spinning cylinder yanked in the pant leg, chewing up more and more of the material—and Buster's leg along with it. Harry frantically tried to jerk Buster free from the churning wheel. Seeing his attempt futile, he bolted to the back of the gin and tripped the electrical switch. The machines grinded to a halt. By that time, Buster's leg was mutilated up to mid-thigh.

"Except for the grace of God and Harry Hutchinson, your daddy would have died," Eva's friend Lela Session told me. She recorded the day in her memoir:

> *It was a sad day in Berkeley County when young Buster Williams got hurt. Everybody loved Mr. Russell. The whole county turned out to give blood. The line ran out of the hospital, down the steps, and into the street . . . black and white.*

History was made in Berkeley County that heartrending day. Heretofore, blacks were not allowed to give blood to whites. With tears streaming down his face, Harry Hutchinson headed the line.

Machine that snagged Daddy's pant leg-shown here with a shield

By the time LaClaire was born, Buster Williams sported the very latest prosthetic wooden leg in the U.S. His stump, a round mound of pure muscle, expertly controlled the wooden leg, hinged at the knee and ankle. Each morning he sat on the edge of his bed, covered the stump with a thick woolen cap, stood on his good leg, and strapped on a wide leather belt that supported the artificial limb, wood polished to a high shine. He put on his trousers, long hose and shoes on both legs.

After choosing a cane from his collection, he walked to the front of the house with a slight hitch . . . out of the house going about his business as usual. We children never knew him before the accident, so we thought nothing of Daddy's having only one leg. A school friend once asked me, "Does your daddy have arthritis?" To most, it appeared Buster only used a cane as a flourish to a dignified walk.

Mother was amazed by Daddy's resilience. He didn't talk about the accident or complain of any inconvenience.

"It didn't keep him from doing anything he'd done before," she said. He never changed his fun-loving, outdoor-living lifestyle. The psychological toll he hid well—for a time.

What a struggle climbing the tall Pinopolis stairs must have been during those years after the accident. Yet Buster's jovial spirit never wavered. He kept running in high gear, hardly out of the hospital before designing a low-slung, modern house for his new family. Only one step up to the front and side doors. He built it in Moncks Corner only a couple of blocks from Williams Farm Supply.

The modern brick house sat on five acres slap dab in the middle of Moncks Corner. His dream did not come cheap. At the time, the average house cost about $14,000. With all the extras, Buster paid almost twice that. True to form, Daddy installed the finest materials like cedar-lined closets and tiled porches. By the time he finished all the add-ons, the house had seventeen rooms, seven doors that opened to the outside, four porches, plus a room and bath for live-in help—thank heavens.

The new house Buster built for Clara Lee in Moncks Corner had the latest kitchen equipment including the first dishwasher and garbage disposal in town. Ten years later, we enjoyed one of the community's first central air-conditioned houses.

For the baths, Buster chose large square tubs with two seats on the sides. Marble panels divided the children's bathroom so three could have privacy—LaClaire could bathe, I could brush teeth, and Rusty could tinkle, all at the same time. The cedar closets had little buttons that automatically turned on the lights when the doors opened. The sun parlor where the piano sat on shiny wood floors had floor-to-ceiling windows that Eva kept gleaming.

As to interior furnishing, Buster filled his house with antique desks, love seats, dining table, silver service, platters, bowls, as well as water, wine, and martini crystal from his friend George Birlant's antique shop on King Street. Nothing was too good for his Clara Lee.

And those lovely furnishings from Birlant's Antiques? They took a beating as the three of us grew older. It was all Eva could do to keep us from breaking something or other. "Lawdamercy," she'd say, when I broke the delicate wooden carving off the top of the Victorian love seat for the umpteenth time. Eva deftly glued it back before Daddy got home. Did they ever use the felt-covered gaming table that unfolded in triangles? They *did* use the poker machine that Buster bought when the law shut down Carolina Yacht Club's gambling. The machine became a focal point at some of the parties. Later it took up residence in the guest room closet.

Buster's generosity won Clara Lee's heart time and again. He reveled in the smallest details, like designing Clara Lee's dressing table with large, three-sided mirrors.

"A heap of cleaning," Eva said. On the wall facing the dressing table, drawers and cabinets with shelves reached to the ceiling. The top shelves were filled with boxes upon boxes of hats, some with feathers and sashes, others plain cloches. Two deep, wide drawers held stacks of sweaters, lush cashmere pullovers and prickly wool cardigans.

Long, filmy nightgowns, nylon and satin pastels, filled the bottom drawer. Eva washed the gowns by hand and hung them to dry on the wire line outdoors so they smelled fresh. "A man like a sweet smellin' woman, Baby. Like your mama. Memba that," Eva said. Mother wore lace bras, subtly padded. She needed the boost because she was flat as a fried egg. I wondered if I'd need pads when I grew up. I wanted Eva's bosoms. Thick, round . . . and warm.

There was never a question of who was in charge during the building—Clara Lee would have followed Buster to the moon long before that seemed possible. "I was just grateful to have a place of my own," she said when I asked how they decided to build a modern house so different from the ones they both grew up in.

He built the house on Library Street—right in the middle of town. Library Street dead-ended into Piggly Wiggly grocery on Main Street. The picture show and school were just down the street. Baptist, Christian, Methodist, and Presbyterian churches stood within a block or two. Up Main Street was the 5¢ and 10¢ store, the Trolley Car and Rexall Pharmacy with Dr. Lacey's office in back. Read's and Barron's dry goods stores beside the pharmacy. Piano lessons two blocks away at Mrs. Spann's, dance lessons three houses up Church Street at Mrs. Knight's studio. Through the back woods was Williams Farm Supply. Everything within walking and biking distance. From the hub of our house we could spoke out to all the important places in town. All we had to do was let Eva know which direction we were headed. Eva was home base.

Mother, Daddy, LaClaire, Eva and I moved into that house two years after Daddy's accident, the very week I was born. Between Eva and Chester, our house and yard stayed immaculate. Chester Davis was hired to take care of the large grounds that stretched around the house. A creek ran all the way down Main Street—a natural playground for children. Our yard was the coolest place in town, one of two houses on our block, a wide circular drive curved the full length of the low brick house. The drive filled with small, brown and white rocks that we used for money when playing store. It had an expanse of grass and a big hickory tree out front. We smashed the hard beige nuts between bricks in order to tease out the bits of sweet meat. A sea of pansies surrounded the tree, hundreds of yellow and purple velveteen faces lifted to the sun.

We each had inside and outside jobs, and one of my yard jobs was to pick pansies. The more I picked, the more they bloomed. Multicolored lantana lined the driveway. The walkway to Mother's rose garden began where the cars nosed in.

Getting out of a car in most any weather, something or other piqued our noses . . . perhaps from wisteria that dripped its grape clusters from the giant pine tree, or magnolia blossoms behind the rose garden, or silver bells, narcissus and daffodils that bloomed near the porch. The purple Japanese magnolia bloomed at the end of February when the camellias browned and fell to the ground. But the blazing yellow forsythia won the prize for being the first to announce the end of winter. I ran shouting the news to Eva. She said the same thing every spring, "Ain't God a wonder, Baby?"

In the far side yard, a moss draped oak tree sprawled. Eva was forever calling LaClaire and her book out of that tree for supper. I never did climb the tree, more evidence to support my "scaredy-cat" tag. Beyond the side yard was a big field for throwing the football, playing catch, or shooting basketball, which lured all the boys within a three-block radius. Out back was the playhouse, a real house with brick steps and windows, where we played store for hours on end. Rusty was "Mr. Man" who sold his sisters pyracantha berries, acorns, hickory nuts, and gumballs—all picked up from our yard. Beside the playhouse was Buster's camellia breeding ground and off limits. Nobody kicked balls in that direction, for sure. Behind the playhouse was a fig tree that we covered with netting every summer to keep the birds from eating the fruit before Eva could make her scrumptious fig preserves. The grass beyond the fig tree sloped toward several acres of dense hardwoods. These woods served as the backdrop for playing cowboys and Indians and building tree houses.

Besides tending the grounds, Chester also served as a butler, driver, and handyman. Chester and his buxom wife Victoria first lived behind the warehouse. When their children came along, they moved into in a frame house behind Gathers Funeral Home on the other side of the railroad tracks. A lanky, handsome man the color of whole wheat bread crust, Chester came on board with an attitude. Eva dubbed him an "uppity" black man and tried to keep him "in the yard where he belong at." Unfortunately for Chester, the distinction between house servants and field hands was still alive among the black community in the Lowcountry.

Eschewing the yard work, Chester traded his army uniform for a butler's outfit and wore it proudly whenever possible. He boasted having a metal plate in his head from the war. Eva claimed he was "teched in the head" from that injury. He had traveled in Europe where acceptance of black soldiers was taken for granted, and he told stories about the war, including ones about the elite Tuskegee Airmen, the first black aviators in the military, and Edward Gibson, a decorated black South Carolina soldier. He didn't mention the part about Gibson's returning home wearing his uniform and being arrested on the spot in Charleston for impersonating an officer. It took his mother's white employer to get him out of jail.

Did Chester know about Sergeant Isaac Woodard's debacle? Woodard served as a longshoreman in the Navy, winning three medals for unloading ships under fire in New Guinea. Returning home, local police pulled him off a bus in Batesburg, South Carolina, dragged him in an alleyway and jabbed him repeatedly in his eyes with a Billy club, and jailed him. In the trial in Aiken, the defense attorney told the jury that "if you rule against Shull [the accused officer], then let South Carolina secede again." Shull got off scot-free. The South Carolina incident led President Truman to promulgate an executive order in 1948 to ban racial discrimination in the Armed Forces, over the objection of senior military officers.

Heaven forbid! All this going on while I'm skipping to the library, ringlets bouncing.

I avoided Chester whenever possible. He gave me tight-lipped smiles I didn't trust. When I stepped in a flowerbed, he'd order me to pick a switch from a nearby forsythia bush and strip all the leaves except for a few at the tip. He ceremoniously held out a hand for me to turn over the switch, then unceremoniously blistered my legs till they stung like fire. If Eva caught him in the act, she dashed out of the door, snatched me up, and sent him running with blazing words.

"Get your black hand off my Baby!" On Eva's watch, nobody touched her Baby.

Mother probably had mixed feelings around the time of my birth. Sorry for not delivering the boy she and Buster wanted; excited about moving into a new house; anxious about running a household, chasing a toddler, and tending a newborn without the help she'd been used to in Pinopolis. But her knight presented his queen with a most generous gift—Eva. By the time Rusty arrived two years later, the young couple had long entrusted their children completely to her care. Besides, Eva's presence allowed Buster's indomitable spirit and Clara Lee's unswerving love to keep riding a wave of delight for almost ten more years.

Life still seemed honey coated. It's little wonder Buster captivated the reserved Clara Lee. He was charismatic, easy on the eyes and passionate about life. This passion didn't slow one whit after he married. He grabbed for it all—adventure, money, position, and women. He was a debonair fellow with wavy walnut hair and bright brown eyes, a sensuous man who splashed on Old Spice each morning and kissed ladies' hands soft and slow.

An engaging smile coupled with his verbal smorgasbord drew in young and old. Language, politics, and people stimulated him. On his bed-side table, he kept a blue college dictionary. Another beige unabridged version rested on a podium nearby.

He could dispatch wit on the latest political news or tell a hunting tale that made folks hold their sides. He read extensively—Winston Churchill's speeches, Thor Heyerdahl's *Kon-Tiki*, Robert Penn Warren's story of Louisiana politician Huey Long, and *The New Yorker*. He woke to the radio beside his bed playing Puccini operas or Glenn Miller favorites like "Chattanooga Choo Choo." He enticed Clara Lee and friends to fly to New York, a town he'd painted red often with his mother. They saw the latest Broadway plays like *Annie Get Your Gun*. Little wonder he initiated scintillating conversation.

When Buster walked into a room, attention drifted his way. He appeared taller than his five-feet-eight because he carried himself like a Roman centurion—straight back, squared shoulders. A valued customer at Berlin's in Charleston, Buster wore a tie and a three-piece tailor-made suit every day, whether to the dusty warehouse and lint-filled cotton gin, to the county courthouse to do his Clerk of Court duties, or to visit farmers who needed money to tide them over until cotton season.

Regular trips to the Charleston Hotel barber shop kept Buster's thick hair trimmed and nails manicured. Chester polished Daddy's row of lace up shoes, taut with jointed wooden shoetrees. We liked to play with those stringless foot marionettes when Chester wasn't around. Hunting clothes and fishing boots never touched the master bedroom closet; they stayed in a sliding cabinet in the foyer along with his guns and shells.

Buster Williams

He also sported an array of intriguing walking canes. A black one with a silver band and JRW initials, one—a gun—had a concealed trigger near the top. Another hid a flask that unscrewed at the crook. When fully dressed, Daddy hooked his walking cane on his left wrist and smoothed back his damp hair with his right palm—ready to charm the world, and Clara Lee.

"You sho do look *fine* dis mornin, Mista Buster," Eva said as he stopped by the kitchen to say good-bye, a daily ritual. Eva washed, lightly starched, and carefully ironed his long-sleeved white shirts with JRW monograms on the pockets. She proudly sent her young man into each day looking his best.

"How about some of your *fine* fried chicken for supper?" he replied. He loved to play with words and with Eva. And you could be sure she'd rustle up some of his favorite okra gumbo too. As with Harry, Buster enjoyed an ease with Eva. Their admiration was mutual. She respected this young businessman who appreciated and supported her and her family, and Buster appreciated Eva, the seasoned house-keeper whose skills helped his world run smoothly. Besides, she concocted the finest chicken purlieu and banana pudding in the Lowcountry. From the day Buster and Eva met at the hospital, their affinity for each other was evident. Their loyalty never wavered, even in the later years when it was tested.

Clara Lee Peeples Williams

In the early days of their marriage, while Buster charmed, Clara Lee sparkled. Everyone acknowledged Clara Lee to be a beauty. Big-boned but slender, almost as tall as Daddy, she carried herself well. She dressed in chic but conservative suits and walked with long, sure strides. When she entered a room, heads turned. Taken apart, her physical features seemed unremarkable: a prominent Peeples nose, scant eyebrows, brownish-green eyes, thin lips. But, ah, her smile. She stunned those around her with a combination of her olive complexion, high cheekbones, and double-divot dimples. Clara Lee's smile was her crowning glory.

Years later I met Dr. Jack Rhodes, a Charleston pediatrician who grew up in Estill with Mother. "Well, aren't you a pretty little thing," he said. "But you'll never be the beauty your mother was. Those Peeples girls had the best bones in Hampton County." And Superintendent of Schools Henry Bonner knew Mother well when she taught school. "Your mother had the most radiant smile," he told me at her funeral. And it was true. Mostly for my daddy.

Around Buster, Clara Lee radiated an aura of intangible joy. At a party, she'd look people in the eye, cock her head, nod a time or two, seeming to give full attention, then glance over her shoulder to cast that brilliant smile to Buster across the room. Balancing a martini glass in one hand, a cigarette holder in the other, poised and graceful, listening. I never heard her tell a joke or start a serious conversation. She spoke with her smile. An observer, she beamed in Buster's presence, adding to the glow of the limelight he needed.

To me, she seemed like a foreign countess, just out of reach—an apparition. I longed to be with her inside the bubble of light that floated effortlessly. But there was no room for anyone but her Buster.

And he knew how to treat a lady. He opened her door, helped with her wrap, lit her cigarette— all with a touch to the hand or shoulder. He lavished her with gifts. Her jewelry box overflowed: gold loop earrings, inlaid ivory miniature dog earrings, a black onyx necklace. In later years, she seldom wore jewelry except for a rectangular white-gold watch outlined with tiny diamonds and a large ring with a cluster of diamonds bunched like hydrangea petals.

Buster lavished Clara Lee with the kinds of things that he himself needed in order to feel valued, to feel loved—the things his parents had showered on him. He never realized that he didn't need to buy Clara Lee's heart—he already had it. From her own Baptist upbringing, Clara Lee knew all that glittered wasn't gold. She nonetheless made an effort to appreciate Buster's way of showing his affection because it brought him so much joy. In the end, though, his appetites overwhelmed us all.

Buster loved parties and surprises, and he elicited Eva's considerable help one May 17, 1948. The two of them plotted a surprise birthday party for Mother. He swooped her out of the house for an all-day fishing trip near Pooshee, property he owned on the lake across from Pinopolis. Eva packed a picnic lunch. Buster invited everybody and his brother to the party that evening, arranging for them to park their cars behind the house next door. He asked Mrs. Spann, our piano teacher, to play for the occasion.

"Gots some turnin' to do today," Eva said anytime the couple hosted a party. And this day was no different. First, she vacuumed every inch of carpet and cleaned everything from the windows to the highball glasses. She checked the flower vases for water. Mother always kept fresh flowers in the house. Eva puffed the sofa pillows, and laid out cocktail napkins and plates. Next, she hit the kitchen and began fixing the hors-d'oeuvres—cheese squares on toothpicks, little chicken salad sandwiches with sliced olives on top, toasted pecans, and hot crab dip from *Charleston Receipts*. And shrimp cocktail. Her Buster wanted the shrimp cooked quick like, so she scooped them from the boiling water when they had barely turned pink. No rubbery shrimp out of *her* kitchen. Deveining took some time, and by day's end, her face glowed from the kitchen's heat.

As the sun set, Chester put on his white coat and brought out the scotch, bourbon, gin and vodka from the pantry, Eva accusing him of taking nips himself. She surveyed the bar. All the fixings lay near the silver martini shaker, the two-cupped jigger, and glass stirrers. To the side, stemmed martini glasses and gold-rimmed highball glasses with hand-painted quail, woodcocks, and ducks. She polished the silver silent butler to be at the ready for Chester to empty the overflowing ashtrays. Everyone smoked like a chimney back then. Long before filtered cigarettes made it to the market, my parents' crowd used filtered cigarette holders, which lent an elegant air to their parties.

Eva then stepped into her room behind the kitchen, bathed and put on a fresh uniform. Sometimes Eva solicited help from her relatives for the bigger parties. Her niece Marie Motte helped out in the kitchen this evening. She asked Eva exactly what a "cocktail party" was. Eva replied straight-faced, "I not sho, but I think dey cock dey leg and sho dey tail," and they both had a good chuckle.

Satisfied with everything, Eva bustled to the back of the house to dress LaClaire, Rusty, and me in our best clothes and remind us to welcome folks as they flowed in the front and side doors. The women wore high heels with their calf-length party dresses; the men wore suits and ties, even though the heat was stifling—there was no air conditioning yet. The living room, sun parlor, and dining room were packed with friends. Lights out. We watched expectantly as the green Oldsmobile pulled in the circle drive at dusk.

Buster opened the car door for Clara Lee, and they walked to the side porch together. Clara Lee opened the door to a chorus of "Happy birthday to you!" Face flushed from the sun, body exhausted, boots and trousers covered with mud and fish scales, her eyes enlarged with surprise. She shyly looked over her shoulder to Buster, delight shining in her eyes, and his. The piano played on, the glasses clinked far into the evening. Buster and Clara Lee stood at the front door, arms around each other's waists, waving goodnight as laughter wafted through the spring air. I loved them so much that night.

In the dead of winter, Eva unexpectedly commandeered another birthday party on January 14, 1951. Our parents were in New York when LaClaire was about to turn twelve. She was clearly disappointed that no one had planned a party. Eva picked up on LaClaire's glum mood. She realized our parents would not be home in time for the birthday. This just wouldn't do. She started "cogitating."

"Ain't it somebody's birthday coming up?" she said to LaClaire.

"They forgot my birthday," she whispered. Eva jumped into action. She picked up the phone and called LaClaire's friends. She invited them to a celebration of cake and ice cream under the oak tree in the side yard. Eva saved the day. One of her countless saves. My parents bounded in the door days later with a wonderful present—a navy blue velvet ice skating outfit trimmed in white fur. Mother bought most of our clothes at Best and Company showings in the Charleston Hotel or from the Best catalog. This outfit, however, came straight from the New York store. LaClaire adored it. She wore her birthday outfit to school the next day.

Buster and Clara Lee thought their joy ride would never end. They became the core of a young couples' group that embraced a fast life full of intelligent, varied, high-spirited friends who frequently filled the house. Highballs at the end of each day. Cocktail parties and house parties on the weekends.

Eva spent those evenings walking among the guests offering trays of sandwiches and cheese biscuits that she'd prepared in the afternoon. She smiled her bright smile, saying, "How you doing, Miss Zada?" and "Good evening, Mista Algie." She moved with ease among the couples, engaged in light banter, always looking folks in the eye. Neither Mother nor Daddy felt the need to check on things in the kitchen or remind Eva to serve this or that. Eva was an efficient, caring hostess; these were her guests in her house, and she welcomed them. Those late nights added to long days for her, but she never complained, just rubbed her sore feet with alcohol before bed.

But eventually I came to complain, only to Eva, of course. In the early days, I looked forward to the mandatory "Say hello to everyone" because I liked my parents' friends. They treated me as if I had good sense—never called me "sweetie," "honey," "sugar," or "dahlin'." Some nights, however, I dreaded being dragged out of a dead sleep by Eva to play the piano when too much Scotch fueled Daddy's natural exuberance.

Most of the time Eva adroitly kept us under her wing, out of the way, yet always near enough to quickly put me in a dress to play a piano piece for party guests. Shaking me, she whispered, "Hurry up, Baby. Get up. Yo daddy want you to play for the folks," she said as she shook me awake. In two shakes of a cow's tail, she stripped off my pj's and slipped me into my favorite brown-checked organdy pinafore. Looking in the mirror, I noticed my teeth still had a gap. The dentist promised it would close.

Angie wearing her favorite pinafore

"Go on now," she'd push my bottom down the long hall, still tying my sash as I stumbled toward the noisy sun parlor.

The Pinopolis crowd were Episcopalians, the men professionals, the wives homemakers—no disparaging occupation to create lovely, inviting homes, and keep husband and children happy. All lived on Lake Moultrie. The William Martins brought sophistication and amusement to these social gatherings. Uncle Dooley Martin was the first President of the Bank of Berkeley that he and Daddy started. Aunt Bettina was one of the old Parker family from Charleston; she always relayed the latest news from the city. (It was the Southern custom to call close family friends "aunt" and "uncle.") They held broad worldviews and voiced their non-provincial social and political opinions with tactful zest. When I married, the Martins hosted the rehearsal dinner at their home on the lake in Pinopolis, a nice affair.

Eva and I both kept savings accounts at Uncle Dooley's bank and walked the length of Main Street to make our deposits, Eva lifting me up to the tall window. Lela Session told me that she co-signed numerous notes for other blacks who couldn't get outright loans themselves. "All I had to do was call Mr. Dooley and say I'd be in tomorrow to sign, and he'd grant the loan," she said.

Zada and Philip Morgan never missed a party either. Philip's insurance office operated out of a small house on Daddy's property by the railroad. Zada and Mother were superb bridge partners, winning often. When visiting the Morgans on the lake, we played with their children, Zee and John.

And many Sundays found me at the Ball's lake house water skiing or playing tennis. Peach and Moultrie Ball were truly like an aunt and uncle to us, their daughter Moonie like a cousin. Peach was Doc and Miss Anne Fishburne's daughter and my brother Rusty's godmother. The tale is that at Peach's birth, the round and pink baby was declared a "Peach" by her nurse; the name stuck. Moultrie, Berkeley County Hospital administrator, hired me for summer work during college. I have the book he wrote about his World War II exploits. He entertained the crowd with those stories. In Flatrock, North Carolina, where the Balls hosted summer house parties and bridge gatherings, the bullbats flew at dusk, a signal to make the first drink of the evening.

"It's bullbat time!" someone announced with verve, and the drinking began. Buster and his friends loved their toddies.

During this sometimes frenzied fellowship time, one of my parents' favorite watering holes was in Charleston. If Buster got bored, he'd whisk Clara Lee down to the Carolina Yacht Club on Charleston Harbor, where he was a member. The old Charlestonians, mainly white Anglo-Saxon Protestants, belonged to this exclusive club, its black-balling ceremonies legendary. Located on the tip of the city's peninsula on East Bay Street, it was one of the oldest yacht clubs in America. For much of its history, the club was the center of the Charleston social scene where local and non-resident members like my dad wined and dined, sailed, and played poker. The Back Bar, where women weren't allowed, was replete with seven "one-armed bandits" (slot machines). During my teens, I spent many nights dancing across the slick wooden floor of the Yacht Club's upstairs ballroom and many days watching from the club's dock as my boyfriend won regattas. That story's coming later.

Around the corner from the Yacht Club on Church Street lived Cheeka and Ben Scott Whaley. Cheeka was Peach's sister, one of the Fishburne girls. The Whaleys and their three girls—Miss Em, Angie, and Marty—traveled from Charleston to Trinity Episcopal Church in Pinopolis every single Sunday. The girls called it "going to the country." Here they visited their Fishburne grandparents, who lived next door to the church. Sunday afternoons, "the other Angie" and I rode horses in the woods behind the Fishburne house. Angie and I also played tennis on the Balls' clay court, joined by Moonie, Marty or Miss Em.

Pinopolis boys fell like pinecones from the trees when the Whaley girls came to the village. Richie and Heyward Porcher, Eddie Davis and Pard Walsh groomed the red clay court and outlined the lines with lime to get ready for the gaggle of girls who appeared after church. We arrived unscrewing the nuts of the wooden presses to free our Wilson racquets. White balls tossed, play began. Moonie's daddy stood on the sideline shouting instructions: "Racquet back! Turn your side. Watch the damn ball!" "Good forehand, Angie." I admit it was usually the other Angie who received the compliments.

Out-of-town friends visited Buster and Clara Lee often, especially during hunting season. A number of Buster's college buddies started the Atlantic Hunting Club at Moss Grove Plantation, property he owned a couple of miles outside of Moncks Corner on Highway 52. The word "plantation" conjures up oak-lined avenues with white-columned mansions. In reality, plantations come in various forms. As long as there was dirt with a dwelling, animals, and some crop or another, it warranted being called a plantation. Houses ranged from Tara in *Gone with the Wind* to modest hunting lodges like the ones at Hanover and Moss Grove. Berkeley County boasted well over three hundred plantations before the lakes came. Hanover, miraculously saved by my grandfather's ingenuity; Moss Grove, fortunately out of range.

We often visited plantations that dotted the banks of the Cooper River between Moncks Corner and Charleston. The naturalist artist Edward von Dingle was a family friend. He lived in Huger at Middlebury Plantation, an unpretentious wooden structure built in 1693. Amazingly, Mr. Dingle allowed

Middlebury Plantation

us children to touch the colorful feathers of the hundreds of taxidermied birds. He kept them in chests with shallow pull-out trays barely deep enough for the birds to rest. He used them "to get the colors just right," he said, for his popular bird paintings that adorned many Lowcountry walls.

At The Bluff Plantation, another modest building, we rocked on the porch with Mother's old friend, Mrs. Albert Storm. She gave me a Windsor desk from The Bluff when I married. As we rocked, her clouded eyes stared into the darkness. She talked about her dream of restoring sight to the blind—a dream that became

Mulberry Plantation

a reality with her gift in 1961 that made possible The Storm Eye Institute of the Medical University of South Carolina.

The house at Mulberry Plantation was elegant by Lowcountry standards. Built in 1714, it perched on a knoll overlooking the western branch of the Cooper River, all brick with majestic steps. The Williamses were no strangers there either because Mother's good friend Fanny Brawley lived there. Her son Willie Islin and my brother Rusty became hunting buddies.

We spent a lot of time at Wappaoola Plantation (editor's note: commonly misspelled as Wappoola or Wapoolla), named for the nearby creek, meaning "sweet water." The Anthony J. Drexels became like family for a time. The Philadelphia-based family of distinguished money brokers and entrepreneurs kept residences in Paris and London . . . and the Lowcountry. Aunt Helen, Uncle Tony and their three children enjoyed the large house with white columns outside and wide winding staircase inside when they moved near Moncks Corner. Their children were about our ages, so we looked forward to gatherings at Wappaoola or the Drexel's Daytona Beach home.

Wappaoola

But our family spent most weekends at our own Moss Grove Plantation. Plantation land was imbued with a rich earth that yielded abundant crops—everything from cotton to timber—and lots of acreage for prime dove and quail hunting. In the 1940s and 1950s, sharecroppers plowed and planted the bulk of the twelve hundred acres of Moss Grove. But for Buster, Clara Lee and their friends, it was primarily a hunting paradise—the women as keen on hunting as the men, oftentimes better shots.

So in the fall, the Williams family, including Eva, trooped to Moss Grove for long, lazy weekends. There was a main cabin, a barn, and a few odd outer buildings like sheds to park the tractor and store farm equipment. We went along on quail and dove hunts, roamed the woods, and rode horses. Eva cooked and played host inside. Buster played host to the crowd outside. In his element at Moss Grove,

Buster was always riding high in a jeep or on a horse.

After his leg accident, sitting camouflaged in a field to shoot dove wasn't a problem for Buster. Driving the jeep, he'd disperse the hunters around the field. Always gracious, he'd give his friends the hot spots so everyone could shoot the limit. Once he settled himself on his canvas stool under an oak's tips at the edge of the field, he'd send sister LaClaire on horseback through the cornfield to scare up the game. The galloping horse sent a thick cloud of mushroomed-colored dove into the sky. The shooting sounded like a 4th of July celebration! LaClaire also served as her daddy's retriever. He was a crackerjack marksman, so by sunset LaClaire amassed a mound of silky doves beside his stand. And accolades from her daddy. Love and doves aplenty filled those heady days.

When quail hunting, Buster, Clara Lee, and the other hunters rode on horseback. Was that a concession to Daddy's mobility or simply something expected in those days, like riding to the hounds when deer hunting? Horse and rider navigated under miles of canopied pines while the bird dogs picked up scents from Bob Whites. Willie Mullinax trained Buster's pointers, and they outshone all the other dogs. Noses to the ground, legs churning over the scrubs and pine needles, tails whipping the air. Freeze! The lead dog sniffed a covey, his tail stiff as a pencil, his body in a point. All the dogs stopped dead still imitating the pose. The next move, a blur of dogs rushing the brush. A covey of six or eight quail burst in the air so quickly that hearts stutter while shots explode overhead. In the quiet aftermath, the dogs retrieve the downed quail, gingerly carrying each to his master.

Back at the cabin, Eva plucked feathers, gutted, and cooked birds by the dozen. Quail and dove sizzled in the frying pan; others wrapped in bacon and baked until breasts fell off the bones. Add grits and gravy, a bowl of succotash, and a pan of biscuits, and she had a meal of wild game ready to eat. When hunters walked in the door of the cabin, a mixture of smells whetted their appetites. After they wet their whistles, of course.

Once a tinge of autumn touched the air, Uncle Charlie Gold, Daddy's best buddy from Chapel Hill days, and his wife Aunt Alice made a beeline to Moss Grove from North Carolina. Like family for many years, even today we say the Moravian blessings the Golds taught us.

> Come Lord Jesus our guest to be, and bless these gifts bestowed by thee. Amen.

Squat as an elf, Aunt Alice was. Her small eyes twinkled. Her full breasts rested on a rounded tummy where she propped one hand while she waved the other around with a cigarette holder. Sometimes the cigarette was lit, often not. Her hair was short, frizzed and the color of a barely tarnished penny. A ruddy flush covered her apple cheeks and freckled face. Her mouth stayed open in a half laugh because if she wasn't laughing right then, she was getting ready to or had just finished.

She giggled her way right into my heart. I might have been her pet because one day Aunt Alice suggested to Mother that they make a canopy for my new four-poster bed and a matching skirt for my dressing table. That entailed a trip to Charleston's Read

Aunt Alice and Uncle Charlie in their yacht

Brothers on King Street to select the fabric. The two returned with a mini-print of red-white-blue flowers, which I adored. The project took longer than expected because Aunt Alice and Eva had to do all the work. Mother had no idea how to use the new sewing machine. As it ended up, Aunt Alice taught

Mother and me enough to get by in later years when we needed it. The canopy turned out beautifully. Only once did I get fussed at for jumping so high on my bed that my head hit the top and dislodged one of the wooden cross pieces. The canopy fell with a crash on my head. Thank goodness Eva made everything hunky-dory before Daddy got home.

Uncle Charlie matched Aunt Alice in buoyancy. With his bald head, portly belly and jolly personality, we viewed him as our very own Santa Claus. He made paper birds magically "fly away" and "come back home" on his fingertips; he found quarters behind our ears. Eva adored him because of his effusive compliments on her cooking as well as the bills that crossed her palm as he headed back to North Carolina.

"Mista Charlie is a sport, now," she said, shaking her head.

More than "a sport" to our family, Uncle Charlie gifted each of us children with a slice of waterfront property on Lake Moultrie when we were born. The land was across the lake from Pinopolis, part of Pooshee Plantation owned by Daddy's friend Dwight Porcher. Our family ended up owning the far end of Pooshee, a lakeside bluff where Daddy planned to build a summer home. No one can say my daddy wasn't a dreamer. We spent many afternoons picnicking on the lakeshore and riding around in our boat. While the adults fished, we looked for minnows in the reeds and dug in the sand at Jack's Hole. Uncle Charlie and Aunt Alice came down to fish at Pooshee in the spring too. Or they brought their yacht to Charleston for off-shore fishing.

The Golds also invited our family into their world in North Carolina. Once when we were having dinner at Greensboro Country Club, Uncle Charlie said we could have anything we wanted for dessert. "I want a nickel's worth of chocolate ice cream," Rusty announced. He was so darling, the only one of us blessed with *both* of Mother's dimples. At the Trolley Car in Moncks Corner, a nickel translated into two big scoops. Uncle Charlie's raucous laugh echoed across the imposing dining hall. "Give this boy a *quarter's* worth!" he told the waiter.

Another trip to North Carolina I remember well because I had my first driving lesson. Uncle Charlie decided to indulge me, although Mother insisted I was too young. He put me behind the wheel of his Cadillac on the wide sandy road leading to Camp Brian and showed me two counter-intuitive things I remember to this day: how to *speed up* around a curve and how to focus on the *right shoulder* when meeting a car.

I remember that vacation well too because Eva and Chester came along. It was an icy winter night as we drove to Uncle Charlie's hunting club where the adults shot ducks and geese, and the children chased each other in johnboats through a maze of cypress trees. In Buster's Oldsmobile phase, he and Clara Lee took the lead in the silver sedan. Behind, Chester steered the green convertible. He and Eva rode up front; LaClaire, Rusty and I sat in the back seat (a reversal of sorts). A Marine stopped the Williamses' two-car caravan as we rode up to Cherry Point Naval Station's check point. After waving the first car on, the guard peeked in our car's window, smiled at Chester and Eva.

Daddy had a low license number because of serving on the Santee Cooper Board, and the guard mistook him for the governor. "I assume you're with the South Carolina governor's party. Go right ahead," he said. He saluted us through the gate. Eva lifted her chin a notch. A smug smile eased across her face. She could have been mistaken for the aristocratic Mrs. Astor, if you didn't know better. What a satisfaction it must have been to be treated with such deference—possibly a first for Eva from a white man in a position of authority. Chester, of course, took the scene in stride. Well, perhaps with a little smirk toward Eva.

Buster also enjoyed close relationships with a number of high-powered politicians. Senator Strom Thurmond and his first wife Jean became friends. Thurmond, the longest serving senator in US congressional history, switched from Democrat to Dixiecrat, and finally to Republican. When the then-bachelor Thurmond was Governor, he became enamored by Jean Crouch at her high school graduation where he gave the address. He declared she had "the prettiest eyes" he'd ever seen. She declared he was "too old." He promptly called the press and walked on his hands across the front yard of the governor's mansion to prove his vigor. Everyone hooted and hollered. Jean eventually acquiesced when she finished Columbia College and turned 21. Thurmond was 45. She became the love of his life. The two couples stayed close friends for over ten years. Sadly, Jean died of a malignant brain tumor at thirty-three.

One day Eva was cleaning the guest room after a visit from the Thurmonds. Walking out to find Clara Lee, holding two brown lace-up shoes by her index fingers, one in each hand, she cocked her head, "Mista Strum done left he shoes."

Mother replied, "He knows better. Put them back in the closet until he comes next week." Eva did. And he did.

Years later in 1963 when LaClaire married Charlie Laffitte, Jr. from Allendale County, Thurmond attended the wedding. Charlie's father, like Buster, was a friend and staunch supporter of the then democrat. For Thurmond, this wedding was a "two-fer." Used to guests of all stations in her house, Eva wasn't intimidated by the likes of Strom Thurmond. At the reception on the lawn of Berkeley Country Club, Eva left the serving table and marched up to the tall, still-formidable U.S. Senator. She extended her hand with a huge grin.

"Welcome, Mista Strum. We glad you come," Eva greeted him with grace.

Eva greeted with grace the Thurmond she knew as friend of our family. The same Thurmond who ran for President of the United States as a Dixiecrat, a states' rights party organized to preserve the Southern racial status quo in 1948. Eva greeted with grace the Thurmond who also authored the Southern Manifesto against the 1954 Supreme Court desegregation ruling. The same man who, a year later, filibustered for twenty-four hours and twenty-eight minutes against passage of the Civil Rights Bill in the U.S. Senate. And this was the same Thurmond who after receiving five battle stars and eighteen decorations, medals, and awards for his service as an Army general in World War II, announced his candidacy for Governor of South Carolina with these words:

Senator Strom Thurmond and his wife Jean after his filibuster.
(AP Photo/William J. Smith)

> *I wanna tell you, ladies and gentlemen, that there's not enough troops in the Army to force the Southern people to break down segregation and admit the nigger race into our theaters, into our swimming pools, into our homes, and into our churches.*

Did Eva ever hear those words? I surely didn't. Did she know his staunch segregationist stand as she called him to a hot breakfast or pressed his wrinkled shirts when he was a guest in our house? Probably. But what I know for certain is that Southern hospitality and manners prevailed. Eva, ever the lady.

Yes, Eva knew "Mista Strum" up close and personal because Strom Thurmond was Buster's friend. If anybody loved politics, it was this Berkeley County boy who grew up hobnobbing with the movers and shakers in local and state politics. Working for his father at Williams Farm Supply gave Buster time and resources to engage in politics as well as civic affairs, just like his father and grandfather before him.

Like his father, Buster was a visionary who helped get several ventures started in Berkeley County. He and Uncle Dooley founded The Bank of Berkeley. He helped finance Dial Funeral Home, the first mortuary in the county. He was a charter member and president of the Lions Club. For many years our garage stored clusters of brooms made by the blind, which the club sold to raise money. He also served as director of the Chamber of Commerce. Fingers in many pies, my daddy.

But politics particularly engaged his passion. In South Carolina, heavily Democratic at the time, Buster served as secretary of the Berkeley County Democratic Party executive committee. He led the political machine that campaigned vigorously for close friends like Rembert Dennis (SC Senator and Rusty's godfather), Mendel Rivers (US Congressman and Chairman of the House Armed Services Committee), Jimmy Byrnes (SC Governor, US Secretary of State, and US Supreme Court Judge), and, of course, Strom Thurmond. After working as a colonel on Governor Thurmond's staff, Daddy earned a coveted appointment to the Board of the South Carolina Public Service Authority. He served on that Santee Cooper board for fifteen years.

LaClaire rode all over the back roads of Berkeley County in Daddy's jeep as he persuaded both white and black to vote. This a far cry from Buster's youth when Governor "Pitchfork" Ben Tillman from North Charleston called on constituents to shoot every black man who tried to vote. Blacks could vote in the 50's, and Buster believed it right and fair. He mustered all his charm to garner votes for the Democrats. Eva, aware of Buster's goings-on, was a willing convert. He smoothed her path to register, not easy for many blacks who were denied their rights because of revision of voting rules after Reconstruction. Aside from intimidation by individuals and groups like the Ku Klux Klan, the payment of high poll taxes, complicated literacy tests and evidence of owning property made many blacks ineligible to vote. But savvy, caring people like my daddy knew how to get around the racist Jim Crow laws.

Clara Lee attended most of the political affairs with Buster, and she participated in many social and service activities as well. In fact, at one point after she stopped teaching, she worked for the Welfare Department. With dignity and competence, she met the expectations for the wife of a prominent young man. She also had free time because after the three children arrived, she no longer worked full time. And she had Eva.

Many a day we'd get home from school to a gathering of women playing bridge or having a meeting in our living room. Clara Lee led the Moncks Corner Garden Club and Book Club, hosted showers and wedding parties, and arranged flowers for the church. And she took Eva's pies to the sick. She didn't have to remind Eva to polish the silverware, clean the windows, wax the porches.

"Miss Clara Lee like things just so," Eva said, rubbing a fork with vigor or giving the tile an extra coat of wax.

Clara Lee and Eva functioned contentedly as a team. In the early days, Clara Lee taught Eva the fine points of serving a meal, polishing silver, setting a table, putting on a party. Eva showed Clara Lee the skills of making a proper bed, cleaning a house from top to bottom, but especially cooking and tending children. Both glowed with the richness of their lives. Eva, living in a fine home with a family who needed and appreciated her gifts and enough money to help her aging parents live comfortably. And Clara Lee, basking in the freedom to embrace her husband's world and love.

And how my daddy delighted in enlarging her world! And, oh, how she longed to please. Gardening became Clara Lee's joy. Before her marriage to Buster, she probably had not put one finger in the soil. Was there a flower garden in Estill? I never saw one. My daddy appreciated beauty of all kinds and was naturally drawn to flowers; therefore, Clara Lee took an interest. Buster focused on showy camellias. He gibbed hundreds of plants to create hybrids that won ribbons in Charleston Camellia shows. Eva arranged the best blooms for travel to the show, wrapping each stem with soaked cotton and placing them on trays to put in the back of the station wagon. Yes, Oldsmobile came out with one.

Clara Lee's garden yielded the more common azaleas, chrysanthemums, roses, gladiolas, and daffodils. In spring, the scent of sweet peas drifted in my bedroom windows. In late fall, velvet-faced pansies greeted visitors in the driveway. Fresh flower arrangements filled the living room, dining room, and bedrooms. Chester turned the ground, fertilized, moved a brick walk here or there, but Clara Lee insisted on doing the planting, pruning, cutting and arranging. She won ribbons for her designs at flower shows and was delighted when people asked permission to pick blooms or greens for special events.

In the yard Clara Lee seemed at home. But in the kitchen she struggled like a bream out of water while Eva swished through the current with ease. Day in, day out, Eva produced three full meals a day—no cold cereals or sandwiches. Men in the Lowcountry, city or country, always came home for "dinner" at midday. "Supper" was the evening meal. No such thing as "lunch." In downtown Charleston, private schools let children out to run a few blocks home for dinner with the family, then back for afternoon classes.

Clara Lee cooked occasionally in Eva's kitchen, the math major following a recipe's exact specifications. No improvisation. Homemade mayonnaise her specialty, she rarely resorted to buying Mrs. Duke's popular new dressing made in Greenville, all the rage back then. Wanting to please Buster, on special occasions, she produced a new dish without a dry run, which made both Eva and Buster a bit nervous. Her drive for excellence often made her the winner of the veiled cook-offs for the desserts for Bridge Club. She eventually became known in our family for crab and eggplant casseroles, mazetti chocked with extra beef and sharp cheddar, and heavenly hash salad, which we children loved because of the baby marshmallows. Eva worked at her side, separating the white from the yoke or chopping the onions so Mother wouldn't tear. Eva liked helping Clara Lee make Buster proud.

Yes, Buster liked the finer things in life, but it was people he treasured. Eva in particular. Ready with a compliment and effortless conversation, he kept Eva happy. He'd also slip her extra cash from time to time without Clara Lee's knowing it. Some blacks called Eva an Uncle Tom, but her friend Lela claimed those came from jealous folk. The black community generally thought Eva's working for the respected Williamses was a blessing to both. Eva didn't "go to work" each day. Eva was family.

Mother and Daddy were living a wonder-filled life, always on the go—fishing, hunting, partying, traveling. And laughing. They laughed a lot. Life was grand, exciting for the young couple so in love with each other and life itself. Clara Lee had little time for mothering, at least for this second child, and another girl at that. Besides, there was always Eva, encouraging her.

"Go on now." She went.

"Have a good time." She did.

"Don't you worry none." And she didn't. Because Eva was there.

While Clara Lee sipped cocktails and flirted with Buster, Eva nurtured me. In the early years, I don't recall interacting with Mother. It was always Eva and me. She didn't stint on LaClaire and Rusty either, but I believed she was all mine. Mother, I watched from afar, catching glimpses of swishing skirts, high heels with ankle straps. Or she and Daddy would be headed out to hunt quail, and her boots or the butt of her twelve-gauge would catch my eye. I'd stand behind Eva's apron, snatching a glance from her that glinted over me like the sun peeking through a cloud.

Perhaps it wasn't just *time* but also *touch* that drew me to Eva. A hugger and a patter, Eva patted my head, my cheek, my rump . . . whatever struck her fancy as I ran through the kitchen. It was Eva I hugged goodnight, Eva who smoothed my tears with her thick hand when I stumped my toe. I can't recall my mother's touch. Would I have run to her had she

bent down with open arms? Who begins such rit-
uals, the mother or the child? I was always a little
wary of rumpling her dress should I sit in her lap.

"She's a fine one, yo mama," Eva often said as
she pulled my head to her leg with her palm. Eva
and Clara Lee seemed to have mutual respect for
their roles: Clara Lee took care of Buster, Eva took
care of the house and children. In truth, Eva took
care of us all. We appeared the perfect family—as
long as Eva was present.

I'm not sure when the dis-ease began, when we
started being afraid. LaClaire, the eldest, perceived
it first. When Eva was absent even for short times
to go to church or check on her family, something
seemed amiss. One Sunday when Eva was visiting
her parents, seven-year-old LaClaire got a notion.
I was five, Rusty three. Neither LaClaire nor I can
remember what prompted the bold escape to Eva's
house, a couple of miles away. LaClaire woke us well
before sunup. Nervous as a hen, she had a heck of
a time putting on Rusty's shoes. Finally all dressed,
we sneaked out of the house and hit the sidewalk
hand in hand—running away to Eva.

Just two blocks into our walk, we saw the town's
police car driving toward us. We ducked behind the
boxwood hedge in front of Butch Howard's house
next door to the school. Officer Peagler spotted us
and slowly pulled over to the curb beside the hedge.
Leaving his motor running, he cranked down his
window and looked straight through those bushes.
My heart zipped up and down. I knew he'd put us in
jail. I started crying. LaClaire squeezed my hand so
hard that I shut up.

"Who's there?" he called.

LaClaire stood up, resolute as our spokesper-
son. She looked him in the eyes.

"Where you children off to?" he asked.

"We're going to Eva's," LaClaire said without a
blink. When LaClaire made up her mind to do something, it'd take a bulldozer to push her off course.

I reckon he saw her resolve. Rusty stood glued to her leg. I whimpered a little. She didn't budge, just stared him down.

He looked the three of us over real slow like.

"Well, ya'll be careful now," he said, and leisurely pulled his cruiser away from the curb, no doubt turning at the next corner to let Buster Williams know his three children were on the loose.

We made it to Eva's steps just as the sun cracked the sky over Whitesville Road. "Well, do Lawdy, look what we got chere. Come on in out de cold." She swept her arm wide as she pushed open the screened door. After a powerful fine breakfast, the four of us trudged back to Library Street, taking turns holding Eva's hands. The minute we opened the door to our house, Daddy showed his face.

Before he could say a word, Eva met his eyes. "Now, Mista Busta, look what I done found on my doorstep dis morning. Dey's plum tuckered out," and she pushed us down the hall to our rooms telling him, "Now I gona rustle up some breckwus fo' you," which she did. Eva knew how to handle Buster Williams.

Eva dealt with many changes that affected our family, which often meant taking on more responsibility than she bargained for. The Drexels of Wappaoola Plantation were part of fun times, until the end. I have a picture of the couple from Philadelphia, Mother and Daddy and other friends in our living room, men in their suits and vests, women in long dresses, high heels and smiles, all raising martini glasses to the camera. A snapshot of the glory days.

The first drop-dead gorgeous woman I'd seen up close, Aunt Helen Drexel was almost six feet tall, with thick black hair caressing her wide shoulders. She wore red dresses and black gowns. Her smooth, slender hands with long red fingernails were the model for Pond's hand cream. Before a party one evening, I saw her paint herself with an artist's flare. "Let me put on my eyes," she said, as she drew broad, black eyebrows, added violet eye shadow, thick black liner, and multiple layers of black mascara. Then she smoothed on bright red lipstick. Aunt Helen looked as if she belonged on the front of *Harper's Bazaar,* which they say she once was. She dotted perfume on her wrists and behind both ears. I closed my eyes as I sucked in the sweetness. Mother never used scent because once when double-dating in college, the other girl wore such heavy perfume that they had to stop the car for Clara Lee to be sick. That cured *her.*

Mother merely dusted her cheeks with powder, smoothed on some lipstick, fluffed her hair with her fingers, and she was ready to go. Her wardrobe looked like the woods—soft greens, browns and beige—no vibrant colors. Her simple classic style spoke not as loudly as Aunt Helen's but just as eloquently. Eva and I loved Aunt Helen who embraced us easily and laughed with us often, unlike the reserved Clara Lee, who saved her affection for Buster.

Uncle Tony was as handsome as Aunt Helen was gorgeous. Way over six feet, lean yet broad-shouldered, black hair and dark eyes. You'd think he was the ultimate Southern gentleman, if you didn't know he was from Philadelphia. A tinge of sophistication hinted he'd been around. For sport, he dressed in jodhpurs tucked in tall leather boots. And in the woods, Uncle Tony was as good a shot as my daddy, which is saying something.

The Drexel children, young Tony, Howard and Diana were fun-loving, attractive people as well, and we spent many carefree days with them. We didn't know we weren't supposed to cotton to Yankees. The Drexels' older son Tony missed the northern snows. One weekend he hitched up their snow sled behind a pickup truck used by Blackie, the Wappaoola overseer. There were wild sled rides through plantation fields that day. Not scaredy-cat me, of course. Another time someone found a thin, small beige-colored rubber tube on the floor of Blackie's truck. Can't remember who picked it up, put it to his lips and blew it up like a balloon. When we ran inside to show it to the adults toasting their martinis—they went speechless. I had no idea why. That night I learned about condoms.

My favorite activity at Wappaoola was jumping on the joggling board—a long, limber pine board about sixteen feet long suspended between two upright supports with curved bottoms. You could rock back and forth sitting down, or jump high as the sky standing up. From the early 19th century, Lowcountry children "joggled" on the boards. Courting couples sat on opposite ends until they bounced their way to the middle. There's an old saying that no home with a joggling board would ever have an un-married daughter. We had one in our side yard

Joggling board

under the oak tree in Moncks Corner. The board at Wappaoola was set up on the rough brick porch. So LaClaire, Diana and I were covered.

Four of my twelve stitches came because of jog-gling at Wappaoola. Normally we each took turns, but one day I obstinately refused to get off the board. Impatient Diana grabbed my arm and jerked me right off onto the porch. I popped my eyebrow on a brick, which sent a rush of blood down my face. Everyone thought I was dying or at least had lost my sight since the blood puddled in my left eye. I screamed bloody murder (histrionics evident), and Daddy rushed me to the hospital amidst much hubbub.

Eva wasn't at Wappaoola that day. If she had been there, it wouldn't have happened—I just knew it. But she *was* there when I got home. She took off my bloody blouse and helped me into my pj's. She checked my bandage as I slipped between the bed-covers. In a few minutes, she brought me a bowl of chocolate ice cream. She sat on the edge of my bed until the last spoonful, then tucked me in for the night. As I popped my two middle fingers in my mouth and began twirling a strand of hair around a finger on my other hand, Eva patted my head.

"You res' now, Baby. Everyt'ing gonna be awright," she said.

Not long after my mishap, we received dreadful news from Wappaoola. Uncle Tony had been sitting in his den cleaning a shotgun from his collection, something he did regularly. He didn't know this particular gun had a bullet in the chamber, and he accidentally shot himself—dead. It shocked everyone. Aunt Helen fell apart and needed time to gather herself. Young Tony went back to boarding school. Aunt Helen, Howard and Diana moved in with us for a while. Eva handled the extra family in our house with aplomb, whether fixing meals or washing and ironing stacks of clothes. Aunt Helen eventually went to their Florida house alone. Diana and Howard lived with us until the end of the school year.

Angie, LaClaire and Diana

Eva then had five children to keep up with, and Diana was getting too much attention as far as I was concerned. I became jealous of her crisp Northern speech, her long limbs and luxurious dark hair that she casually but constantly brushed out of her eyes. I felt colorless in comparison and brooded unattractively. Both twelve, we shared my bedroom, my special canopy bed, and it seemed we were always at each other for one thing or another. (Let's just say I wasn't my best self that year.)

"Chile, she don't want nothin' what's yourn. I speck you to 'have yoursef. That girl daddy be *dead*. You yere Beba? Now, come long. Supper gettin' cold." Eva shamed me into being nice to Diana. After all, her daddy *was* dead. When the family eventually resettled up North, I missed them.

The Drexels were a symbol of all those glorious days when Daddy and Mother glided together, glittered with friends, grabbed at life and love. They experienced life like children at the county fair. They wanted to do everything—rock the swing when the Ferris wheel stopped at the top, cling to each other when the roller coaster made their stomachs leap to their throats, laugh when he won a teddy bear for her on the first ball toss. Like the hub of the cotton candy machine, they swirled layers of pink clouds, their sweet stickiness touching all those within their sphere.

For a glorious time, Clara Lee and Buster Williams lived the fairytale. Uncle Tony's death destroyed the illusion that all couples live happily ever after.

Chapter 5

No Time fo' Grievin'

Steal away, steal away,
Steal away to Jesus
       –Negro Spiritual

Uncle Tony's shooting himself was not my first experience with death.

When I was eight years old, I killed my puppy. Petty was her name. Before the killing, my third-grade year had been about hearing "Red rover, red rover, let *Angie* come over!" About playing hopscotch with the girls and marbles with the boys. About crossing the monkey bars without stopping. Swinging on the swings so high that the pipe legs lift off the ground and give you a scare. About sitting on the library floor listening to Mrs. Matthews read Peter Rabbit tales, and calling someone a "nincompoop" without stumbling.

That same year, Ceille Baird, a feisty classmate challenged Jeanenne Smith to a fight in the school yard. Ceille was being pummeled by this country girl who "had feedsack dresses and dirty feet and clumpy stuck hair." On the losing end, Ceille "whined, struggling to get her mouth out of the dirt" when Jeanne, still on top, stopped everything. Ceille wrote this ending to her story, "How Angela Williams Saved my Life":

> It was then I noticed Jeanenne was paying not one iota of attention to me and I realized my pleadings had nothing to do with anything.
>
> Angela Williams had skipped by and Jeanenne had glanced up, mesmerized.
>
> "She always smells like fresh folded cotton," Jeanenne said. "Even at the end of the day."

Jeanenne raked herself off me. "How do you think she does that?" she asked as she squatted beside me in the dirt.

I righted myself. "I've always wondered."

Angela had short light braids tied with dark ribbons. She had a freckle or two and a white Peter Pan blouse and a dark skirt that never lost its pleats. She had a Mammy-maid named Eva who waited.

Jeanenne worked a strand of my dislodged hair from between her fingers. "Do you think she washes her ears?"

"Eva would see to that," I said. "Feet too, I bet. Toes and all."

"Bottoms too?"

"Probably."

"What you reckon she does in summers?" Jeanenne wondered.

"I think she plays singing games. And has macaroons and ginger tea that Eva serves to her on a little white cloth. And they talk a lot while Eva presses things that really don't need to be. I think she eats a lot of cherry suckers that her Aunt Maude brings her."

. . . Angela and Eva crossed the street holding hands. Had our arms been a little longer, Jeannene and I might have touched them.

"I bet the cool tree shade follows them all the way home," Jeanenne predicted.

But life isn't always the way it appears.

The year before my puppy died, I thought the worst already had happened. In first and second grades, Eva walked me as far as the schoolyard. I looked forward to those morning walks with Eva's thick hand wrapped around mine. This November morning, a quick knee hug at the school gate, and I raced to Mrs. Speer's second-grade classroom to jostle for position around the pot-bellied stove— the same stove she took me behind to paddle me for talking out of turn later that spring. When the bell rang, we scattered to our desks. My new navy pleated skirt flared prettily as a bare bottom hit the chair. I froze. *Was I naked? No. But where were my panties?*

Eva taught the dressing routine. Lay out clothes on the dresser stool the night before, put a nickel for a recess treat in a shoe, socks on top, and slide the shoes under the stool. Excited over my new navy skirt that swirled when I twirled, this morning I forgot my underwear. Discombobulated then panic-struck by my discovery, I agonized. *What should I do? Stay seated all day? Beg off at recess?* Coming out of my terror, I realized Eva would know; she always knew what to do. I eased out of the chair and tiptoed to Mrs. Speer's desk. "May I please go to the bathroom?" I whispered.

Lickety split, I ran the two blocks home and burst into tears when I hit the kitchen. Eva listened to the problem between my heaves. I'd been a cry-baby from the get go, but Eva never did cotton to my extra crying, so in short order she patted me into silence. "Let Beba study," she said. The next thing I knew, underwear pulled on, Eva had whipped on a fresh apron, and we were hotfooting it back to school.

Eva marched up the steps of the two-story brick building of Berkeley Grammar School, strode through the front door, walked down the wide hall-way, straight into my classroom without so much as a howdy do. All six feet of Mrs. Speer stopped in mid-sentence, staring at all five feet of Eva in her uniform and cap. Eva looked Mrs. Speer square in the eye. "You have to scuse Miss Anjul this morning, she had a mergency," she announced. She dropped my hand, turned around, closed the door behind her, and swished right back down the hall.

That incident was pretty awful but nothing as terrible as what came later.

The Williams family loved dogs, all kinds of dogs. Cocker spaniels and boxers for pets, pointers and setters for quail and dove hunting, Labradors for ducks. Cats were another thing altogether—they ate birds. I never warmed to cats. Neighborhood kids knew Mister Buster would pay a quarter for each cat hit with a BB gun. Every boy in the South got a BB gun on his sixth birthday, a four-ten on his tenth. A quarter equaled two Saturday movies and a Hershey bar—good pay.

Having a secret passion for dogs, I slept not with doll babies but stuffed dogs—fuzzy brown ones, shiny black ones, big ones, little ones. I longed for a dog of my very own. Naturally, LaClaire got one first. Thad was a brown boxer, a brute of a dog whose furrowed brow frightened me a little. By this time my siblings had added the "scaredy-cat" title to "cry baby," but I tried to be brave around him because I wanted a dog *so bad*. I needed Daddy to think I could care for one. I watched LaClaire with envy.

LaClaire's dog Thad retrieved sticks and pinecones over and over for her, chased behind her when she rode her bike, and snuggled beside her on the grass while she read a book. She vociferously defended Thad when the Markums down the street accused him of eating their chickens in the dark of night. Turned out he did, but LaClaire's loyalty to Thad never wavered.

Pestering Daddy finally paid off. He brought home a precious beagle puppy and placed her in my arms. I almost cried from happiness. Liver spots dotted her white coat that felt like glass when I stroked her. I called her "Petty" because that's all I ever wanted to do, pet her.

Rusty with Angie's dog Petty

Eva reminded me of the responsibilities that came with Petty. Wake early to feed her. Keep a bowl filled with fresh water. Wash her with the hose by the back steps so she wouldn't smell like dog. And give her plenty of hugs and scratches behind the ears so she wouldn't be lonely. Rusty loved dogs too, so I let him play with Petty when I was in a generous mood.

I delighted in my duties, feeling grownup and important, like LaClaire. No more cutting out paper dolls. LaClaire was the true tomboy, but neither of us was much into dolls. And Eva let us do our own leanings, not pushing us into girlish things the way Mother sometimes did. Both masters at shaping us children, they employed different styles. Like a potter, Eva wet her relaxed hands and let the clay ooze through her fingers, take its own shape. Mother held firm hands around the clay, shaping it into a preconceived object.

One of the worst tongue-lashing I ever got from my mother was when I cut off the long blonde hair on my designer bride doll. The doll *came* with long hair, so it should *keep* its long hair. When I cried to Eva over the reprimand, she put her hands on her hips, looked all around the shorn doll, and gave her assessment. "It's awright, ain't nothin' but hair, Baby." Then she paused and said, "She sho look sassy with a new do."

Petty's arrival relegated dolls to the attic. She became the impetus for bounding out of bed in the morning and racing home in the afternoons. Eva watched for my homecoming and released Petty just in time to meet me at the end of the drive. When Petty saw me coming, her little tail stuck straight up like an antenna and switched round and round until I scooped under her front legs and lifted her to my face. I closed my eyes anticipating the wet licks. She gnawed playfully on my fingers, chased me around the yard, let me try to knot her drooping ears. How I loved that puppy!

This particular morning, the morning of the killing, seemed like usual. Eva had already brought in the milk from the porch and poured off the cream from the neck of the bottle. Paper, inside too. "Gotta get the wake-up coffee to Mista Buster and Miss Clara Lee," Eva mumbled as she woke the three of us to get dressed. If we dawdled getting dressed, we'd hear the last call, "Time for breckwus!"

I got to the kitchen side of the house in time to put the newspaper in the side slot of Daddy's footed tray. Then I rushed to the front yard to pick purple and yellow pansies for Mother's tray. Eva trooped off with first one tray then the other, hitting the swinging door with her hip as she left the kitchen, working her way through the dining room, across the sun parlor, down the long hall past Rusty's room, our bathroom, my room, finally across from LaClaire's room to the master bedroom suite at the opposite end of the house. She planted the trays firmly across each lap with a nod and a "Good morning, Miss Clara Lee, Mista Buster," and trekked back to the kitchen.

Clara Lee and Buster woke listening to the radio beside the bed. If "The Wippenpoof Song" played, Daddy called us to his room through the intercom to sing the "ba, ba, ba" part. It was one of his favorite songs. Mother and Daddy ate breakfast, read the paper, drank coffee and smoked cigarettes. Meanwhile, Eva was whipping up the same full breakfast so we could "soak up learnin'" at school.

Eva was the best cook in town, especially her breakfasts with hot biscuits. Of course grits was a staple, with a touch of butter and a dollop of cream. Always "grits," not "hominy" or "hominy grits." Cooked long and slow, not too runny, not too stiff. On occasional winter mornings, hot oatmeal with brown sugar and cream substituted for grits. Along with grits came sizzling hot sausage and over-easy eggs that slid from the curved edge of the pan and landed with a soft plop on the mound of grits.

About once a week Eva mixed up creamed salmon or salmon cakes, my favorite. Canned salmon with the bones flecked out, diced onions, a few crushed Ritz crackers, salt and pepper— all pressed into patties, dusted with flour and browned quickly in spitting butter. Eva's other specialty in the mornings was fish roe and eggs. It seemed magical as the dots of fish roe fatten when they hit the hot iron skillet, getting puffy and firm. Eva then threw in whisked eggs, stirring them into the roe before they got too hard. A royal breakfast—served with grits, of course.

Every morning we were bound to have some kind of fruit. Half a grapefruit with sugar sprinkled on top was a treat because Eva broke out the sterling silver serrated grapefruit spoons. She cut around the outer edge and along the membranes between each segment so that with one easy scoop the cool morsel slipped on the spoon. A true labor of love. I liked figs picked from the backyard in August too.

Stewed prunes, however, I dreaded. I knew they were coming. Eva insisted we needed prunes on occasion "to keep reg'la." Each morning I just prayed it wouldn't be this morning. But on this day, a mound of dark, warm prunes stared at me from the fruit bowl. My mouth turned down. I knew the rule. Eat all until it's gone, the starving children in China being the theme. Usually compliant, aiming to please Eva, *this* morning I bowed my back as an inner voice shouted.

No. No prunes!

By this time I'd acquired a third nickname, "Miss Goody Two Shoes." Refusing to eat those prunes may have been my first conscious act of defiance. When Eva left us to go to her bedroom behind the kitchen, I slid out of my chair, grabbed my bowl, scooted to the back porch, and dumped the prunes into Petty's food dish. By the time I sat back down, Eva was none the wiser. And Petty plowed right through those prunes, long ears brushing the bowl with every lick of her tongue.

That crisp fall morning I walked out of our driveway onto the sidewalk heading for school. All alone, no Eva this day. After all, I was in third grade now. I wore Mary Jane shoes and white socks with lace on the edges. Halfway down the block I felt something nip at my socks. My brand new puppy Petty was following me to school, chasing after me with a weak "yip, yip." I turned around to see her at my ankles, legs churning to keep up, teeth snatching at my socks. I'd catch all kinds of grief later for leaving a crack in the door so she could sneak out. Secretly delighted by her devotion, I nonetheless fussed at her, calling her "bad dog" in my sternest voice. I laid down my books on the sidewalk so I could pick her up to take her back to the house.

As I leaned down, she suddenly stopped snapping at my socks and froze like a bird dog in point. She quivered slightly. I watched the quiver turn into a shake, a shake so hard that she looked like a broken wind-up toy vibrating like crazy but not going anywhere. I watched open-mouthed as the shake eased into a shiver, and then . . . her legs collapsed. Petty lay at my feet in a heap. Dead.

I don't remember how I ended up in Eva's arms. The memory remains a blur. I do remember Daddy's saying he'd take her to the vet to figure out why she died. I don't remember how I learned that prune pits had blocked her small intestines. I do remember diving into Eva's apron when I heard the news. It was all my stupid fault. I killed Petty. My heart broke twice—from losing the precious dog I'd adored and from feeling my first guilt. The crying just wouldn't stop.

And Eva was there. Kneeling down, she crushed me to her chest, stroking the back of my head with her broad hand, rocking me back and forth, back and forth till I shushed. "It's awright. You didn't know no better. Hush now, Baby." She held me for the longest time. "Dying ain't no time fo' grievin'." Just the same, she made sure that we planned a funeral so her Baby could mourn proper.

Carrying Petty in a Buster Brown shoebox to where the woods took over the back yard, I felt as if we entered a deep forest. My small hands gripped the shoebox with Petty inside. "Lemme tote the shovel," Eva said. Behind the thick stand of bamboo we cleared leaves and sticks off a flat piece of ground. I stood silently while Eva stepped down on the edge of the shovel biting into the ashen earth. With each toss of her wrist, she slung the dirt aside. Bite and toss, bite and toss. "I don't want to put her in the dirt," I whimpered.

Eva didn't break her rhythm. "We ain't nothin' but dirt, Baby. Sho as dere's a Jesus, this dog goin' back where she come from." She took the box from my hands and placed it in the shallow grave. We both kicked the dirt back in the hole, my effort half-hearted. Head cocked back, Eva looked up toward the sky.

I was as sad as an eight-year-old can be. Yet Eva seemed strangely happy. She raised her chin, lifted her arms, and in a deep, rumbling tone she sang, "On Jordan's stormy banks I stand . . . I am bound for the Promise Land." Then in her softest voice, she ended with "steal away, steal away, steal away to Jesus." After that she set me down on her knee and rambled on and on about "gloryland," "meeting Jesus," "crossing to de other side," and "going home." She talked about heaven, saying that Petty's "body done turn loose her soul." She talked about the angels and the pearly gates. "Hit's a place of joy!" I didn't know what all the words meant, but the flood of words, the far away look mesmerized me. After a long pause of silence, Eva tilted her chin sky-ward again.

"Petty done put on her wings, Baby. Look up yonder, you see em? Look, Baby!" She threw her head back, teeth gleaming . . . and sure enough, I saw Petty floating on the clouds, standing on her hind legs, white tummy showing, wings on, outstretched paws flying high, looking down. Smiling. We sat right down in the crunchy fall leaves, me in Eva's lap, both of us watching Petty winging her way home, Eva and me singing and grinning to beat the band.

We played with our dogs outside, never inside. LaClaire climbed trees and hung out with Rusty and the neighborhood boys. In fact, most of our time was spent outdoors, though Eva had to regularly push me out and lock the door to "give that young 'un some fresh air" because I didn't want to leave her side.

One day when I was in fourth grade, I paid the price for not playing outside, for staying inside to tend my little cousin Stevie. Not a happy tale. It was shortly after Mother brought baby Stevie home to live with us. When the doctor told Mama Lillian that her daughter Sara wouldn't be able to care for her newborn baby because of the brain tumor, a phone call set up a chain of events. Mama Lillian called Daddy Van, who called Clara Lee, who talked to Buster, who spoke to Eva. The deal was done. Stevie would come to live with us. Eva declared it a joy to have "one more of God's churren to tend." That's how Stevie came to live with us.

"I know 'bout family takin' care o' family," Eva said. "Didn't my mama take in baby Miriam when cousin Lucille had trouble? And didn't Miss Lillian take in little Van when his mama lef' him?" That's what families do. Eva rolled with the tide, seeing the baby as yet another gift from God that the waves washed up on her shore. Stevie's assimilation into our family was seamless. Knowing he was in Eva's capable hands, everyone rested easy—his mother, his grandparents, and his aunt and uncle who'd taken him in.

Angie and Stevie

Stevie arrived in our household not too long after Petty died, so Eva wisely shifted my focus to Stevie to lift my drooping spirit. "I needs you to help Beba take care o' this sweet baby," she said. Stevie became my excuse to stay inside.

When school let out, I'd rush home to see whether Stevie was awake, or I'd hit the swinging kitchen door with a thwap. "Is it time for his bottle?" I asked. Eva placed a cool bottle of milk in a pan of water, and I'd pull up a stool beside the stove to watch impatiently for the bubbles to rise. Eva instinctively knew when to lift the bottle out. I sniffed the milk's sweet warmth when she shook a few drops on the inside of her wrist. "It just right, Baby," she declared and handed the warm, glass bottle to me.

I attached myself to the wriggling bundle like a kangaroo tending her joey. His feet rarely touched the floor. He was *my* baby. Eva wasn't stingy. She taught me how to hold, feed, and change him. We stayed inside except when we sunned his little naked body on a blanket in the back yard.

One hot summer afternoon, Eva put me in charge of watching Stevie on the side porch at the back of the house. He was napping in his crib that Eva put out there to catch the breeze. The bed was encased on all sides with a fine screen. A screened top folded back and one side unlatched to make lifting him out easy. No gnat or skeeter ever touched my baby Stevie.

Baby Stevie

Well, this afternoon, a tall man with thin brown hair appeared out of nowhere on the side porch steps. I didn't know him from Adam's house cat, but he smiled politely, asked my name. "I'm Angie," I answered, just as politely, like Eva taught me. He opened the screened door and came on the porch.

"Angie, I'm Steve's father. I've come to take him for a ride. We won't be long." I thought nothing of it when he lifted the crib's top and scooped the sleeping infant into his arms, walked down the steps, and got into his car.

Eva was ironing in her room behind the kitchen when I rushed in with the good news. "I met Stevie's daddy. He's taking him for a ride!" I sang. Her back was to me, and in one motion she unplugged the iron, set it on its haunches, took two steps around the corner and dialed 310. "Mista Busta, the baby done gone," Eva said. Calm as you please.

The next days were nightmarish—police at the house asking questions, Mother and Daddy looking at me hard, saying nothing, LaClaire asking, "What were you *thinking*?"

Sequestering myself in my bedroom, away from the accusing words and disappointed looks, I wept for what seemed like days. Someone stole Stevie on my watch. *My* watch.

And Eva came.

"Hush, now. It's awright, Baby. You didn't have cause to know. Hush." She made me a grilled cheese sandwich slathered with mayonnaise on the inside and butter on the outside. She stirred chocolate syrup in my milk, usually saved for a special treat. She ran my bath water, something she'd stopped doing a while back. My big pitcher ears had not picked up that Steve's mother Sara and her husband were estranged, that he was mad as a poked pit bull that the Williamses had taken his son.

But nobody messes with Buster Williams, especially not in Berkeley County. He could stop trains and buses, garner a posse of highway patrolman, and get the sheriff out of bed at 2:00 a.m. It took two days, but the police found Stevie and his father in a motel in Florida. A highway patrolman drove Stevie all the way to Moncks Corner. He arrived home smiling and cooing. We never heard from his father again.

Stevie's joyous presence lasted three years—years I savored. Since birth, Rusty had toddled after LaClaire, who happily took him under her growing, graceful arms. Eva bequeathed Stevie to me—gave me my own live baby to tend.

My bliss ended abruptly. Out of the blue it seemed, my parents sent Stevie to Estill—to Mama Lillian and Daddy Van, to his grandparents, to that peaceful household. Why? Nobody told me anything. I was distraught.

"If I'd taken better care of him, they wouldn't have sent him away," I cried to Eva.

"Baby, ain't nonna your doing," she said as she pulled my head to her. She knew more than she was letting on.

Well, whose doing was it? I thought, as I buried my head in her apron that smelled of onions and chicken.

"Bad can turn to good, Baby. You listen to Beba now. This fo' the best. Wait 'n see. It'll be awright." With this ray of light gone, a perpetual overcast sky stretched across the Williams house—from the kitchen where Stevie sat in the high chair to the bedroom where he bumped his head to sleep every night. So I went outside, outside to the playhouse, outside to read, outside to walk among the flowers, outside to delve into the woods where we buried Petty.

Eva's father Daddy Bill died several years later. Oh, he was a favorite visitor. When I heard Daddy Bill's wagon wheels and Agnes's hooves crunch on the rock driveway, I dashed to the side porch. "Good afternoon, chile," he said, pulling off his hat. He climbed down from the wagon to unload corn, tomatoes, black-eyed peas, or pole beans that grew in his garden. "I'll jes carry dese wedge-a-tubbles round back," he said. He never set a foot inside the house nor approached the front door. If Eva's cousin dropped by for a visit, Eva would step outside and usher her in the kitchen through the back door. But Eva lived there—she used all seven doors any time she pleased.

When Daddy Bill visited, I sat on the front porch watching sweet-faced Agnes swish flies with her tail. Sometimes I'd scrape the metal chair across the tile floor just to see the mule's big ears flinch. Daddy Bill's leaving was a captivating ritual. He'd haul himself up to the seat, turn with a look, nod his head and touch the tip of his hat with two fingers. Body still, leather reins lifted, eyes fixed on Agnes, he paused. With a flick of the wrist, the reins slapped against the mule's haunch, and the wagon lurched into motion, rocks crunching. "Click, click, giddyup." Daddy Bill and Agnes headed home.

When Daddy Bill died, the whole Williams family went to the funeral at Rock Hill Baptist Church. The church was a small white building with a bell hanging in its steeple, a wooden cross on top. A rope hung inside the front door to ring the bell, and I had an urge to pull on that rough rope right then and there. Eva always said that those devilish thoughts were "meanness popping out. Let em go, chile." I let it go. Inside a sea of white shone—white dresses, white hats, white shirts, pants, and coats. Is this a funeral? I thought, *Where's all the black? Oh, there, there in the choir, about a dozen folks robed in black.* I was struck by so many dark faces lined up in rows, ranging in tones from coal to caramel. *Why are they all called 'black' people?* I wondered.

A man dressed in a black suit ushered us to a pew at the front where the preacher sat in a high-backed chair. I spied Eva and relaxed a bit because she wasn't crying or carrying on. As usual, a white handkerchief poked out of the edge of her cuff, handy to dab perspiration off her forehead or wipe her glasses. She was calm as the water at low tide . . . until the tide started to turn.

A low humming rolled in as the choir began a lazy sway. Ever so slightly the volume rose. The pace increased. The swaying lengthened. The congregation and the preacher joined in, gradually filling the church with a sound like a train revving up to roll up a mountain. And sure enough, out burst a noise that made me jump in my seat. "Go down, *Moses.* Let my people *go.*" While clapping double-time and stomping to the rhythm, their voices boomed like an orchestra of different instruments playing the same song. Then they'd soften and sing, "I'd rather have Jesus than silver or gold . . . ."

After a while the reverend preached long and hard about Daddy Bill's going to heaven, being at peace, seeing Jesus. He stretched his arms wide, and the people raised their hands and said, "Praise God!" His Bible flip flopped as he shook it above his head to make a point, holding it with thumb and forefinger, pacing side to side. He didn't read a word. "In my father's house are many mansions," and the crowd called out, "Yes, Jesus!" People talked about Daddy Bill's goodness punctuated with "Amen!" and "Tell it, brother!" People shouted with joy that Daddy Bill was "goin' home to Jesus. Hallelujah!"

I caught the spirit right then and there and began clapping too—until Mother grabbed my arm and brought it down with a jerk. We stayed for several hours, long enough for Daddy Bill to get to heaven. At Trinity Episcopal Church in Pinopolis, we were in and out in one hour flat on Sundays, fifteen minutes max for a funeral.

Eva told me that Daddy Bill's funeral heated up right good after we left and lasted till nightfall. The last sounds I heard coming from the church were Eva's favorites. "Steal away, steal away, steal away to Jesus . . . steal away home. I ain't got long to stay here." I had a pretty good inkling of that home they were talking about. But I didn't want to go to my home right then because I knew I'd be in for it for getting carried away during the service. And Eva wasn't gonna be there.

Daddy Bill was dead, Uncle Tony was dead, Petty was dead. But Eva said that nobody you love ever dies "cause you carry em round right chere in yo' heart, Baby," and she thumped her chest with her fingers. Death was the curve on Eva's full, ribbed lips, a far-away look, a lively spiritual, and a winged pup yipping from up there somewhere. It was dressing in white, not black, and clapping and shouting— and crying. Yes, tears. But tears of joy, not sorrow, cause "dying ain't no time fo' grievin'." Eva said so.

I was not aware then of *another* kind of dying . . . a slow death seeping into the fabric of my very own family.

Chapter 6

Summertime

Summer time, and the livin' is easy.
Fish are jumpin', and the cotton is high.
Yo' daddy's rich, and yo' ma is good looking.
So hush, little baby, don't you cry.
　　　　　　—George Gershwin, composer

Eva and I sat on the back steps shooting watermelon seeds across the grass, eating the cool pink flesh, juice dripping off our chins. She taught me to roll my tongue around the slick black seeds and spurt them out with a *thoosh*. Afterwards, I washed my fingers and face under the spigot at the foot of the steps, inhaling the mint that grew rampant under the dripping faucet. I picked the winged-tipped leaves to float in iced tea at suppertime. Other summer days I'd sit on the porch helping Eva nurse the ice cream churn, turning the crank till my arms got sore, refilling the ice, sprinkling it with salt to make the ice cream firm. We added strawberries or peaches at the end.

Eva insisted we "tend to bidness" on that back stoop too. Summertime brought bushels of peas to shell and beans to snap, as well as crocus sacks stuffed with silk-bearded corn to shuck. Side by side, Eva and I tackled a bushel basket of butter beans. I'd run my thumb from one end of the pod to the other, popping out green beans until the bowl in my lap overflowed. I eagerly awaited Eva's praise.

"Now ain't you a helper, chile."

Other times Eva watched from the kitchen window as LaClaire, Rusty, and I fooled around in the back yard before bedtime. I didn't feel left out then, when the three of us gathered at dusk dressed in our pj's playing Simon Says or swing-the-biscuit, or we lay on our backs spotting dogs and doughnuts in the drifting clouds. Sometimes we'd tie a string around a June bug's leg and watch it fly in a circle or clamp the dead shell on our nose, squealing with delight. At twilight we'd catch fireflies in Mason jars. Eva poked holes in the tops with an ice pick and let us take them to bed. Many summer nights the iridescent green twinkles blinked me to sleep.

Those early years of our family were like riding the wave of a Debussy symphony—each movement a surprise that delights. Given Daddy's zest for living, there were regular crescendos, high adventures. Some impromptu. Some planned. Daddy conducted activities with a confident hand, Mother assisted with awe and grace, and Eva directed the show. Eva was behind the scene assuring the family functioned with precision. The occasional cacophony that threatened, Eva smoothed over. It was Eva who dealt with the sugar rationing and the ban on pre-sliced bread during war time. Later it was Eva who pushed us out the door to make our piano lessons on time. It was Eva who packed up the family for vacations, and Eva who sewed nametags on our shirts, shorts, and socks for summer camp.

Eva and family at Pawley's Island

Our summers in those days were idyllic mostly. The whole family took off to Pawley's Island for a month. We filled up both cars with a few clothes and "a heap of food," as Eva would say, and headed to a rambling house at the old beach resort north of Georgetown, South Carolina. We drove up highway 17 reading Burma Shave signs, waving to the chain gang clearing

the roadside in their black-and-white striped overalls. We couldn't wait to get to the beach! Everyone
called Pawley's "elegantly shabby," and we loved it.
We arrived at the shore where shrimp, crab, and fish
teemed in the creeks. Daddy and Mother fished; Eva
and we three children walked the beach and crabbed.

My first lesson on sex came from Eva when we
went crabbing. Carrying a bucket full of crab lines,
LaClaire, Rusty and I trailed like puppies behind
Eva to the tidal pools brimming with fat blue crabs.
The female crabs wear aprons on their underbellies,
she explained. Sure enough, one of the crabs was
a mama crab with orange eggs bulging out of her
apron. Eva told us to throw her back so she could
have more babies. Male crabs, also called "Jimmys,"
sported pointers embedded in the shell that covers
their bellies. Jimmys were keepers. I didn't yet grasp
Eva's explanation about the male's pointer hiding
under the female's apron. All I really wanted to do
was catch the scampering bug-eyed creatures.

Eva showed me how to wind the thick cotton
cord around a sturdy stick. At the other end of the
line of about eight feet, I tied a double knot around
a squishy chicken neck. I liked hearing the plop
of the neck as it disappeared beneath the murky
water. "Skretch the string good 'n tight, wait to feel
a nibble," Eva said. Crabs were prolific, so the latch-
ing-hold part was easy.

The hardest part was dragging the neck s l o w l y
so the crab wouldn't let go, and getting it close enough
to scoop it up with the long-handled net without the
crab's seeing me and scooting away, leaving a dust
trail beneath the water. That happened a lot. I'd turn
pouting toward Eva, who was catching them hand
over fist. She patted my head and pulled me close to
her wide bare feet at the edge of the water. "Patience,
Baby. Patience. You smarta 'n that crab," she said.

LaClaire always found a special spot away from
us, Rusty at her side. She had a knack for pulling in
the crabs fast and steady, never a loose line. Besides,
her long arms stretched the net way out to scoop
the crabs before they caught sight of her shadow.

She was a natural. To this day LaClaire remains the Crab Queen. We'd catch a bushel before suppertime. Eva made sure I caught a few. "Didn't I tell you, chile? Jes take patience."

One day we walked down the beach laden with our crabbing gear and met a young black woman strolling hand-in-hand with a blonde-haired toddler. "Mind your manners. Say 'hello'," Eva said before striking up a conversation with the woman about the fluctuating tide.

"Do it always flush back 'n forth like that?" the woman asked as she stared out at the breakers.

"Yeah, it do that right reg'lar," Eva said, adding, "Crabbing best when it flush out." My heart filled with pride—my Eva was so smart.

Another place our family enjoyed in the summer was Wampee, a spit of land at the tip end of the Pinopolis peninsula that had once been a thriving plantation. "Wampee" was the Indian name for chickweed. When the lake was low, remnants of pottery and arrowheads reminded us to respect the Native Americans who lived there first.

At one time the Wampee plantation house, built in 1842, was home of Charles Macbeth, Esq., Mayor of Charleston. The house itself survived by a hair when the surrounding lands were flooded to make Lake Moultrie in the 1940s. Big Wampee included the original spruced-up house plus a large building for meals and meetings, with a wide porch overlooking the lake. It became the entertainment and meeting center for officers of Santee Cooper, their board, and other state officials. Lucky us, we had ready access to this recreational paradise because Daddy served on the Board of Santee Cooper.

A short walk down a sandy road was Little Wampee. It had a mess hall and a cluster of cabins originally constructed for the workers during the building of Lake Moultrie. Situated on a two-acre cove the land looked out to three small islands a couple of miles out into the lake. We named the islands Snap, Crackle, and Pop for our favorite breakfast cereal that came in little boxes. LaClaire as a teenager became enamored with Esther Williams, America's mermaid, and swam out to those islands regularly. So afraid that she wouldn't make it back to the cove, I stood on the shore watching her image shrink to a speck, disappear, and then miraculously reappear on the swim back. Always independent, LaClaire rarely ran to Eva in distress, and I never saw her cry. Eva gave LaClaire her space. "I gots my eye on her. So do de Lawd. Don't you worry none," she said. Eva had the faith. I worried anyhow.

Little Wampee became home base for the family many summers. I felt free as a weed there. The army-green cabins matched the color of the tall pines that lined the shore. We each enjoyed a separate hut with two built-in beds, an unfinished table between them, and a naked light bulb overhead. Another cabin only a ten-second sprint behind the first row served as the bathroom for everyone. Eva and Chester too.

At Wampee I gravitated to the mess hall where Eva spent her time. It had a screened porch with rocking chairs and a main room with an open fireplace, win-

*Rusty and Eva
at Little Wampee*

dows all the way round and a table that could seat twenty diners. A wide doorless opening led to a kitchen almost the size of the big room. Everything in it was king-sized—the black stove, the commercial refrigerator, and tall wooden cabinets. Even the pots and iced tea glasses dwarfed ours at home. Eva and the Wampee kitchen seemed to go together. Big and buxom, she needed plenty of room to do her turning in, and Wampee suited her just fine.

Mostly I tagged behind Eva in the kitchen or in the berry bushes nearby.

"Beba hankerin' for a blackberry pie," she announced out of the blue, and off to the brambles we'd go, picking buckets of berries for pies and cobblers. The prickly bushes grew over my head and stretched as far as my little eyes could see. Eva made me wear long sleeves and long pants for berry picking. The hard, red berries were "bitter as gall," she said. I had no idea what "gall" was, but I was taking no chances. The two-toned ones "ain't quite ripe," and the juicy black ones "is just right." Fingertips, mouth and tongue stained purple, I ate as many as I put in my tin bucket. In no time we were both slick from heat, but I never missed out on these escapades with Eva.

Chester, who also went to Wampee, warned us to be on the lookout for snakes that liked the blackberry bushes. Eva paid him no mind, but once inside the patch, she'd whisper, "Watch out for mista rattler, chile," and we marched right into the thickest part to get the fattest berries. No snake would scare off my Eva.

But one day a snake scared the living daylights out of *me*! Every day after lunch Eva sent us children to separate cabins for rest and reading hour. No swimming after lunch. You'd cramp and drown if you swam right after eating, so went the old wives' tale. As I was walking through the unmown grass to the bathhouse during rest time, barefooted as usual, the instep of my foot curved over a round, hard object. I looked down. Under my arch lay a huge black snake. I screamed but couldn't move. Eva bounded out of her cabin shouting for Chester to bring a hoe. He came running.

"Kill it! Kill it!" I yelled, still immobile. Chester raised the hoe and chopped the snake's head off in one sharp blow.

I shook all over afterwards, and Eva tended to me in my cabin. Daddy arrived after work and heard my tale of woe. "What kind of snake was it?" he asked. Now, we Williams children knew our snakes.

Daddy made sure of that because South Carolina had the largest variety of poisonous snakes in the United States. The Lowcountry was crawling with snakes like the deadly water moccasin and diamondback rattler. Pointy heads—poisonous. Round heads—friendly. I racked my brain for a lie he'd believe. I couldn't think of one.

Looking to the floor, I mumbled, "A king snake."

He looked over at me with sad brown eyes. "You know better than to kill a king snake, Angie. They eat rats and other varmints. They're our friends," he reminded me.

He slipped off his belt, wrapped the buckle around his knuckles, and slapped the loose end against my bottom while I cried.

Afterwards Eva took me aside, patted my head, and leaned down to whisper in my ear. "It okay, Baby. Never you mind. You didn't know. The head can shet off when we gits scared." I wore sandals the rest of that summer.

A blackberry cobbler was the reward for a hot, sticky afternoon's work. Eva bumped the sifter against the butt of her hand as a sprinkle of flour drifted like snow across the glass dish, readying it for the fresh berries. She reminded me that I was her best helper when I turned the little wooden crank with my small fingers. Other than fresh blackberry and peach desserts, meals at Wampee were filled with Big Boy tomatoes, corn on the cob, butter beans, biscuits, fish, and more fish. Breakfast, dinner, supper. Fish. Eating Eva's fried fish was the best part of summers at Wampee.

One morning when the sun was barely peeking over the horizon, I heard Eva talking to herself. "I gots to cold do some turnin' dis morning to get breckwus on fore Cap'n Busta get back." I was already perched on a high stool watching Eva cook. She kept glancing out of the window over the sink that looked on the dull grey-green water of the lake. An aluminum speck rounded the bend. "Oh, Lawdy! Cap'n Busta done comin!" and with increased shuffling and slamming, she started to moving twice as fast.

She was a little behind this morning because she'd taken me fishing earlier. As I listened to the grits pop and watched the specks of perspiration appear on Eva's forehead, it seemed that the day was half gone. Eva made me hit the sack early the night before. "I want you to be bright eyed and bushy tailed for fishin," she said. We'd already been up since five o'clock. Daddy had left earlier while it was still pitch dark, heading to the dam across the lake to fish for rockfish (striped bass) once the sun came up.

Eva and I didn't have to go far, just a few steps to the edge of the cove. Slick mud caked to our bare feet like brown moccasins as we walked to her favorite fishing corner. The fog hung thick with promise. I rubbed the sandman from my eyes with one hand and clutched a thin bamboo cane with the other. Eva checked the hooks and clipped small red-and-white bobbins on each line. Plump earthworms wiggled in a peach can. We had dug them up under the pines the evening before. Eva did most of the digging, but I put in the black dirt for them to squirm in. Just before bedtime I sprinkled them with water so they wouldn't feel like sandpaper when we put them on the hooks. Eva always made me bait my own. "Tech em. See? 'E won't bite. Just de Lawd's creature, Baby," she said.

Eva's respect for living creatures from worms to roaches never ceased to amaze me. When a housefly blended into her dark arm, she didn't flinch. "Don't pay it no nevermind," she advised. Eva taught me to hold still during the feather steps of a fly, a bee, even a wasp—me cool as a cucumber. Imagine that! Mosquitoes were another thing. I always smacked them, bringing tiny smears of blood to my arm or leg. This didn't set well with Eva. "Dey ain't doing you no harm, chile. Just bresh em off. Don't gots to *kill* em." This morning Eva simply shooed them away with a swat of her dish towel and checked her bait.

Cool mud oozed between my toes as we stood ankle deep in the still water of the cove. I shivered. My fingers fumbled several worms until I found a juicy one. The hook easily pierced the head. I pushed the rest of the corrugated body down, around, and up until it formed a perfect crook. Eva smiled as I dropped the unleaded line in the water with barely a ripple. *This* morning I was going to catch a fish big enough to eat. She said Jesus wouldn't like it if we fried up baby fish.

In no time Eva had strung six hand-sized bream. She poked a stick through their gills and pursed mouths and lay them at the water's edge. An occasional feeble flap of a tail splashed her leg. Finally I felt a tug on my bait. Once on shore the shiny fish measured about five inches. "Big enough to eat," Eva declared. Then off to the kitchen she gave me a one-armed hug. Proud as Punch, I knew Daddy would eat my fish for breakfast this morning.

Though I loved fish, it was biscuit making, not fish frying, that triggered the best memories—just Eva and me singing and getting messy. With a big metal spoon, Eva dug out three or four wads of shortening, which she plopped into a pottery bowl. Some people used butter or margarine, but it had to be Crisco with the blue and white label. "Nuttin' else fit to eat," Eva said.

She rapidly sliced the globs into pieces with the side of the spoon. Then she poured several cups of Red Brand self-rising flour into a metal sifter. My job was to hold the sifter over the bowl, turn the handle and sprinkle the flour over the Crisco chunks as Eva continued cutting them smaller and smaller. Sometime during the process—I never knew when—Eva would start singing and moving her feet to the rhythm while she sang:

Mama's li'l baby love' short'nin', short'nin',
Mama's li'l baby love' short'nin' bread.
Bring out de skillet, bring out de pan.
Mama's gona make it fas'iz she can.

The switch from adding flour to pouring in milk, the exchange from metal spoon to wooden spoon and stirring all happened without a break in rhythm as Eva blended the three white ingredients into a doughy mass. She powdered the table and both hands with flour then scooped the sticky glob from the bowl and rolled it around in the flour until it became a ball the size of a cantaloupe. A yeasty smell drifted to my nose as I anticipated the next step.

Eva pushed into the rubbery mass with the heel of her hand. Down and out, she stretched the dough, pulling it back to fold over itself, forming another mound to bump down, push out and fold over. Bump, push, fold. When the dough got tacky, she dusted her hands with more flour without skipping a beat. The rhythm continued until the texture was "jes right so de air still in 'em. Make 'em light 'n a feather," she'd say.

My turn! A splash of flour around the rolling pin and the flattening began. I pressed and pressed the dough until it made a circle the size of a lazy Susan. With a small juice glass, I spun the lip into a hill of flour, pushed down on the dough and twisted the glass. When baby circles filled the giant circle, I poked my fingers in my flour pile, picked up each biscuit by its edge and placed it in a neat row on the baking pan.

Biscuits in the oven this morning at Wampee, I perched on the stool to watch my fish crackle in the shallow grease of the cast iron pan. Eva had saved it for last. The corn meal turned crisp and tan. Daddy would just love it! I heard him on the porch whistling to the bobwhites the way he did every morning, killing time until Eva called for breakfast. These days lately, he seemed more quiet.

"Breckwus, Cap'n Busta." When he came in and sat at the head of the long table, I raced in with my fish on a plate.

"Daddy, look! All by myself! *You* eat it!" He fluffed my matted curls and piled it on the platter with the others—on top. I scooted back to the kitchen with Eva. Daddy called for more coffee and shouted how good the fish was.

"Yep, yourn was the sweetest o the lot. Could tell by the way the tail curl—a sign of a *real* sweet fish!" Eva said. My cheeks flushed from the steamy grits, the warming sun that poured in the window, and pride. Waiting for Daddy to finish his meal, Eva started heating a big pot of water to fix my favorite summer snack—boiled peanuts. They soaked in the heated salted water for half a day until the hard shells turned supple enough to pry open to the soft nut inside. How I loved boiled peanuts! But it'd be a while before these would be ready.

Breakfast over, I jumped off the stool and ran to help Eva clear the table. I picked up Daddy's unused spoon to put in the drawer behind the table and glimpsed the large white platter bare, except for crisp crumbs and two small fish—one with a curled tail. I dropped the spoon and darted to Eva. Clutching her knees, I cried, "He didn't *eat* it!" Tears poured while she patted my shoulder.

"Your daddy gots lots on his mind dese days, Baby. Hush now."

I sniffled to the kitchen with Eva. She split my fish from gill to tail, lifted a sliver of white flesh exposing a delicate skeleton. She separated the backbone and placed the tiny fillets on two small plates. I sat immobile on the stool, eyes flooded. Eva picked up a section with her thumb and forefinger and placed it gently on the inside of her lip where it turned pink. "Umm . . . um! Just like I said, sweetest fish in the lot. Open your mout, chile." And morsel by morsel Eva placed the fish on my tongue. Soon it was gone. My eyes teared again. My oily fingers reached round her neck as she swooped me up to her broad shoulders. Dodging the light string overhead, I smiled to hear her say again, "Yes, *suh*, that sho was a *sw-e-eet* tasting fish!"

Another summer at Wampee I woke early too. I was about four. When Daddy returned from fishing, he called for me to take a spin around the cove. Eva shook me awake. I wondered, *me? With Daddy? By myself?* I ran to the shore waiting for his boat to come in, crust still in my eyes, wearing one-piece yellow pajamas with red buttons and red piping down the front. Daddy nosed the boat in, and I scrambled over the bow barely wetting my ankles. Daddy's invitation issued with good intentions, I accepted with benign ignorance. Daddy had decided I needed to learn to swim. LaClaire and Rusty already knew how, and it was LaClaire and Rusty who went fishing with Daddy in the boat. As usual, I was a step behind, or a step inside, with Eva.

We flew around the cove in a wide circle as I crouched on the triangle of the bow. Blonde tangles flying, the spray stinging my cheeks with each slap of the boat. My fingers gripped the gunnels with fear and delight. About fifty feet from shore, he cut the engine and called me to come to the back, the boat still swaying from the quick stop. I teetered unsteadily from bow to stern.

When I reached his outstretched arms, he stood, lifted me high, and flung me like an anchor far out into the dark water.

"Swim!" he shouted, and pushed the throttle out of neutral into forward, leaving me in his wake. I was terrified—first from the shock of the water striking my chest, then from the water rushing up my nose and down my throat. My nose stung, my throat closed. I choked, coughed and sputtered. I flailed my arms. My head went under. I kicked my legs with all my might. Hard. Harder.

My head surfaced and I gulped precious air, frantically pulling at the water with my hands. With both feet and hands in gear, I dogpaddled toward my father, who stood cheering me on.

"Come on. Kick! You can do it. Paddle! That's it!" When my toes finally touched the mushy bottom, he said, "I'm proud of you, Angie." It was a red letter day. I learned how to swim . . . and to not trust my daddy.

Watching from the kitchen window, Eva met me at the mess hall steps as I ran to her. But she didn't kneel down to hug me as Daddy observed the scene. She pulled my head to her thigh and said loud enough for him to hear, "Never you mind. Your daddy done right to teach you. To dis day, your Beba can't swim a lick. You way head of me, Baby."

Eva knew who buttered her bread.

As I got older, I increasingly wandered from Eva's side. But Eva was always present, looking out of the kitchen window or watching us from her fishing corner in the cover. My first taste of real freedom came at Wampee. We had a little johnboat with a 15-horse-power motor which we were allowed to drive anywhere in the cove

. . . once we could swim and were strong enough to pull the rubber-handled crank rope. And we could run until the gas ran out. It did almost every day. We kept that motor humming.

One day I was strong enough to pull the thick cotton cord quick enough to start the engine myself. To celebrate I putted to the middle of the cove, turned the motor's arm level with the transom, and spun in

Angie and Rusty at Wampee

circles till I got dizzy! On shore, I ran to sing my triumph to Eva. She didn't look up from peeling a potato. "I know you can do wut you puts your mind to. But if'n you think ridin' 'roun' and 'roun' is gona git you somewheres, you gots another think comin', missy." Eva always set the record straight.

As LaClaire, Rusty and I got older, part of our summers we spent away from Wampee at camps in North Carolina where the Whaley girls and other Charleston children spent their summers. LaClaire and I went to Rockbrook Camp near Brevard, Diana Drexel went too, the year she lived with us. Rusty went to Mondamin nearby. LaClaire adored camp; in fact, in college she became a swim instructor there. I, on the hand, extracted a negative: I imagined that Mother and Daddy shipped us off for two months so they could get rid of us, so they could be free.

They aren't home half the time anyway. It's Eva who takes care of us, I thought. The real test, especially that first summer, was being away from Eva for eight weeks, fifty-six whole days! The idea made my feet drag while Eva helped pack a foot locker full of green and white uniforms with red ties, riding jodhpurs, a poncho and stationery.

I wanted to write to Eva, but Mother dismissed the idea. "She can't read," she said. I knew better. I saw her writing the grocery lists, copying the letters carefully from the labels. I saw her reading her Bible at night; she knew it by heart. Looking back, I wondered if Mother simply wanted me to write to *her* when she knew Eva was the one I'd miss the most. At Rockbrook I learned how to cry without making a sound. After lights out. And only because I missed Eva so much that I couldn't help it.

Charleston area girls, Rockbrook Camp, Brevard, NC
(Angie the second row; Diana and Miss Em back row)

Up through ten years old, I wasn't especially keen on all the outdoor living that my family enjoyed, but I eventually came around by eleven or twelve. Rockbrook helped. Everyone was required to do everything—from archery to hiking. We earned white and red beads for our accomplishments. I wanted my necklace to have more beads than anyone in my cabin, and it did. *Eva would be proud*, I thought.

I liked canoeing. The graceful paddle maneuvers seemed like ballet—feathering the droplets across a silky surface. Learning to breathe in the pocket of air underneath an overturned canoe helped me push through a fear of drowning since my first swim at Wampee. Winning the Prize Canoe

Trip was a dream come true—a week of canoeing the French Broad River. I enjoyed it all—the adrenalin rush while riding the rapids, the relief after a hard push, my arm and back muscles tight with fatigue. When the day's trip ended and we took a dip in the cool river before collecting firewood for the camp, I thought of Eva, Eva who brought me that same calm refreshment of spirit. I missed her.

Horseback riding, on the other hand, was a challenge. Always a bit scared of horses, big animals with sharp hooves and snorting sounds, I, nevertheless, was determined not to let the fear show. Horror of horrors, one year I was chosen for the Prize Riding Trip where campers galloped through thick forests and jumped logs and streams for a week. Shocked and petrified, I approached the instructor to beg off. She said, "Angie, I chose you not because you're the best rider but because you tried so hard," she said. I went. And I fell. And fell. Each time the horse jumped anything over six inches, I was brushing dirt off my bottom, eager to get to the part I enjoyed back at the campsite—currying and feeding the tired animal.

Camping under the stars at night, I prayed to God to keep me safe. And talked to Eva. What was she doing back home? That first year of camp, she told me not to be sad. "Just 'memba we bof lookin' up at de same sky. I ain't far, Baby. Sides, you got Jesus." Making it back to camp in one piece that week was a credit to Jesus and Eva, not my equestrian skills, for sure.

Once back at camp, I made a bee line to the infirmary. A trace of blood appeared on my underwear, so I asked for a band aid, thinking I'd bruised something on one of my falls or rubbed the saddle wrong. The nurse set me straight. "You have the curse," she said.

That was my initiation into womanhood until I got home the next week to Eva. "It ain't no 'curse,' chile," she declared with a broad smile. "God made you special so you can have babies, and that sho as shooting ain't no curse. You a woman now," she said as she pulled me into her. A couple of weeks later, Mother left a pamphlet on menstruation by my bedside. Women like my mother didn't discuss personal things like that. Through LaClaire I learned that Mother forbid the use of tampons "until you marry"—the mere idea horrifying. Thank goodness for LaClaire and Eva, or I wouldn't have had a clue about what was going on with the changes in my body.

The previous summer when I was twelve, I'd become envious that my friends had begun wearing brassieres. Our family had planned a visit to the Drexels' house in Daytona Beach. Before the trip, Eva took me to Barron's Department Store on Main Street. Though whites shopped mostly at Barron's and blacks at Read's, Mr. Bennie Barron always welcomed Eva and put our purchases on Daddy's tab. That day Eva helped me buy a new bathing suit—my first two-piece suit. Granted, I didn't *need* a top, but for the first time I *had* a top, and it resembled a bra. I was tickled pink.

Once in Daytona, the adults flew off to the Bahamas. They left LaClaire, Rusty, Tony, Howard, Diana and me in the care of Mrs. Dooling, an older, anxious, pasty-faced woman. She was *nothing* like Eva, who would not have put up with our shenanigans for an instant. We six ran circles around her while she yelled, cajoled, or begged for orderly behavior. Behind her back we called her "the old biddy." She swore that we gave her shingles, and I don't doubt it.

One overcast day LaClaire, Diana, and I decided to go swimming in the ocean in front of the house. "Don't go beyond your knees," Mrs. Dooling said. She couldn't swim and didn't go down to the beach with us.

Eva would have been upset that we were left alone in front of all that water. "It go clean to China," Eva told us when we vacationed at Pawleys Island. She always went on the beach with us, wearing her uniform, letting the waves wash over her bare feet as they pressed into the sand, watching us out of the corner of her eye. At Wampee on the lake, Eva was there, barefooted on the shore fishing for bream, keeping one eye on us while we swam in the cove.

This day in Florida, no Eva. The sky still gray from a fierce northeaster the day before, the beach was deserted. Giddy with freedom after a rainy day cooped up inside, LaClaire, Diana and I ignored the knee guideline. The waves kicked up pretty high because of the earlier storm. The water tugged at our legs as we waded.

Out of nowhere, a big wave knocked the stuffing out of us, turning us upside down. A powerful force sucked me under with the churning shells. Eventually I was lifted off the bottom, but I couldn't tell which way was up. My chest burned. I grabbed at the water, reaching my arms up, stretching for the top, for air. *I'm dying,* I thought, lungs ready to explode.

At that moment, I burst through the surface with frantic flailing, heaving in the thick air, tasting the salt with each intake of breath and water. My lungs stretched then released like an accordion— expanding, contracting. In. Out. Alive, breathing, eyes stinging. I saw grayness everywhere—the expansive sky overhead, the undulating waves. Treading water furiously, I turned myself around to discover that the undertow had dragged me far away from LaClaire and Diana. Yelling and waving in panic, I called to them, called to Eva.

Daring to wade out to their chests, LaClaire and Diana made a chain with their arms and reached toward me as the current pushed me farther and farther out until Diana and LaClaire became mere spots—like turtle heads on the lake. LaClaire charged out of the water and ran down the beach to the first person she saw, a man with a little boy. She held the child's hand at the water's edge while the man raced to rescue me. His strong arms eventually reached me. He hauled me to shore and lay me face down on the beach to pump water out of me.

Eyes closed, breathing hard, I could hear people gathered round making incoherent noises. I wanted to turn into liquid, ooze into the sand, disappear. My body was intact, but I was so embarrassed. I felt my bare nipples pressed into the rough sand. *Please, God, let me die. I can't get up,* I prayed.

The sea's turmoil had ripped away the top to my bathing suit. I wore only my bottoms. Tears mingled with the sea's salt as I silently called for Eva. She could save me, make everything all right. But she wasn't there, and I'd almost drowned. And, worse, I had nothing to cover my budding breasts.

It was time for summer to end, time to go home—home to Eva.

Chapter 7

When Father Knew Best

*It doesn't matter who my father was; it's who I
remember he was.*
                    —Anne Sexton, poet

Going back home to Eva felt like falling into
a hammock. Whenever I returned from camp or a
family vacation, I flopped into Eva's easy embrace
and let out the breath I didn't know I'd been holding.
Truth be told, our household was structured for us
to feel safe, with or without an Eva.

Mother and Daddy were good, if often absent,
parents. They established rules and routines that
gave us a sense of order and security, a feeling that
someone was in charge—and it wasn't the children.
They presented a united front on acceptable behav-
iors and polite manners, as well as consistent discipline with appropriate consequences. In my parents'
absence, Eva carried out the rules and at the same
time reinforced her own values. She made it clear—
"Ain't no question who driving de bus." No spoiled
children on her watch.

The house rules made life predictable. No
backtalk or sassing adults—including appropriately
respectful tone of voice. No name calling—a careless
"stupid" put me in my bedroom for the rest of the day.
No grades below "Satisfactory" on report cards—an
"S minus" elicited a scolding. No chewing gum in the
house—wads of the rubbery substance lay under the
azalea by the front door. I usually swallowed mine
until Eva said it would close up my bottom.

Household routines included adhering to bed-
times, cleaning plates at mealtime, finishing school
work before play, being home before dark, putting

up our bikes, completing chores, and conserving resources. Daddy once restricted us to four squares of toilet paper per use because of "excessive wadding and balling" of tissue. He ordered it by the case and stored it at the warehouse until Eva requested replenishing. Daily chores were required and charted—emptying the trash, cleaning our bathroom, pulling weeds, polishing silver. Posting my check marks ahead of LaClaire and Rusty brought me great satisfaction.

"You a good girl," Eva commented encouragingly.

I dreaded, however, the Saturday morning inspections. Daddy was adamant about our not leaving the house until we passed inspection. Eva knew Daddy's ritual and taught us everything required to pass inspection—everything from making hospital corners on our sheets to using newspaper to clean the window panes. Daddy bounced quarters on the sheets for tautness and inspected closets and drawers for neatness. He wore white gloves to check for dust on Venetian blinds, baseboards, and tops of doors. Make no mistake, these were serious military inspections. To please him, I kept my room spotless.

LaClaire, on the other hand, often didn't pass inspection. Saturdays found her floor strewn with clothes she'd worn all week. As I scurried to make sure everything in my room looked immaculate, she sat on her bed reading a book. Even when she started dating, punishment didn't faze her. Boys called her from throughout the Lowcountry: from Summerville (sweet boys), from Walterboro (wild boys), from Charleston (refined boys), and from Estill (country boys). LaClaire didn't hesitate to cancel or turn down a date if she'd gotten it in her noggin not to clean her room. LaClaire taught me about a different kind of power, the kind I'd learn more about later from Eva's people, the non-violent protest—the sit-in. Her silent refusals rendered authority helpless. On the sideline, I secretly cheered, suspecting I'd never muster such courage.

The reward for my diligence was the Saturday matinee. When I finished chores and passed inspection, Daddy placed a shiny dime in my palm for the cowboy picture show at the theatre on the corner—nine cents for a ticket, a penny left over for a pink ball of bubble gum that usually ended up under the seat when the gum lost its juice and turned into a rubber clump. *Bugs Bunny, Daffy Duck, Roadrunner,* and *Elmer Fudd* cartoons warmed up the main attraction with the Lone Ranger and Tonto, Johnny Mack Brown or Lash LaRue and his bullwhip. I melted when Gene Autrey played his

Cowboy movies every Saturday

guitar or Roy Rogers sat on Trigger singing a duet with Dale Evans. And because I followed Eva's meticulous cleaning instructions, I rarely missed a picture show.

I tried to finish inspection early so I could go roller skating on the smooth concrete in front of the theatre beforehand. Eva made sure I wore oxfords with thick soles so the clamps would hold after she tightened them with the clunky skate key. I wore the key on a shoe string around my neck so that if I fell and a skate came off, I'd have the key handy. I loved those times, skating in wide circles, speeding past the slow pokes with the wind blowing my hair back. I felt free as the breeze on my face on those Saturday mornings.

It wasn't like me to buck house rules. But for chocolate, I did. One school morning LaClaire and Rusty dared me to leave my bed unmade. They handed over their nickels for a recess snack. I was ecstatic. Sitting in homeroom, I envisioned my choices: an orange dreamsicle, an Eskimo pie, grape or orange double-sticked popsicles, a Nutty Buddy? But I didn't waver from my all-time favorite. This meant not one, not two, but *three* fudgesicles!

Not ten minutes into Miss Fultz's fourth grade class while she was still collecting lunch money from students, Chester appeared at the doorway. Dressed in his white coat, scrawny neck stretched high, he announced smugly, "Miss Angela has to come home to make her bed." Eyes to the floor, I left with Chester. It irked me when Chester showed off his snooty speech by calling me all three syllables of my full name: "An-ge-la."

Eva greeted me with hands on hips, head dipped in disappointment. "Yo daddy gonna have a conniption if he knowed what you done. Now git on in dere and make yo' bed." Chester drove me back to school, more humiliation. Still, I bought *three* fudge-sicles from the canteen at recess that day.

Eva, who never let us get away with a blooming thing, managed to protect us at the same time. She made sure the rules and routines were carried out in our household, but her presence engendered a feeling of comfort and caring that went beyond the regulations. Eva band-aided scraped knees when I fell on my skates and listened to my whines when LaClaire ignored my pesky persistence to let me play with her. Eva shooed me out the door to go to ballet and tap lessons if I lingered. "Skeedaddle outa here, chile," she said. And I'd bounce to Mrs. Knight's studio half a block away.

And when LaClaire was grounded for skipping piano lessons for a year, it was Eva who made sure LaClaire adhered to Daddy's punishment. For a whole year LaClaire brazenly rode off on her bike each week with music books in the basket heading for her lesson. Every day she practiced more diligently than ever. Clever deception, but she got busted when Mother called to ask Mrs. Spann why she'd not received a bill for LaClaire along with mine. She got grounded a *long* time for that one.

Daddy relied on Eva to carry out the discipline he meted out. Eva was proud to have Buster's confidence. Early on, she taught him about rearing his babies, about firmness and fairness, things he had not learned in his own household growing up. True, he may have added his military spin with the Saturday morning inspections, but we were none the worse for wear with those demands, especially since Eva taught us the ropes.

And there were those glorious summer times at Pawley's Island where Daddy let us run free with Eva on the beach and in the creeks. He planned family picnics to our part of Pooshee Plantation, where copious springs ran through before the lakes came. We swam and fished untethered in Jack's Hole many Sundays after church. At Moss Grove Daddy let us steer the jeep and organized hayrides just for us.

In the best of times my daddy was a wonder-filled father. Fun and funny. He turned the radio up and encouraged us to sing, "I was waltzing . . . with my darling . . . to the Tennessee Waltz." He spouted lines from *Alice in Wonderland.* "Off with their heads!" "Righto, gov'nor." "Are you Tweedle Dee or Tweedle Dum?" he teased me. He pretended to be the White Rabbit saying, "I'm late. I'm late. For a very important date," as he left for work.

Language fascinated him, and by extension, us. It seemed there wasn't a word Buster Williams didn't know. A college dictionary beside his bed spilled over with additional meanings or nuances he'd write in with his small, neat hand. At the foot of his bed, an elephantine unabridged dictionary stood at attention on a podium. He paid a quarter if we could spell and define "spurious" or "mendacity," and he explained scientific basics like surface tension by floating a dime on a water glass at suppertime. We marveled. Eva stood to the side, watching with amusement and pride as her Buster delighted his children—her children too.

We all, Eva too, were eager to please my daddy. He expected a great deal from us. He usually meted out consistent, logical consequences for errant behavior. But not always. We might get a spanking for carelessly spilling milk at the table on the evenings when he was tactless and tight. Yet, in the day time, sensitive and sober, a larger transgression might yield a surprising response—like the time I lost Mother's ring.

Mostly removed, Mother abdicated rules to Eva and punishment to Daddy. Eva tried to make sure we steered clear of the master bedroom suite, knowing little good could come of our plundering in Daddy's closet to play with his walking sticks or shoe trees, or rifle through mother's dressing room drawers for lipstick or powder. Mother's dressing room was off limits. A small picture hung beside her mirror. An odd little man in a frock coat and top hat holding a hoop and a stick was pictured above this saying:

> *Never take the property of others.*
> *If you wish people to respect your own property,*
> *Respect that of others.*

When we transgressed, Mother prompted us to read the verse aloud. No further discussion.

But I forever longed to try on Mother's jewelry. If Eva thought I was headed for temptation, she'd say, "Curiosity killed the cat." Not sure what that meant, it nonetheless deterred me on many occasions.

One day I succumbed to temptation and opened a velveteen box that I'd been eyeing. Three matching bands snuggled side by side in the soft cloth. A rectangular ruby sat in the center of each ring, with two flat diamonds on the sides. The smallest ring fit my middle finger perfectly. I blithely walked out of the house and downtown wearing that diamond-ruby ring. Later that day, I arrived home with no ring. "Missy, you done ruint yourself," Eva said. She looked heavenward and said, "Lemme cogitate what to do."

At dinner time, Eva greeted Daddy at the door. "Mista Busta, you ain't gona *believe* what dis chile done when she *know* better." (Eva's way of softening the bad news.) He threw Eva a long look. He received a *longer* look from her that indicated she expected the best from him. Then she delivered the awful news.

He sighed and clasped me by both shoulders, "Taking other people's property without asking is just like stealing. I know you didn't lose the ring on purpose," he said, "but when we do things we shouldn't, bad things often happen." He suggested we retrace my steps. Daddy, Eva and I paraded down the sidewalk and took a left at Main Street, past the wall in front of the bank and two more blocks to the Rexall drug store where I'd stopped and ordered a cherry coke. No ring.

The only place we couldn't search was beneath the drainage grate by the sidewalk in front of the pharmacy. In a last ditch effort, Daddy called the town's maintenance crew to remove the heavy grate. They gladly responded because my daddy was known for his friendly, generous nature. With a group of curious people watching, workmen searched in the debris of mud and leaves. No ring. No one talked on the way home. Once inside, Daddy spoke to the air, "I'll tell Clara Lee," and went to the back of the house.

That was that. Eva looked down at me. "Baby, it's time to thank yo' Jesus." And I did.

My covetous nature obviously was not confined to Mother's jewelry because not long afterwards I transgressed again on a family weekend at Moss Grove. Sometimes my jealousy of LaClaire's attention from Daddy inexplicably reared its green head. It was LaClaire he praised for shooting the most tin cans off the fence post, for scattering dove on the hunts, for riding well. LaClaire could do anything— and everything better than I.

One day I strode out of the cabin at Moss Grove wearing my favorite riding dungarees. Eva's eyebrow lifted quizzically, "Now what you fixin to do, missy?" Her words trailed me. How she could always tell I was up to mischief is beyond me. I walked to the barn and ceremoniously saddled LaClaire's horse, Blaze. A big sorrel, face marked with a slashing white flame. That horse could streak like lightning. My horse's name was Molly and all the name implied—ordinary, docile, slow. A plug. I had to kick her ten times before she would take a first step. What I liked about Molly was not *riding* her but brushing and currying her smooth back and feeling her spongy lips lift grain from my palm. I loved to close my eyes and run my hand from the hard bone between her ears to her nose, fingertips lingering on the velvet cushion.

Goodness knows why I thought I could ride Blaze. Maybe I'd just read *Black Beauty*. Maybe I became bold because it seemed LaClaire always got the best of everything, like the sky blue bicycle at Christmas while mine was a dull navy blue. I saddled up Blaze and led him beside the stall in order to climb into the saddle from the stall's railing since my feet couldn't reach the stirrup from the ground. That's how *big* Blaze was.

The instant he felt my weight, Blaze shot out of the barn like a wasp had stung his rump. I barely had time to grab the reins. The stirrups loose, my feet banged like Raggedy Ann legs against his side. Neck stretched forward and ears back, Blaze was flying, churning up dirt. And I was yelling, clutching the reins, holding on for dear life on the back of a runaway horse.

I saw it coming, the fence ahead. In my panic, the reins fell limp. All I could do was cling to Blaze's neck and twist his mane around my fingers. He rounded the corner of the fence at full speed, cutting so close that the post swiped my leg and flipped me off to the ground in one swift move. Whop! Breath gone and stretched flat, I couldn't move. I imagined a broken leg, an arm at least. As I lay on the hard ground, I looked up to see Blaze galloping around the fence, a brown blur hightailing it back to the barn.

Though nothing except my pride was damaged, I shook from fright. I never wanted to see a horse again. I staggered back to the barn. Blaze stood by his stall, quiet and pretty as you please. So did my father. I got lucky; it was well before toddy time. He didn't chastise me for riding alone or for not asking permission to ride LaClaire's horse.

"Get back on" was all he said. I balked. He looked at me. My eyes pleaded with him as they filled with fearful tears. He didn't flinch. I still didn't move. His eyes didn't deviate. I took a timid step, then another. He held the reins with his left hand and offered his right hand for me to step into so I could reach the stirrup. I slowly lifted a foot to his palm, and he hoisted me up in the saddle. After adjusting the too-long stirrups, he led Blaze and me out of the barn into the sunshine.

After the runaway incident, it took a cute boy with copper hair to lure me back to the horse barn. But I wasn't interested in the horses this day. Herbie Dumeresque was the son of one of Daddy's North Carolina friends who descended on Moss Grove during hunting season. Freckles dotted his cheeks, and his dark eyes shone. Eva caught me staring at him earlier and said with a twinkle, "Now dat's a fine one." Nothing got past my Eva.

Horse mania in young girls usually subsides at about fourteen. They say that petting, grooming, and caring for horses serves as a great transition to boys during those awkward middle years. I was right on schedule. I easily shifted from horses to boys, and my experiences at Moss Grove hastened the shift.

On this warm fall day, the adults scattered over the farm to hunt dove. LaClaire, Rusty, Herbie and I paraded to the barn to saddle our horses. I had trouble tightening the girth on Molly. She liked to puff out her belly so I couldn't cinch it in enough to keep the saddle from slipping once she let the air out. I asked LaClaire for help. Big mistake.

"You're such a baby," she muttered as she walked over to help.

"I'm not a baby," I shot back. Everybody looked up.

"Oh, yeah? Then why do you still suck your fingers? Huh?" she said.

"I don't suck my fingers!" Now that was a story— a *big* story. (We weren't allowed to use the word "lie.") I had just spoken a flat-out lie, in front of God and Herbie Dumeresque.

Most of my growing-up years, I sucked the middle and ring fingers of my right hand, generally accompanied by hair twirling with the left hand. And here I was thirteen years old! It annoyed Mother that Eva didn't join her in the finger sucking battle. "Baby, you kin suck your fingers til the cow come home," she told me. This is the only time I recall Eva's not falling in line with one of Mother's directives. Mother was adamant that I stop "the unattractive, unladylike habit." Equally adamant, Eva simply said, "In Gawd's time, Miss Clara Lee. In Gawd's time." Mother tried everything from making me wear gloves to bed to painting my fingers with a peppered liquid that scalded my tongue. Still, each morning I'd awake with fingers in my mouth. And after years of sucking with two Bugs-Bunny front teeth resting on the middle joints of my fingers, they sported two large calluses. The nickname Bugs didn't bother me as much as those hard knots.

"You do too suck your fingers. Let me see your hand," LaClaire said in a calm voice, moving steadily toward me. Terrified, I darted out of the barn, all three of them chasing after me. I crossed the dirt road and started running across the nearest field— my favorite, the one with the majestic mushroom-shaped oak tree in the middle, the tree that Daddy planted around and wouldn't let them cut down.

The loamy ground made it difficult to keep my footing. Running unevenly, I stumbled over clumps of gray earth trying to stay in the ruts made by the plow. I ran until my nose and throat turned dry. I ran until my legs felt like noodles. Making it almost across the field to the woods, I finally collapsed in the dirt. Within a few desperate breaths, they fell on me, holding me down, victoriously lifting my hand skyward.

Their high voices drifted away as they jogged back to the barn. Dirt and tears mingled into mud as I lay face down. I cried for Eva. Where *was* she? If she had seen them from the cabin window, she would have chased the pack away with a quick yell, "Leave her be!" A green bottle-fly buzzed near my ear. Something pricked at my nose, a familiar musty smell. Eventually I stood up, brushed off my britches, kicked a dirt clod across three rows and trudged back to the barn.

I never sucked my fingers again. "Can't beat God's timing, Baby," Eva told me a couple of days later. *God and Herbie Dumeresque*, I thought to myself.

I never saw Herbie again. And that next summer, Daddy gave me a surprise birthday party hay ride at Moss Grove. The horse pulled the wagon laden with sweet-smelling hay and awkward pairings of young people. I snuggled in the hay holding hands with another cute red-headed boy who never even noticed the fading knots on my fingers.

From the time I can remember, boys always hung around our house. Only boys lived near us, and our yard was the biggest and best to play in. The field beside the house was full of boys playing football or shooting hoops; we were usually right in there with them, especially LaClaire. The back woods were thick with boys playing deers and hounds until dusk dragged everyone home or Eva called us in for supper.

If it rained, we'd gather on the side screened porch, all boys except for LaClaire and me. One summer day someone suggested we have a cussing contest. Now, none of the boys went around cussing, certainly not in front of the Williams girls. Not being a cusser myself, I was all ears. At first it was "shucks," "fiddlesticks," "swannie," "darn," "dog-gone-it," "blast it," and "dad-gum-it." Then they got warmed up: "damn," "hell," "shit," "crap." They threw in "Jap," and "coon" for good measure.

I was shocked when a friend called Brazil nuts "nigger toes." In our household, the word "nigger" or "coon" was never uttered. I'd never heard a curse word from my parents or their friends. (I was forty years old when I said "shit" for the first time. It felt so surprisingly good, I laughed out loud.)

When it seemed they were all cussed out, someone whispered, "fuck." Dead silence. I'd never heard the word. No one ventured to say the worst word of all—"goddamn." We all knew lightning would strike if you took the Lord's name in vain. When I asked Eva about the "F" word, she dismissed it with a flip of her wrist. "Dey is some words ain't worth learnin', much less sayin', chile. Memba that."

LaClaire and I had lots of boy playmates, not necessarily boyfriends. But that changed for me one rainy afternoon. I sat on my bed doing homework. I looked out of my window and saw John Dangerfield walking on the sidewalk by the house. He lived one block up Church Street and was heading to the library. His mother worked there and drove the book-mobile all over rural Berkeley County where children clamored to expand their narrow world. John was in LaClaire's class. Cute as a cocker puppy, he had hair the color of a toasted biscuit and a face full of freckles. Raindrops ran down the window panes puddling into tiny pearls. I kept my eyes on John until the window fog swallowed his figure. That's when I felt a flutter in my chest, a flush to my cheek. I thought I was having a heart attack.

LaClaire probably had experienced dozens of crushes by then, but she seemed more interested in reading than romancing. She was in the eighth grade, I was in sixth. I didn't say anything about my flutter to anyone, but the doodles on the front cover of my 4-H Club Song Book bore witness that something stirred inside. I fervently pledged . . .

> *My HEAD to clearer thinking*
> *My HEART to greater loyalty,*
> *My HANDS to larger service and*
> *My HEALTH to better living.*

And I loved singing the songs like "Dixie," "Old Black Joe," "America," and "The Battle Hymn of the Republic." Between songs, however, I drew hearts with AW + JD inside and wrote in fancy script "*Angela + John*" all over the cover.

I wasn't exactly sure what the hearts and the flutter meant . . . until the day I came home from school and found several boys in our yard. That week LaClaire and her girlfriends were suspended from school. LaClaire, Margaret Bradley (the principal's daughter), and Linden Spann (our piano teacher's daughter) were caught shooting spitballs in class. *Major* offense. Daddy, showing his creative flare, assigned his daughter jobs to do around the house and yard during her home vacation. Mowing the lawn, raking the leaves, weeding the gardens, trimming the bushes. I felt so sorry for her, imagining her hating to miss school, plus having to work so hard.

Until I walked in the driveway to see LaClaire sitting on the porch, book in her lap, feet propped on the brick wall. Stunned, I looked across the yard. Four boys had skipped school that day and were doing LaClaire's yard work. I thought what a clever Tom Sawyer scene, until I noticed my John . . . on his knees pulling weeds! Astounded by my visceral response and without thinking, I blurted out the worst thing I could think of. "You're a . . . a . . . a whore!" I shouted at LaClaire. She looked stricken. Slamming the porch door, I stomped to my room amazed at my flagrant abuse of the name-calling rule. How could she do this to me? She had a million boy friends. Couldn't she leave *one* for me?

Eva opened my door before suppertime. "Your daddy want to see you to de back o' the house," she said. Never good news. Punishment usually was metered out in the back master bedroom.

Dragging my feet, I entered the room.

"I hear you called your sister a name this afternoon," Daddy said.

"Yes, sir, I did."

"And what was it?" he asked.

I hesitated. "A . . . a whore," I said, looking at the rug beneath my feet.

"Oh? And what is a whore?" he asked.

I became flustered. I wasn't sure *what* a whore was.

"Well?" he prodded.

"It's someone who likes boys a lot!" I blurted out.

"Hmmm," he said. "Why don't you look it up to be sure?"

Buster Williams, wordsmith of the highest order, motioned me to the tall podium where *Webster's Unabridged Dictionary* rested. No matter how hard I looked, I could not find the word. Patiently, Daddy let me search at least five minutes.

"Try looking under 'w' instead of 'h,'" he said. Mortified, I continued my search. Found it.

Sexual? Intercourse? Promiscuous? Prostitution? None of those words were in Mrs. Wofford's English class vocabulary list or the Episcopal *Book of Common Prayer*, which had the biggest words I knew.

"Why don't you read the definition to me," he coaxed.

I read the words, stumbling and sputtering over the unfamiliar terms.

"And is this what your sister is?" Daddy asked.

"I have no idea," I whispered.

"Then I suggest you not call people names unless you know what they mean," he said dismissing me with a wry smile. I don't recall apologizing to LaClaire. I hope she forgave me.

When I sheepishly told Eva what I'd done and Daddy's response, she lifted her wooden spoon and pointed toward the heavens. "Member this day, Baby. This your daddy fo' true—them other times, bury 'em."

We sat down at the kitchen table while she talked about how plump and handsome he was when she first met him at the hospital and saved her from the bedpans, how he loved my mother and built us all this fine house, and how generous he was with handouts to "poor folks who's beaten down." How he fixed Daddy Bill's roof when it leaked and made sure Miss Hattie got the best doctor in town. How he cooked us fried bananas and sang us songs. How he gave us bicycles, dogs and horses and hayrides and trips to the Pawley's Island, summers at Wampee, and Sundays at Pooshee. She said my daddy was a good man with a big heart. I wondered if she was talking to me or to herself.

When she paused, I thought of how he'd let me off the hook that very day when I deserved a double whipping for name calling. Eva rose from her chair, walked over to the sink and stared out the window. It was starting to drizzle rain.

"Gawd know your daddy kin be the best," she said.

Photo Gallery

Van Peeples

Lillian Gray Peeples

Francis Gray
Lillian's mother

Jacob David Gray II
Lillian's brother

Young Clara Lee

Clara Lee and baby Rudy

Van and Lillian Peeples' Estill House

Van Peeples workers in Progressive Farmer

Daddy Van and Mama Lillian

The Williams' Pinopolis house

Thomas and Carrie Williams

Russell "Daddy Grand" Williams

Downtown Charleston, SC

Berkeley County Courthouse in 1900s—Mt. Pleasant, SC

Olive's father Isaac V. Bardin

Martha Washington Exum Bardin

Isaac and Martha Bardin
Magnolia Cemetery

The Bardin home, 214 Calhoun St.,
Charleston, SC

Olive Bardin, on Converse College golf team—Spartanburg, SC

The House that Buster Williams built in Moncks Corner

LaClaire - three years old

Angie in ringlets - four years old

Rusty at Wampee

LaClaire, Angie and Rusty

LaClaire

LaClaire and Clara Lee in Estill

LaClaire Williams

Charlie and LaClaire
at The Citadel Hop

LaClaire at Converse College

Angie missing front teeth

High School Homecoming

Dowse and Angie at the prom

Angie at Queens College

Angela May Queen at Queens College

Rusty Williams

Clara Lee and Stevie

Daddy Van and Stevie

Cousins Sammy and Stevie

Sue Roach and Rusty

Rusty at Military School

Buster and Clara Lee

Daddy and Uncle Charlie fishing

Daddy and Aunt Ginger

Partying—Aunt Helen with Daddy in the center

Dr. Kershaw Fishburne
Angela's Godfather

"It's Eva who is prominent in the wedding photographs."

Eva at Moss Grove

Miriam Edwards

Mark, Queen Esther, David,
Miriam and Sam Taylor

Eva and family
at NAACP convention

Eva at Mount Zion Baptist Church—Albany, Georgia

Chapter 8

Gathering Clouds

*Any woodsman can tell you that in a broken and
sundered nest, one can hardly find more than a
precious few whole eggs. So it is with family.*
—Thomas Jefferson

Eva knew the magic was over long before anyone
else. What she didn't physically see, she surmised
from her gift of intuition. Eva noticed. She noticed
Buster's nights out, heard the car come in the driveway just before dawn. He didn't wake singing to the
radio. He picked at his breakfast, even when she
fixed his favorite fish roe and eggs. A blight grew on
his camellias, and Chester's yard work included frequent runs to the red dot store. The house no longer
rang with the laughter of his friends, and the children stopped having slumber parties. He and Clara
Lee gradually splayed in separate directions, often
converging at days end with silent passings in the
hallway or muffled rows in the bedroom. Yes, Eva
knew what went on in our house—her house.

I was in the fifth grade before my antenna
detected the unraveling. I'd either refused to see,
been sheltered from by Eva, or allowed Mother to
explain away the increasing incidents. It all pointed
to one thing—Buster had a drinking problem.

We became used to the late-night whippings.
They began sporadically, then continued more regularly. The ominous sound of Daddy's walking stick
thudding down the hall made my eyes open wide in
the dark. Even if I was already asleep, the thump
woke me full alert. Waiting, waiting . . . hoping he'd
pass us by on the way to his bed. When he stopped,
Rusty's room was first, then mine, and finally

LaClaire's. I'd hear cries from Rusty and know that none of us would be spared that night. Each of us pulled from our beds and spanked for some infraction, real or imagined. I sometimes carried blood blisters on my behind from his belt into the next day.

Eva saw my marks. She'd hang her head, and without a word against my daddy she'd say, "Gawd be your strenth, Baby." Other times she'd say, "Call on Jesus," or "Take your burden to da Lawd, chile." I took her advice to heart and tried talking to God or Jesus after the whippings, and by morning the memory dissolved enough to welcome the hug and food that Eva dispensed to feed my hunger. I ate and I cried.

I don't remember LaClaire or Rusty ever talking about Daddy's beatings. I was the tattle tale, but only to Eva. Mother surely knew about them, even though Daddy delivered the belt beatings alone. Always the belt, never the hand. But no one spoke about what happened when Daddy came home drunk. The beatings just became part of our lives. And Mother bore her own pain. When her muffled cries drifted through the heating ducts or intercom, I covered my head with a pillow or said prayers aloud to drown out the sounds. Yet the beatings persisted for us all.

It's little wonder Buster turned to alcohol to dull the pain. First, there was his mother's erratic behavior and eventual abandonment when he was young. He virtually grew up away at boarding schools. The Depression hit the country, and he and his buddies scrambled for jobs. Then he lost a leg in a gin accident soon after marrying his Lowcountry queen. Perhaps he saw

Buster home after the accident

his perfect marriage flawed by this accident, his Camelot world blemished. Yet there's a picture showing his usual bravado the day he arrived home from the hospital—dressed in a three-piece suit, flirting with the nurse on one arm and balancing on a crutch with the other. What energy it must have taken to gallantly wear the warrior's wound all those years.

Shortly after the gin accident came another wound. His father, the core of the small family, died suddenly of a heart attack. Grandfather Russell told Clara Lee before he died, "I'm worried about my boy." Still awash with Buster's charm, she didn't know what he meant at the time.

Buster was left with more responsibility than he could handle—a large business to run, hundreds of acres of land to manage, clerk of court and Santee Cooper duties. Additionally, people expected his considerable support: his political friends, a fiscally dependent mother and aunt, as well as his wife, three children, Chester and Eva.

A few years after Daddy Grand died, Buster was diagnosed with an "ulcerated stomach," perhaps because of suppressed stress. Once Dr. Walsh removed two-thirds of his stomach, the young father couldn't seem to hold his liquor—a couple of drinks, and he got tipsy. Granted, he had a head start on alcohol use beginning in his teenage years, which accelerated in college and gathered speed living the fast life in the Lowcountry.

Another disappointment came during World War II. His buddies signed up to fight in a battle he would have relished—the military regimen, the male camaraderie, the broad travel. Not qualified for the draft because of his leg, he must have been devastated, especially given his penchant for excitement and risk-taking.

Even Chester bore war wounds and talked about the war, how the United States Army made an effort to treat everyone equal yet trained black soldiers separately. In spite of that, groups like the Tuskegee Airmen, the Army's all-black air unit, broke barriers in the sky and on the ground.

Over sixty years after the war, I heard an NPR interview with one of the living airmen who said a War Department spokesman claimed blacks "weren't intelligent enough, not coordinated enough, and couldn't be taught." So the determined pilots had to be ten times better to show they weren't the "dumb black niggers" they were called by some of the training officers. Those determined airmen paved the way for integration of the US Armed Forces. After World War II, the March on Washington Movement, the black press's Double V Campaign (victory over Jim Crow at home and fascism abroad), and the NAACP pressured the federal government to abolish separate racial units in the US military.

Perhaps as compensation for his son Buster's not being able to volunteer to fight the traditional way or because of true patriotism, Daddy Grand Russell gave to the war cause in a big way. In 1944 he sold sixty acres of land near the railroad trestle to The United States to be used as an army warehouse. Sale price: $1.00. Interestingly, the check was made out to J. Russell Williams, Jr. and Clara Lee Williams. The framed check hangs on the wall of Williams Farm Supply to this day.

While all the excitement took place abroad, Buster led Berkeley County in the war effort at home by selling war bonds. I can imagine he was quite an effective salesman. He also served as a fierce watchdog for the blackouts. LaClaire rode with him throughout the county to remind black and white families to keep their houses dark after sunset so enemy planes could not find their targets. A far cry from fighting the enemy up close.

The losses and disappointments took their toll on this once vibrant Lowcountry young man. For about ten years after the war, Buster unsteadily steered the helm of the family business. His father had left the largest, most lucrative farm supply business in Berkeley County in the hands of his only heir. Growing up with no restraints and few responsibilities, Buster spent much time keeping up with local and national news and helping people and

businesses in the community and, of course, hunting, fishing, and partying with friends. That Buster
had neither an aptitude nor a passion for business
exacerbated the financial strain. Then came the rav-
enous boll weevil, eating away at the South's most
valued commodity—cotton, the staple income for
Williams Farm Supply.

By and by, wealthy Northerners bought up
area plantations and used them as hunting retreats.
And large companies like Continental Can, Georgia
Pacific, and Westvaco purchased thousands of acres
of Lowcountry land for growing timber—leaving less
land for farming and less business for Buster.

As life in the Lowcountry changed, life in our
family changed too—for me and for Eva. Although
the alterations happened gradually, like gray clouds
sneaking across a blue sky, the turning point came
like a cloudburst out of nowhere. The setting sun
glinted through the trees early one evening as Clara
Lee and Buster drove over to Santee, a town some
seventy miles from Moncks Corner. Friends were
hosting a gathering at Santee Country Club; the couple rarely missed a party, near or far. They chatted
and listened to the radio as they crossed the Santee
Bridge, the very bridge Buster's father had helped
bring to fruition when the Santee and Cooper rivers
joined in the lake project. They arrived at the club in
good spirits. Maybe they both had high hopes that
this night would end differently, that Buster would
abstain or restrain his liquor intake as he promised
many times over.

But after an extended night of partying and
excessive imbibing, Buster insisted on taking the wheel
of their new Oldsmobile for the long, late-night drive
home. Mother's offer to drive, rebuffed. Buster drove
erratically at high speed toward home. Clara Lee lay
across the front seat. The careening car approached
the dark and desolate Santee Canal causeway, deep
water on both sides of the narrow road, the speedom-
eter registering one hundred miles an hour. WHAM!
The car slammed into the back of a huge oil tanker
with no tail lights lumbering on the back roads.

The entire front end of the car crushed like an accordion. Then silence. No one knows how long before a Greyhound bus eventually came upon the scene. The driver pulled over and stopped. When he looked through the smashed window, he saw two limp, bloodied figures. *Surely they had to be dead,* he thought. He and a couple of passengers struggled to pull Clara Lee and Buster from the twisted wreckage. Blood poured from both but each had a pulse, so they carried them up the bus stairs and laid the bloodied and broken bodies on the floor of the aisle.

Buster was unconscious. Clara Lee, barely coherent, mumbled to the driver, "Hospital. Orangeburg." The bus sped them to the nearest hospital while passengers stemmed the bleeding with their shirts, jackets, scarves. Once at the hospital, nurses and doctors worked on the couple for hours. The impact put a hole in Clara Lee's forehead from the radio dial, and she bit off a part of her tongue. Her leg was crushed too. Buster received severe internal injuries and a broken kneecap on his one good leg.

The next morning, Nannie, my aunt Maude, came to the house and announced that Daddy and Mother had been in a wreck. That's all I remember her saying. Eva stood at our side. "It'll be awright," she said, pulling us close. Eva knew these things. The news frightened me nonetheless. At night I imagined their dying, winging their way to heaven, our burying them among the bamboos in the back yard beside Petty. Circles appeared under my eyes. I ate a puny breakfast, according to Eva, and dragged myself to school. Eva prayed aloud as she tended LaClaire, Rusty and me, allaying fears with close hugs and whispered words. Somewhere in there, I heard her say my daddy was "lost." What did that mean? Couldn't they find him?

Days passed. Weeks passed. One afternoon doing my homework sitting in the kitchen with Eva, I noticed the downturn of her mouth, the red in her eyes, the curve of her shoulders. And I felt *her* sadness, not just mine. I wondered, *Are Daddy and Mother Eva's children too?*

It was over a month before Buster and Clara Lee were transferred to Berkeley County Hospital. The same hospital where all of us were born, I had my tonsils out and Daddy recuperated from his leg accident. It was a block from our school on Main Street, two blocks from home. Doc Fishburne had raised money to build it.

Berkeley County Hospital

More days passed before we were allowed to see them. Everybody talked about wanting to see them. In my naiveté, I wasn't sure what that meant. Was it a viewing like when someone died in town and people went to "see" the deceased lying in an open casket? I could hardly sleep the night beforehand. And by then we'd seen the car after it was hauled to the filling station on Main Street. How could anyone survive in that tangled metal? Would Mother and Daddy be alive or dead?

Dr. Walsh had taken my tonsils out earlier that year in the same hospital. My teddy bear and a corsage from a fifth-grade classmate, Dennis Noonan, rested on the hospital pillow. Mother teased that I'd no longer be Eva's "Baby" if a young man was sending flowers. I smiled, delighting to be the center of attention *and* to be eating my fill of chocolate ice cream to soothe my raw throat. This pleasant hospital image soon was replaced with a less amusing scene.

Eva walked with us from school to the hospital the day Principal Wofford gave the three Williams children permission to visit our parents during recess period one Friday. I ran ahead and pushed open the heavy hospital door thinking they'd be right in front of me. My feet stopped. I looked up at the foyer's high-ceiling while Eva caught up with me and led us down a wide, dark hall to another door. I burst into tears of relief when I saw both of them in beds side by side. They were alive! Bandaged from head to toe, looking like mummies, each mustered a smile. Buster, ever the romantic, had insisted they both be in the same room. He joked about the accident as Clara Lee looked off into the distance.

She spoke to us with a lisp, showed us her funny looking tongue. She looked tired and tense. She ignored Buster, his smiles, his laughter. Something seemed out of sync between them. I felt uncomfortable, confused by two conversations I couldn't follow. One spoken: banter between Daddy and Eva, teasing between Daddy and LaClaire. The other unspoken: solemn looks between Eva and Mother, ignored glances from Daddy to Mother. I was eager to leave the room—the white walls, the white linens, Mother's white bandages, Daddy's white teeth. On the walk back to school, I asked Eva, "Are they going to be okay?"

"De bodies will mend, but your daddy gots some cleaning up to do," she answered softly. Nannie, bless her heart, moved in with us for the weeks Mother and Daddy were in the hospital. That didn't set well with Eva. "I been tendin' dese churren aplenty when Miss Clara Lee and Mista Busta go all over creation. I ain't need nobody to help me now," she mumbled just low enough for Nannie not to hear. Always respectful, Eva nonetheless didn't appreciate someone taking over her territory. Hadn't she been running our household and minding the Williams children for the past ten years? It wounded her pride.

But Nannie, caretaker of the universe, felt the need to come to our rescue, to show the community her Christian benevolence. But we didn't *need* her. Besides, it made Eva increasingly grumpy to be bossed about. She knew very well what to cook for supper, when to change the bed linens. "Miss Maude need to let me go bout my bidness," Eva complained. She wasn't used to orders. And we weren't used to being reminded to take a bath, brush our teeth, lay out our clothes. Eva had trained us well. Nannie also insisted we eat with her in the formal dining room for all our meals, instead of in the kitchen with Eva. That didn't set well with me either. I rejoiced when my parents came home.

After Daddy recuperated from the car accident, he went "on vacation" in the North Carolina mountains for several months. That's what Mother told us anyway. I bought it. The facility was a plush drying-out place near Asheville the likes of Zelda Fitzgerald frequented—a place Uncle Charlie suggested when Mother solicited his help. It specialized in treating alcoholics, a taboo word in polite society. A semblance of emotional equilibrium returned with Daddy away, Eva at the home helm, Mother at the warehouse office.

Even before the car accident, the farm supply and cotton gin business had begun to slide because of Buster's absences and mismanagement. Ever affable with customers, he let folks put feed, seed, and fertilizer on the tab until their families picked cotton each fall. Big-hearted, gregarious, and disorganized, sometimes he documented the loans—often not.

When sharecroppers brought in a wagon full of dirty cotton, dampened by rain or ravaged by boll weevils, he graded on the high side. He stood in the dusty warehouse office in his three-piece suit and tie, pulled apart the sample cotton wad with his manicured hands, weighing how much to pay the farmer who had six or eight mouths to feed and a two-acre plot to till. Knowing it was the only income the man had until the next fall, Buster followed his impulse to be liberal.

And on many Saturday mornings we awoke to a mule and wagon crunching on the rocks of our driveway, a farmer patiently sitting on his buggy seat waiting to ask Cap'n Busta for a handout to tide him over. He never refused. "I sho thanks you, Cap'n Busta," the farmer would say, doffing his hat. The money that crossed those palms didn't show up on any ledger, for sure. And when the seasons changed, our porch was laden with a mess of collards, corn or cabbage from every corner of Berkeley County. (Only a Southerner knows how many fish or vegetables make up a "mess.") Buster carried on the tradition of his father by being generous to those in need. Too generous, it turned out.

After the wreck, with Buster away drying out, Clara Lee spent all her time at Williams Farm Supply. She knew her math and was appalled by the bookkeeping. Worse, the mountain vacation didn't cure Buster's ills. He had sober periods, then relapsed. He met sporadically with Viv Ingle who lived only two blocks away. Viv served as the first director of an alcohol and drug abuse facility in the state. Viv's son Ron, LaClaire's classmate, attests that there were many heated discussions between the two men at his house. Ever facile with words, Buster gave Viv a fit, and vice versa since Viv could more than hold his own with every type of drinker. These were personal, one-on-one meetings, no group gatherings. All on the hush-hush.

Good weeks, sometime months, returned; then Daddy crashed again. As the business continued to fail, Buster gradually abdicated. Eva delivered breakfasts later to him each morning, which he supplemented with a Bloody Mary, while Clara Lee rushed off to open the warehouse. Buster spent less time at the warehouse and more time politicking for his friends, visiting the Carolina Yacht Club or Everett's restaurant in Charleston, and checking by the court house on his clerk of court duties.

Years later when I was in college, my father gave me only one piece of marital advice: "Don't ever let your husband know you're smarter than he is," he said.

I was perplexed by the statement. First, LaClaire was the smart one, not me. Second, marriage was not on my horizon. Did he care about my future? Or . . . in hindsight, did he see Clara Lee's quiet efficiency and confidence at the warehouse as undermining his manhood or playing a part in the unraveling of his marriage? She certainly demonstrated more business skill than he; on the other hand, his interest in others and his interpersonal skills outshone hers by a country mile.

This pattern continued for the next two years

after the wreck, by which time I was in seventh grade. As Eva spent more and more evenings with her parents, things deteriorated. LaClaire instigated another escape that left me behind. Rusty went with her on this final runaway trip. I asked to go. Nope. I watched through my bedroom window as they sneaked into the woods across the street. LaClaire and Rusty were partners in most things—in this case, partners in a family felony. Daddy asked me where they went. Hoping to gain favor, hoping they'd get caught, and hoping they'd be sorry they'd left me behind. I spilled the beans. "They're in the woods behind the Miles' house," I said. Buster ignored Clara Lee's pleas to search for the pair. He slammed and locked all seven doors.

That night I couldn't sleep for the cries and threats coming from my parents' bedroom. By morning, Buster had slept it off. Clara Lee was off to work. And Eva was in the kitchen asking me to help her make biscuits. "What's dis world coming to?" she said, shaking her head as LaClaire and Rusty waltzed in the door after sleeping in the woods all night.

When LaClaire got her driver's license, she continued to push the boundaries. She loved racing cars with the local boys and playing chicken with Daddy's latest Oldsmobile on the Bonneau Beach Road. I can't fathom how I ended up in the car one night when LaClaire left a Chevy in the dust, flooring the car to over 100 miles an hour. Our terrified next-door neighbor Otto curled up in the front seat and cried like a baby. And I, kneeling on the floor of the back seat, called out to Jesus.

She and her friends also sneaked to Charleston at night to race across the rickety old two-lane Cooper River Bridge. The stunt involved stopping with revved up engine on the peninsula side until no car lights were in sight on the Mt. Pleasant side. The challenge was flooring the gas pedal and racing across the long span before an oncoming car touched the bridge. A harrowing two-mile ride. It would take several tries, but eventually she'd be the lone car barreling across the undulating old bridge. These antics were a step up from her younger days when she went to school barefooted. She could find only her Sunday shoes and wouldn't be caught dead in those!

LaClaire's seditious stunts reached a peak with the spitball caper when she was suspended from school for a week for shooting spitballs at the boys. That was it! Mother and Daddy decided LaClaire needed a change of environment. The news jolted me. I couldn't imagine our family without her. She could whip any boy in the neighborhood, climb the oak in the side yard without a boost, swim the front crawl for hours without stopping, bring home perfect report cards and cajole Daddy into doing anything. And, yes, she could be stubborn as a stump. She didn't play with a scaredy-cat or crybaby like me either, but I was afraid to be in our house without her.

Whether I liked it or not, LaClaire was sent off in ninth grade to Ashley Hall School, the girls' boarding school in downtown Charleston. If she resented the change of venue, I heard not a peep. Her loyalty to Daddy remained steadfast. Rusty and I were left at home to receive the full measure of Daddy's spiraling decline.

The baby boy of the three Williams children received the brunt of the pain during those last turbulent years. When Rusty was born two years after me, Mother thought, *Now Buster has his boy.* She felt proud of the gift she'd given him. "It's a shame your daddy was already too far gone to enjoy him, but I didn't know it then," she confided to me years later.

One long night an inebriated Daddy drilled Rusty on his spelling words. "Spell 'apple,'" Daddy said over and over. Paralyzed with fear, Rusty couldn't remember a thing. Daddy whipped. It didn't help. Rusty cried silent tears. For the life of him, my brother could not spell "apple" that night. I thought the session would never end. Upset by the scene, I ran to my room and covered my ears with a pillow. Rusty's muffled cries still sneaked through. Yet I never stepped to Rusty's rescue, not once. LaClaire would have stood up to Daddy. Not me.

One morning Eva found Rusty walking in the

front yard—precariously close to the street. "Do Jesus, keep dis chile safe," she crooned as she walked him back inside the house. "Rusty done walkin in his sleep agin. Mista Busta too hard on dat boy," she said. I ached for Rusty yet kept my distance.

But increasingly Eva was gone at night, at night when the bullbats flew and the liquor flowed. Eva did everything in her power to make life normal in our house, yet she never interfered in the family's domestic dramas. Did she ever want to burst into a room and shout, "Mista Busta, leave my babies alone"? Did she ever cover her own ears to keep from hearing unmerciful punishments of her "churren"? I've always wondered what she would have done had she witnessed such scenes from her Buster. Would she have distracted him with a pull to the kitchen? Cajoled him to go to bed early? Stymied him with a look of disappointment? I don't know, but I can't imagine her sitting on the sidelines while we got hurt.

Whatever she saw, heard or thought, Eva remained calm, and in the morning she appeared. "Get up, Baby. You be quiet now. Your Daddy had a bad night," Or at the end of the day, "Your mama's working late, so let's go on wid supper."

So by the time I was thirteen, I had a father who one day would beat me and call me fat, and the next day give me a gold filigree bracelet with two little diamonds—all depending upon his blood alcohol level at the time. I had a mother I didn't know, a woman who worked "from can 'til can't." A woman who aided and abetted her husband's behavior by covering for him at home, among friends, and in business—all for love.

I created my own system to cope as things spun out of control. Be good to avoid Daddy's anger. Study hard to receive praise. Keep busy to stay away from the home front. And check in with Eva to gauge the day's "weather." Living in our household was like riding the rapids at camp. Nerves on edge as I chose what seemed the best path, paddling like crazy to guide the canoe around rocks, praying I could keep upright at the next rapid, and relieved when the trip ended and my feet hit solid ground—Eva.

Eva took up the slack at home, and Clara Lee took the slack up at the warehouse. They worked in tandem. No words needed. Clara Lee, the responsible and increasingly desperate housewife poured herself into running the business. No discussion. No complaining. Nose to the grindstone—to her physical detriment.

When Doc Fishburne noticed Mother's fatigue and persistent cough the summer of 1955, he suggested that she pay him a visit at the Berkeley County Health Department to take an X-ray. Though it was only a two-block walk from the house, Clara Lee couldn't squeeze in the time.

Cotton wagons lined up for ginning

That August with cotton ginning season at its peak, she wasn't even taking a break for lunch. A nimble worker climbed aboard each wagon as it pulled under the ginning shed and guided a giant aluminum tube over the cotton until it all disappeared up the shaft and into the machines that separated the seeds and packed the cotton into bales. The gin often ran around the clock or until the last wagon was sucked dry. At the crack of dawn, Mother'd be back again to contend with cotton wagons piled high. They lined up from the gin house all the way around the corner down Main Street. The schedule didn't let up until ginning season ended in late fall, sometimes into December.

Uncle Charlie told Mother he intended to put her on the popular television program *What's My Line.* "People in Hollywood would *never* guess the occupation of this beautiful Southern lady—cotton broker," he said. But this particular summer, Mother's dark circles and thinning frame left her a shadow of her former self. No shape for Hollywood.

To stop Doc's pestering, Mother finally dropped by for an X-ray, totally exhausted by this time. The results proved indisputable—the dreaded consumption. Spots on her lungs and no miracle drugs to eradicate the terrible disease—tuberculosis. Doc took control. Nobody argued with Doc, whose friendship with the Williams family went back decades as neighbors and hunting partners in Pinopolis. This was a man who trudged through Hell Hole Swamp on foot or horseback to deliver babies and who brought medicine to a rural Southern county full of poor blacks and whites. His pioneering work was documented in both *LOOK* and *LIFE* magazines in the 1950s. He made day-long buggy trips to Charlotte to convince philanthropist Charles Dana to give money to jumpstart Berkeley County Hospital and later its Health Department.

His physical appearance put the fear of God in anyone who didn't know him. His massive build, his glass eye that didn't always move in sync with his good eye, and his one eyebrow that grew in a bristling, unrestrained way, gave him a ferocious expression. But his heart was as big as the county he served. I remember his rubbing the warts on my young fingers, wishing them away—and they disappeared. He also told me I'd have wrinkles before I turned twenty if I didn't stop squeezing my brows together. Right again. I delighted in being Doc's godchild. The bear of a man enthralled me from the day my warts took flight to the day of my wedding when he hosted the reception in his yard.

A mystique remained surrounding Doc's womanizing and politicking. Were his nurse and my third-grade teacher *really* his mistresses? Was he *really* a part of the conspiracy to assassinate Senator Dennis as a letter to the Senator's widow indicated? All I knew was that he understood our troubled family situation as few did, and his gladiator spirit emerged. All 6-foot, 4-inches of the silver-maned Doc loomed over the 5-foot, 8-inches of forty-year-old Buster Williams and declared Clara Lee must go straightaway to Pinehaven Sanitarium in Charleston. The three children must go to boarding schools. And Buster must stop his drinking and tend to his business with renewed vigor.

So in the late summer of 1955, Clara Lee rushed off to the sanitarium in Charleston. Rusty boarded a train to Daddy's alma mater, Staunton Military Academy in Virginia. I joined LaClaire at Ashley Hall School for girls in Charleston. And Eva moved into a house that Buster built for her.

Our lives altered irrevocably.

Chapter 9

Eyes Wide Open

When a man knows somebody cares, he keeps
some small place, a corner maybe of his soul, clean
and lit.
    —Bryce Courtenay, author

Enclosed by wrought iron fencing and high concrete walls in historic Charleston, Ashley Hall School appeared a safe haven for girls. It wasn't. Not for me. Founded in 1909, Ashley Hall was exclusive . . . in gender and color. Public schools in downtown Charleston were segregated and out of the question for many local daughters. Boarders came from up and down the Eastern seaboard and included the likes of teenager Barbara Bush. My first and only year at boarding school I learned about lying, cheating, smoking and drinking. I learned about sex— boys who tried to "go too far," girls who "put out" for guys, girls who preferred girls to boys, and husbands who cheated on their wives. And how to live away from Eva.

Ashley Hall School

The campus consisted of three major buildings set among oaks draped with Spanish moss. Shell House, a one-room structure embedded with large welk shells on the outside, provided a focus for the main yard and a haven for seniors to smoke. The McBee House anchored the grounds. With its much-photographed winding staircase, it contained a dating parlor and administrative offices downstairs and a ballroom upstairs with a wide, slick wooden floor.

Attached to McBee House loomed another sprawling, two-story structure with classrooms downstairs and boarders' bedrooms upstairs. Through the back

stairway, students could travel from bedroom to classroom in only three minutes— two minutes if we flew. The Purple and White teams battled for accolades from basketball to swimming, in the gym and pool. Across the side street a rambling old building housed Mrs. Brown, the dean of students, and some members of the faculty.

Shell House, Ashley Hall School

Until Buster Williams walked on campus in the fall of 1955, all boarding students had been high schoolers. He met with Miss Caroline "Pudge" Pardue, the new headmistress who would lead the school for almost twenty-five years. Tall and as solid as a punching bag, her full, pale face sat on a thick neck supported by broad shoulders. Her handshake firm and her smile rare, Miss Pardue ran Ashley Hall with rigid rules and high expectations.

But my daddy beguiled her into allowing his younger daughter to become Ashley Hall's first and only eighth-grade boarder. The mitigating circumstances—that her older sister would look after her, that she was a good student, and that she'd be able to visit her sick mother only a few blocks away—may have given sway.

In this elite school for privileged young ladies, I felt *not* so privileged. How could I function without Eva? The tight cocoon I'd woven with Eva's emotional and physical threads was unraveling indeed. Deep down Eva's Baby was scared she *was* a baby— scared to be without Eva, scared that the city girls wouldn't like her, that she'd fail her classes, and . . . scared that her mother might die.

But off I went, silently smoldering from this disruption yet determined not to add more distress to Mother. She had to get well quickly so I could get back to Eva. I felt anxious, not able to imagine breaking up the paired equation that had functioned, however unevenly, in our family for years: LaClaire and Daddy + Rusty and Mother + Angie and Eva = Home. How much I'd prefer to bear the ills I knew than fly to others I didn't know.

Ashley Hall turned out to be an expansive environment for getting an education—an education about real life. A few days after I arrived, I told a bold-faced lie. *Deliberate* lying was new to me. Little white lies, lies to avoid a spanking, or exaggerations to make me look good, I knew well. Eva often chastised me for fibbing. Once out of Eva's reach, it didn't take me long to forget her teaching.

I had just that summer begun going out with boys, always double-dating with LaClaire, a mandate from Mother which I'm sure didn't set well with LaClaire. In Estill, LaClaire and Charlie let me tag along with sweet-talking Bro, Charlie's buddy. At home, we went out with a couple of cute North Charleston boys who came to Thornley Beach pavilion on the lake. We shagged through many weekends. And there was Buckshot Harvey, who drove his dad's cucumber truck to Wampee to visit, embarrassing me by writing little notes signed with XX's and OO's. My dating experience was limited.

An Ashley Hall upperclassman encouraged me to attend a tea dance at The Citadel, the military college not far away on the Ashley River. Afternoon tea dances or evening hops at The Citadel were the social highlights of boarders, so my eyes brightened at the suggestion that I join the girls bussed across town for a dance. There I met a boy who asked me out, well, asked to visit me on campus. No one was allowed to date off campus. The girls sat in stiff chairs in the parlor of McBee House and talked to the boys who called. How a thirteen-year-old managed to get away with dating a freshman in college is beyond me. Eva and Mother would have been horrified. My first date was with a blonde doll-of-a-fellow from Darien, Connecticut, which made him exotic. After fixing his blue eyes onto mine and charming me with his clipped accent, he asked how old I was. "Sixteen," I replied without batting an eyelash. I shocked even myself to hear me add three whole years to my age. How many times had Eva told me, "Lying be a bomination to the Lawd, missy" or "De tongue can be poison, you listenin' to Beba?" That night I prayed that Eva and God would forgive me the lie.

Cheating came next. Funny thing, I didn't *know* I was cheating. Mrs. Irvin, the Latin teacher, was strict and cold as an ice cube. "Dark" is the word that comes to mind. She had short, dark hair; dark, beady eyes; wore dark, tailored dresses; and lived with her young son in one of the shadowy faculty rooms on Smith Street. In class, a slight nod indicated her pleasure with an assignment. Invariably I made 100's on the daily Latin vocabulary tests, getting the nods of affirmation I craved. Midway into the semester, she asked me to stay after class and accompany her to Miss Pardue's office "to discuss a grave matter." Miss Pardue's office? In McBee House? I was petrified.

Once inside the office, in a short, crisp explanation, Mrs. Irvin explained that a classmate reported that I cheated on a vocabulary test. My mouth flew open, stunned. She added that students rarely make 100 on every single test. Silent tears spilled. Miss Pardue ignored the tears, sternly explaining that wanting to please my parents with good grades was commendable, but cheating to get them was not. "I'm sorry your mother's sick, but this is not the way to make her proud." I cried for real then. Mother would be devastated. Eva would be distraught! Lord only knows what Daddy would do.

"How did I cheat?" I asked softly when the cat let go of my tongue.

My first experience with cheating had been in Mrs. Hill's sixth grade classroom when a classmate borrowed my arithmetic homework and turned it in as her own. That was the year my teacher tried to throw herself off the fire escape, my education more than class-room learning that year. An old house had been renovated for classrooms in the old school yard, and our sixth-grade class met on the second floor. The only entrance was a makeshift stairway up the side of the building. Betty Hill was the first teacher I'd ever had who was anywhere near young. I was on the cusp of womanhood, having bought my first bra only the summer before. Tall, slim, pretty, Mrs. Hill had long, silky, light brown hair that grazed my shoulder when she leaned over to look at my work. I'd just cut mine short because Mother insisted it would be easier to keep, but I hated it. Mrs. Hill smiled a lot—unless you messed up. She expected excellence. Mrs. Hill had recently married a popular local hero, a fighter pilot in Korea. The whole town knew Johnny Hill and prayed for his safety. It all was so romantic. I fantasized about their courtship, their marriage, and their letters while apart. I idolized her.

One winter day about mid-morning, Mr. Johnny, the local sheriff and Mrs. Hill's father-in-law, quietly opened our classroom door. He asked Mrs. Hill to step outside on the fire escape. My desk was directly in front of the door, so I had a front row seat. Within seconds Mrs. Hill let out a bloodcurdling scream and flung her body across the banister of the fire escape. It all happened so suddenly that Mr. Johnny almost didn't catch her by the skirt. They struggled. The door shut. It didn't matter. The sobs and cries that followed were deep and hard. I'd never heard such sounds of sorrow. Mr. Johnny's low voice went on and on. It scared me to pieces.

Her Johnny's plane had been shot down over Korea. I grieved for him as surely as she did. I grieved for her, the lover left alone. I wrote her letters, took her flowers. Nothing consoled her. I'm not sure I saw another smile on her face that year, but teach she did, and with a vengeance. Mrs. Hill found a new love, far too soon, in my opinion. That he was tall and handsome as well as kind and caring made no difference. I was incredulous . . . and furious. *How could she love someone else when she'd nearly killed herself over Johnny? What duplicity! What was she thinking? Was she desperate for a man? Surely not. How could she get over such a broken heart?*

In her class I became cold and distant. I moaned to Eva, complained to Mother. I even groused to LaClaire who had "lost it" at Johnny Hill's funeral. Mother said LaClaire should have been paid as the chief mourner.

"I never did like putting people in the ground," LaClaire told me. It never occurred to me that others were affected by the tragedy. It was all about me, *my* feelings. I was inconsolable and angry.

"Jes how long you 'speck to pick at dis sore?" Eva-of-few-words asked me one day. "Forever!" I said.

Eva suggested to Mother that I visit Mrs. Hill. Tackling an emotional issue head on was not Mother's style. "Festerin' don't do that chile not one lick o' good, Miss Clara Lee," Eva said. So Mother drove me to see Mrs. Hill, just around the corner from grandmother Olive's house, the border of flowers not yet dulled by seasons in the elements.

In Betty Hill's parlor I heard about the different kinds of love, how all loves are unique. She explained that she would never stop loving her Johnny. She said that the special love they had couldn't be replaced, that she would treasure it forever, hold it in her heart. Listening to her brought tears to my eyes. I felt immature and ashamed. At the end, she explained that God had sent Clark into her life to bring her joy again. For a long time afterwards, the word "joy" kept jumping out at me. So . . . love is about *joy!*

But back to the cheating. This Ashley Hall teacher didn't seem bent on teaching me about love and joy. That seemed certain. I knew about peeking during hide-and-seek or calling slipsies in marbles, but not about fudging with something as serious as school work. Mrs. Irvin explained that after the last test, I looked inside my notebook to check my answers before turning in the paper. Mustering my courage, I raised my head to Mrs. Irvin black-bean eyes, because Miss Pardue's blue stare was too daunting.

"I always do that," I said. Silence. I pressed on. "I like to know right away whether I missed a word. But I would never change something on my test." Mrs. Irvin and Miss Pardue looked at each other skeptically. Their mistrust, explicit. Their coldness, punishment enough. More silence.

"The *appearance* of cheating is a form of cheating," Miss Pardue said dismissively. Mrs. Irvin never again gave me a nod. By this time *my* mistrust of adults had a solid foothold, except for Eva—thirty miles up the road.

Outside the classroom I learned other things. I had first tried smoking in the backyard with Rusty and some boys a couple of years before going to Ashley Hall. Both Mother and Daddy used cigarette holders to filter nicotine from their cigarettes. We fashioned ours out of the bamboo that grew unbridled behind our house. We cut a four-inch wedge of bamboo, stuck a Winston-Salem in the end, lit it, and had our first smoke. Well, a few minutes of sucking in the bamboo sap and the tobacco smoke made me feel sick—literally. Eva bathed my forehead with a cool washcloth and scolded me as I hung over her toilet bowl. "What was you *thinkin*, chile? You wants to *kill* yoursef?" I promised Eva I'd never smoke again. But I did.

Getting cigarettes? No problem. Eva regularly filled the wooden box on our coffee table in the living room with loose cigarettes for Clara Lee, Buster and their friends. A brass ashtray nearby displaying a nude woman with pointy breasts where people twirled off their ashes intrigued me far more than the cigarette case. Of course smoking was forbidden at Ashley Hall, but that didn't stop girls from lighting up in the bathrooms, beside the windows, on the roofs, behind the bushes or in the grotto. For several weeks I carried a pack of cigarettes in my purse but never lit up one. I doubt anyone noticed either way. Did I want to fit in, feel older? Though not breaking the letter of the law (my promise to Eva), I surely broke the spirit of the law. Hypocrites carry cigarettes with no intention of using them. God and Eva would not have been pleased. It's strange how I lumped God and Eva together when my conscience niggled. Their voices became one.

Even the most sincere and sensible vows can be broken. Not long after my promise to Eva, the smoking issue came up again. LaClaire, Rusty and I were all home for a holiday from boarding school. Eva was cooking up a storm. Mother was resting at the sanitarium. Daddy was in a good stretch. He called the three of us into the living room to talk about the danger of smoking and its connection to Mother's tuberculosis. A conversation with a capital "C." Daddy at his rhetorical best made an impassioned case for steering clear of the terrible weed.

He ended by eliciting a challenge. "If you don't smoke before you're twenty-one, I will buy you a car." Wow! A car, my very own car. LaClaire and Rusty immediately promised to abstain. I remained mute. I had already sworn off smoking. Then why in heaven's name did my hand reach in slow motion toward the cigarette box on the coffee table? I opened the porcelain top with a painted pheasant, lifted a cigarette to my lips, picked up the fat silver lighter and clicked it three times before it held a flame. After one puff I looked my father in the eye. I still have no explanation for my boldness. Suppressed anger at my father? Showing off for LaClaire and Rusty? Tired of being a goody-goody? Who knows. I never took another puff of a cigarette.

Smoking and drinking seemed to go together. And the Ashley Hall boarders loved their booze. Any kind would do—beer, wine, hard liquor, spiked punch. Vodka was the drink of choice because it didn't have a strong odor. Boone's Farm apple wine came next because of the low price. And Purple Jesus at parties! The townies had an easier time of it because their parents' liquor cabinets were amply stocked and easily raided.

No scarcity of ways to get hands on the forbidden substance. Boarders smuggled in alcohol using empty medicine bottles, Coke bottles, mouth-wash and shampoo containers. You name it, they found a way to get their alcohol. Charleston itself was famous for its Southern hospitality, every function requiring a drink in hand. The saying goes that folks in South Carolina ask newcomers different things: In Greenville, "What church do you attend? In Columbia, "Who's your family?" In Charleston, "What will you have to drink?"

Getting high or feeling a buzz—both new terms to me—seemed a rite of passage for many. I watched. I listened. But I knew what alcohol did to Daddy, and it scared me to death. At parties with the day students, my water with lemon passed for a gin and tonic, my plain V-8 juice for a Bloody Mary. I didn't dare dip a toe in that polluted stream.

The year before I went to Ashley Hall, I prayed for my father, fervently, regularly, on my knees during church, in the afternoons or evening in the empty church. And I asked Eva to pray for him too. "Chile, I been doing dat a long time now. He tryin', he tryin'," she said. She told me everybody's got a weakness, some show out front more than others. But all need God because that's where we gather strength.

"He think he can lick the drink hisself. Your daddy ain't yet tapped into the power, Baby." She ended with, "You just make sho the debil drink don't get you. Promise Beba now." We knelt beside her bed on the wood floor of her bedroom, praying for Daddy. The prayer ended with my promising Eva and Jesus never to let alcohol cross my lips. Even the Ashley Hall pressure didn't crack my resolve.

Now sex was another matter—a matter that Eva and I hadn't thoroughly covered quite yet. My fantasy of being a nun, "a bride of Christ," had begun about the time Daddy's drinking escalated. Sunday school teachers and the young priests that the Episcopal Diocese rotated through our Pinopolis church convinced me that prayer could change anything. Bishop Caruthers sent his brightest and best fledgling ministers to Pinopolis, knowing that if they could deal with the sharp, eccentric folks in that village, they could survive anywhere. How I adored those fresh, fervent faces: Steve Scardon, Harold Barrett, Loren Mead. I bought all they were selling. I had secret crushes on the clergy who molded my early theology. The Pinopolis church provided a secure environment that drew this thirsty child to living water. Ensconced in the church I felt I would be forever safe. While in my nun phase, I decided that sequestered religious life would be a perfect world. Christ-like women (nuns) and male comrades (priests). I longed to be pure and unblemished in God's eyes.

Until boys muddied the water. I adjusted my theology a bit . . . and decided that if I chose to marry, I would remain chaste until then, like the high-collared women in Victorian novels. *A compromise*, I thought. The bald truth? I liked boys and often preferred their company to girls. Boys made great friends. They didn't talk behind your back, hurt your feelings or tell you they didn't want to be friends without giving a reason. They didn't say you were a baby for calling your mother "Mommie." They were loyal and straightforward.

So by eighth grade at Ashley Hall, being the bride of Christ took on less allure. Beginning to be interested in the opposite sex, I was ready to broaden my education on this subject. Hadn't a freckle-faced boy walking in the rain past my window made my heart flutter? And at Camp St. Christopher the previous summer, hadn't I felt all tingly when Edwin touched my leg when swimming? Or when Gus held my hand on the boardwalk? It was during this confusing time that I asked Eva about the boundaries between boys and girls.

"Baby, your body be the Lawd's holy temple. It's in de Bible. Don't let nobody tech the temple," she said matter of factly.

"How do I keep them out?" I asked dubiously.

"Chile, you just steps 'way, quick like, and give 'em a hard look," she said, illustrating with aplomb.

"Don't let nobody tech you 'cept the man you marry, Baby." That very day, I promised God and

Eva that I would save myself for marriage. In subsequent years, "my body is a holy temple" stymied many a fellow.

The Ashley Hall girls often talked in puzzling terms about reaching "first, second, and third base," a "hand job," "going all the way," or "teasing." But *nothing* prepared me for the sexual escapade I encountered within the very walls of Ashley Hall. Certainly not my limited experience with a peck on the cheek while playing spin the bottle at Elliott Bishop's house, a hay ride kiss in sixth grade, and some backseat avoidance maneuvers in seventh grade. Nor did my prodigious summer reading of Nancy Drew mysteries before being shipped off to school.

One winter evening my roommate and I fell exhausted into our beds after a long night's swim practice for an upcoming Dolphin Club show. I lay dead-to-the-world, snuggled under a blanket in the cold Ashley Hall annex. In a fog, I gradually awakened to a gentle touch on my breast. Am I dreaming? I stirred and opened my eyes—another body was in my bed. It was an upperclassman from down the hall. I relaxed. She smiled at me.

"It's okay," she said as her hand continued to move. I held stone still, trying to clear my head.

"I've got to go to the bathroom," I whispered, suddenly alert. I took the shortest route to LaClaire's room. Near hysteria, I blurted out the situation. She raced to my room and jerked that girl down the hall so fast that they passed me on the way back to my room. I had never heard about girls liking girls, not even boys liking boys, or the term "homosexuality." After three months at Ashley Hall, I ratcheted up my praying for Mother to get well soon.

Instead of her getting better, *I* got sick. Attacked by uncontrollable coughing spasms—during class (disruptive), meals (nasty), sports (breathless), nights (sleepless)—I concluded that like Mother, TB had found a home in my lungs. I envisioned the worst. I was going to die. No one could know. Mother had to get well first. Then I could die. Mrs. Brown sent me to a doctor who stretched my mouth to almost splitting while he gagged me with a tongue depressor. "Whooping cough," he concluded, "highly contagious."

They sent me packing . . . back home, a place I longed to be. Now feverish and tired, I imagined that Ashley Hall had finagled a devious way to throw out the immature eighth-grade boarder, the one who carried around cigarettes, the one who allegedly cheated. I was upset at their trickery, yet eager to return home, at least for a spell.

Miss Pardue couldn't reach Daddy that day, so she hired a car to drive me home to Moncks Corner. My suitcase and I entered the front door expecting a big welcome, but no one appeared. "Anybody home?" I called. No Eva. No Daddy. I looked toward the side yard. Daddy's car was parked in the driveway. I walked back to the kitchen. No sign of Eva. No pots on the stove, no dishes in the sink. Feeling hot and thirsty, I poured a glass of water, then walked through the house down the back hall to my bedroom. My body ached. All I wanted to do was sleep. But where was everybody?

A sound came from the master bedroom, followed by moans and a thumping sound. Someone must be hurt! I rushed to my parents' room and swung open the door. I saw two naked people intertwined, legs and arms askew . . . and cascading, flaming-red hair. I recognized my father. The other, a complete stranger. Aghast, I stepped backwards, silently pulling the door to.

I don't remember how I got to the front porch or how long I sat in the green French garden chair, rocking back and forth, back and forth, my leg jerking up and down. *Who is that woman back there? Where's Eva? She would know.* When my leg stopped jiggling and my heart took up its regular beat, I decided I knew who the woman was—an escapee from Sunset Lodge, the brothel near Georgetown that people talked about. *But what was she doing in my daddy and mother's bed?* Like a film of gauze lifting from my brain, reality dawned. No matter who it was in the bed with my father, it was not my mother. Not his wife. *How could that be? Mother and Daddy adored each other. How could he be with another woman?*

I sat in the cold, metal chair for what seemed forever. Voices awakened me from my daze. I looked up. Daddy and a long-legged, bosomy red-head pushed through the screened door. Daddy beamed me a surprised smile.

"Oh, I didn't know you were coming home," he said. He turned to the woman.

"This is my daughter." He never said my name nor hers. I rose from the chair as manners required. I heard the metal scrape the tile floor and caught a whiff of rose perfume. Saying a stiff "hello" to the air, I glared up at my daddy and went inside to search for Eva. She still wasn't there.

The weeks that followed remain a haze. I rarely got out of my pajamas, seldom left the bedroom, never went outside. At first all I did was sleep and have fitful dreams. I immersed myself in books. Long through with Nancy Drew, I read *The Scarlet Letter*, and my imagination took flight. *What if someone found out about Daddy and he had to wear an "A"?* I shoved the thought away. Then came Anna Karenina where all was not right with the world and women threw themselves in front of trains for unrequited love. How messy, how frightening this love between men and women.

Divine intervention must have guided the reading material. I began devouring Jane Austen's Victorian novels like *Emma* and *Pride and Prejudice* where I found reassurance. At night I'd read until the book fell from my fingers. In the morning I'd plump the pillows and begin where I left off, safe in a world of fiction where men were gallant and moral women persevered in the face of adversity. I absorbed Austen's insight on social norms and psychological behavior. Good exists; altruism and loyalty, real and possible. My spirits rose from the abyss with Austen's women who flaunted their freedom by daring to speak things unspeakable during their time, not tainted nor sordid but truths, truths about mores and relationships. Though confined to a twelve-by-sixteen room, I traveled a world of wisdom those long weeks of recuperation.

One day I woke to a blustery day, bushes sweeping my windows. Drenching rain pounded the house for hours. *There's not enough rain to wash away the sin in this house*, I thought to myself.

Gradually I began working on my Ashley Hall assignments. To keep my grades up and to make sure there was no space for that afternoon memory to sneak in, I jammed my mind full. But *Eva* did sneak in, cracking the door with a "How's my Baby?" Every day she miraculously appeared to tend me. As far as she knew, she was nursing her sick baby with the whooping cough, not a disillusioned heart. Can you unbreak a heart? Uncry a tear? Maybe Eva *did* know that I had a dual sickness. She came each day to fix meals, wash clothes, and keep everything straight. Did she too realize that nothing would ever be straight again?

Eva knew about Daddy's trysts. Eva knew everything. But she never said a thing. Neither whites nor blacks talked about such personal things back then. I'd wake some mornings with her rubbing my back in long strokes, humming a lazy version of "Jacob's Ladder." At lunch she'd fix a bowl of tomato soup with Ritz crackers floating like rafts and say, "Come on now, Baby. You needs to eat. Let's get some meat on dem bones." She always did like me plump. She didn't spend nights. "It kinda tight for Mista Busta right now, but I be yere in the mornin'."

She sometimes distracted me with her updates on Daddy Bill and Miss Hattie's health or stories of her niece Miriam's church singing. She reported how well Miriam was doing in school, then paused. "Before long, black 'n white be in school together," she commented. *What?* I was shocked. I know now that she had to have heard about the 1955 Supreme Court's decision to integrate schools, but I hadn't. "Long time coming, Baby," she said.

Neither of us knew it would take another ten years to come to fruition. And I had no idea that Eva had her pulse on life outside our family . . . now that she didn't live under the Williamses' roof full time. I still thought that I was the center of Eva's world. I had lots to learn as both our worlds expanded.

I didn't give a happy hoot about such historic news then. So wrapped up in myself, I didn't notice how carefully Eva had begun to talk about things within our family, outside our family. I later marveled at Eva's capacity to hold in what she needed to in order to live in two worlds. She monitored the risks of speaking out in the midst of our family's mess and the country's racial confusion. She knew exactly what those around her needed, and at the same time preserved her dignity and integrity. What a fine line my Eva walked those years.

I don't remember seeing Daddy at all during my six-week convalescence. Maybe I blocked him out. I don't know. I do know that the house was as still as the eye of hurricane Hazel that had hit the Lowcountry the year before. And time stretched like a gray mist around the days, uninterrupted except for silent reads and Eva whispers. Hunks of thinking time, time to extract some of the puzzling patterns of family memories. I struggled to create a soothing Monet from a deranged Picasso. Lacking grandmother Olive's artistic flair, my visions never jelled.

Daddy's unfaithfulness to Mother tugged at the sleeve of my consciousness. How could I know the truth when my family was shrouded in a fog of silence and denial? I didn't know at the time that as far back as when Rusty was born, Daddy's penchant for philandering was already in motion. Everyone knew that Buster had a way with the ladies. He knew just what to say to make them feel good—calling their names, giving compliments, entertaining with wit and charm.

"Helen, what a unique broach. Tell me about it," I'd hear him say.

"My, my Lorraine, you're looking lovely and slim this evening." Always the gentleman, opening doors, pulling out chairs, lighting cigarettes, serving martinis. He paid attention to the smallest detail. Once he reminded me to lotion my elbows and heels.

"Men like their women soft," he said. It would never have occurred to me.

The discovery of Daddy's infidelity, plus my accelerated social education at Ashley Hall, took its toll. I felt as impotent as a fruit fly seeking a place to land. And I landed on Eva—soft as a feather pillow, solid as a mountain. I remember Eva's weight, her depth, her strength. With every hug, her energy imbued my despondent spirit. She cooked me macaroni and cheese, squeezed me fresh orange juice, made me biscuits and banana pudding. During those weeks we hugged a lot, talked in spurts.

"Baby, de Lord don't give us more'n we kin carry," she said. And after weeks of healing, I carried Eva's words with me back to Ashley Hall.

And sure enough, things lightened up.

Chapter 10

Blue Skies

The one thing that can solve most of our problems is dancing.
—James Brown, singer

"Come on and eat a little something," Eva said to Daddy, knowing he would be itching for his first toddy as soon as she left. Eva watched over this middle-aged boy of hers as he struggled to right himself. "You drive careful now, Mista Buster," Eva said, reminding him that he was carrying precious cargo. *When had Eva taken to giving Buster instructions?* Me? I was glad to be leaving those subtle signs of his fall. The mackerel sky gave way to a touch of blue as I stepped into the car. A sober Daddy drove me to Charleston. Eva had refueled her Baby's wilted body and sagging spirit. It was back to Ashley Hall with renewed energy for classes, new friends and extended family—all buoying me for the remainder of the school term. Exams were just around the corner, so I focused on my studies, wanting to make the highest grades so Mother would be proud and Daddy couldn't find fault.

A few days before Christmas break I heard a boarder talking about Rosa Parks stirring up trouble in Alabama. Apparently she was minding her own business sitting in the colored section of a bus when the driver asked her to give up her seat to a white man because the bus was overflowing. She refused. And, boy, did that get those white folks mad. They put her in jail!

Who knew that nine months *before* Rosa Parks became national news, in the same town and the same bus system a shy fifteen-year-old, Claudette

Colvin, LaClaire's same age, staged her own sit-in? Some fifty years afterwards, the elderly Colvin explained on National Public Radio why she didn't get out of her seat when officers insisted. She replied that she'd just come from school where they'd talked of abolitionists Harriet Tubman and Sojourner Truth, icons of freedom in the black community. "It was like Tubman was holding me down on one side and Truth on the other. I couldn't get up. They had to drag me outa that seat," Colvin said. *Where had I seen that Tubman name before?* My only reference was Tubman Creek on the way down to Beaufort. Colvin said black leadership chose the more mature, already-involved Parks over her to be the symbol for the bus boycott movement. Colvin was young and pregnant. It was "politically a wise decision," she said. And right in my own back yard, unsung teenage hero Sara Mae Fleming laid the foundation for the local bus boycott in a courageous stand in Columbia, South Carolina, long before Rosa Parks.

The reality was that young females comprised over fifty percent of activists during the chaotic fifties and sixties. But not me—a little white girl whose history books didn't mention achievements of blacks except Eli Whitney and the cotton gin. Naturally, I remembered him. What the books *didn't* say was Whitney never got a dime from his invention. While black girls my age braved the police, I stayed secure behind wrought iron gates. I focused on the eighth-grade curriculum. Mythology and Latin were required courses. Mythology captivated me—especially the drawings of Greek and Roman gods like naked Diana with a bow and arrow and Medusa with a head of writhing snakes. Eva cut me short when I showed her pictures from my small green book while I was recuperating. "Ain't but one Gawd, missy. You better get that scrate," she huffed.

Latin, my first foreign language, required lots of memorization. I didn't view it as a "dead language" as much as a means to understand English roots. And, like my daddy, I loved words. I made conjugations interesting by creating jingles like "Amo, amas, amat/I love the class a lot." English was a breeze because in the seventh grade back home I'd had Miss Victoria Crawford, whose scathing reprimands for a wrong tense or misplaced comma made me shiver. Students got their revenge at Halloween by stringing rolls of toilet paper in the tree outside her house.

A competitive spirit came to the fore at Ashley Hall, inside and outside the classroom. Before this, I think I studied hard and kept my room clean in order to get praise and keep out of trouble. LaClaire inspired me to my push my own limits and pit myself against others. Ever since the nocturnal advance of LaClaire's classmate, I felt a shift in our relationship. Daddy wasn't around to baby her, Rusty wasn't around for her to baby, and Eva wasn't around to baby me. We had only each other. She became the big sister I'd never had. She showed me the ropes. We were both on the Purple Team and shared a passion to beat the Whites in intramural competitions like basketball or softball.

Behind our gated walls, we had no idea that a few blocks up Rutledge Avenue a group of black baseball-loving boys were pitching curve balls and hitting homers. These Cannon Street All-Stars made it to the Little League World Series that very year. But they played not a single inning of the tournament because South Carolina's "separate but equal" laws prevented blacks and whites from playing together on public facilities. Officials even approached the military bases in the area to let white and black play together, but they were turned down. "Our parents didn't talk about racial things then. We just played. That's all we wanted to do—play the game," reflected Leroy Major, one of the players. Us too. We just played, separated by not only a wrought iron fence but by an invisible barrier.

Black people of that generation attest that very few talked about the unrest. Lord knows the whites didn't want to bring it up either. Everybody kept tamping it down, tamping it down. John Lewis, an Alabama boy who became a leader in the Civil Rights

Movement and a US Congressman, confirmed this view of his childhood:

> *We really didn't discuss the whole question of segregation. It was something that existed and something that we saw when we went to . . . the dime store. . . . You knew not to drink out of the fountain that said White Only . . . [y]ou couldn't go to the soda fountain and get a Coke. Somehow we grew up knowing that you couldn't cross that line, but there was not that much discussing it within my family, not at all. It was a sense of fear, I guess, on the part of my parents, that we must stay in our place.*

I heard about a white boy seeing COLORED and WHITE signs over water fountains and rushing to the COLORED one because he thought the water would be in rainbow colors. His mother practically snatched the hair off his head pulling him away. It seems unbelievable that I was ignorant of these struggles while living with a black woman most of my growing-up years. Eva saw things the way Lewis described it. She had pretty much stayed in her place. We stayed in ours.

It wasn't until I read *The Race Beat* fifty years later that I learned the print media in the Lowcountry harnessed its energy to present the South as a paradise to be preserved at all costs. Likeminded newspaper editors conspired to boycott news of protests, civil rights violations, and integration incidents out of Southern newspapers. The Charleston *News and Courier* editor, Thomas Waring, Jr., and *Richmond News Leader* editor, James Kilpatrick, were among the ringleaders who had a secret meeting in Atlanta to plan their strategy—ignore all incidents of unrest, and pen scathing front-page editorials promoting states' rights and, later, separate but equal opportunities for blacks.

On the other hand, I had no idea that black newspapers had been circulating news about racial strife for decades. Originally there were 2,700 black papers; they dwindled to fewer than 175 by the 1950s when news began traveling by multiple means. *The*

Charleston Advocate, the *Afro-American Citizen* and the *Charleston Free Press* prepared their readers for the battles to come. But they did not show up on the Williamses' doorstep, and *The News and Courier* didn't prepare us for the inevitable conflicts that shook so many.

This was 1955, and Angie Williams was insulated from all sides by parents, the press, and Southern society at large, including Eva, who might have shed light into the dark corners. Bottom Line: Southern whites didn't talk about racial issues because it wasn't polite, blacks didn't talk out of fear of retribution.

So during Ashley Hall days, I didn't know much of anything. I didn't read the paper. I listened to music on the radio on weekends. Ashley Hall had no television. Current news consisted of who was dating whom at the next Citadel hop. We studied and played. LaClaire convinced me to try out for the Dolphin Club, which put on annual synchronized swimming shows. Water was a dubious friend, but I wanted to please her. Swimming to music wasn't as difficult as holding my breath forever as I pointed a leg straight at the ceiling, sculling just enough to sink slowly until the toe disappeared. Among other things, my lung capacity expanded that year.

The Ashley Hall Christmas play enjoyed a long school tradition, a gift to the community. Everyone vied for roles to play Joseph, Mary, shepherds, wise men. The renowned Red Choir constituted an integral component of the pageant. The entire school and many Charlestonians attended the annual musical dramatization at Memminger Auditorium near Grace Episcopal Church. Grandmother Olive belonged to Grace Church when she lived in Charleston, and Ashley Hall boarders marched there every Sunday adorned with hats, gloves, and stockings held up by garter belts with pesky snaps front and back. (Four years later pantyhose arrived, the best invention since sliced bread!) Dress was more informal at Trinity in Pinopolis, but I thought of Eva dressed similarly each Sunday as she left our house, so I didn't mind the dress code one bit.

In the Christmas play, LaClaire played the Virgin Mary one year and the angel Gabriel another, apt roles for the budding beauty. By tenth grade, she was 5-foot, 6-inches, pimples gone, braces off and boxy haircut replaced by long, strawberry-blonde tresses. Eva declared her "sho nuf purty." LaClaire shined as Ashley Hall's poster girl. *The News and Courier* once ran a photograph of her reading a book in the stone grotto on campus. (That was LaClaire, always reading.)

LaClaire encouraged me to be part of the Christmas play. I decided to try out for the Red Choir, the select group who wore red robes and sang carols throughout the medieval play. I loved to sing. Some of the first sounds I recall as a toddler were rhythmic common meter spirituals that Eva sang to me.

> *I got shoes, you got shoes, all God's chillen got shoes.*
> *When I get to heaven gonna put on my shoes . . .*
> *And walk all over God's heaven.*

The image of Eva and me marching all over heaven together made me smile. She often said we needed to "make a joyful noise to the Lawd," and I intended to do just that in the Red Choir . . . if I could make the tryouts.

Mr. Fracht, the conductor of the Charleston Symphony Orchestra and our Red Choir director, was brutal in his perfectionism. An imposing figure with unruly white hair and a barrel chest that bellowed instructions as if firing a cannon—boom, a few bars, then another boom!

"The choir is short on seconds," I overheard someone say. Once I found out what that meant, I spied on the early auditions to discover the songs he used. Every afternoon for a week, I went to the upstairs ballroom and played "We Three Kings" and "Silent Night" on the piano, assiduously memorizing the second soprano parts. I waited until the last day to try out. I prayed he wouldn't select different carols. Like Mother, I had no real ear for music, but I was determined to be in the play. LaClaire would be proud. Eva too.

My prayer was answered. I don't know about LaClaire, but Eva was thrilled. "Ain't that fine. Baby in the choir," she said. I asked her to come. "Beba can't make it, Baby. But you sing real purty now," she said. Eva didn't get to hear her Baby sing a joyful noise. I'm amazed now by my naiveté.

Eva's people didn't go to Grace Episcopal or eat inside white restaurants either. They could be served from a "hole in the wall"—the outside pick-up window for blacks. A friend recalled hitchhiking from his Virginia college to his Tennessee home and being surprised when a black man picked him up. Farther down the road, the driver stopped at a hamburger spot, turned off the ignition, and asked my friend if he'd mind going in to get him a sandwich. No hole in the wall there, I suppose. Jim Crow laws prohibited these same travelers from staying in hotels and motels—they slept in their cars. That's just the way it was in the South.

So, no Eva at the Christmas play, Daddy didn't show, and Mother, of course, was confined to Pinehaven Sanitarium. LaClaire and I made weekly visits to Mother at Pinehaven only a couple of blocks from school near the Medical University of South Carolina. Historically, Pinehaven Camp was started in 1915 to quarantine people with "consumption." By 1920 tuberculosis, with no effective treatment, was the leading killer of young adults in South Carolina. Pinehaven Tuberculosis Hospital opened in 1953, two years before Clara Lee was admitted. By then, TB treatment had changed dramatically with medications, and only about a thousand cases existed in South Carolina.

Mother's bright room included a view of the Ashley River. Sometimes we'd find her "taking air," sunning on the roof, a practice later discarded. Talk was light, mostly about our grades or weekend plans with the Whaley girls. She spent her time reading and cheering up other patients. The Bible, sermons by Peter Marshall, chaplain of the U.S. Senate, and books by Norman Vincent Peale like *The Power of Positive Thinking* rested on her bedside table. Trinity's minister, the Reverend Harold Barrett, visited often from Pinopolis. He gave her counsel and encouraged her to get down on her knees to pray—for her own health and Buster's sobriety. "Miss Clara Lee sho learn how to pray in that hospital," Eva said later.

Mother's health improved. Daddy's abstinence did not. When he visited her after taking a few nips, his eyes sparkled a little too brightly. Mother turned cool and distant, the same look I'd first noticed after the wreck. At other times, LaClaire's Charleston friends mentioned seeing Daddy drunk at the Yacht Club. Sometimes he'd pick us up from school to take us to dinner at Perdita's or the Colony House. Everett's Restaurant was another favorite; he liked to talk with William Deas, the black chef who made the famous she-crab soup that became a ubiquitous appetizer in Charleston restaurants. On those dining out evenings, at first Daddy might be sober yet smell of the previous night's alcohol still oozing from his pores—a smell so regular that I acquired a keener nose than a narcotic dog. By the time we ate dessert, he was tipsy. I'd close my eyes as he maneuvered the narrow Charleston streets to deposit us back at school on Rutledge Avenue.

After an occasional weekend at home, drives back to the city were even worse. Thirty miles of speeding and crossing the center line of the two-lane road left me frightened and breathless. Wild, weaving rides. Eva was right to give Buster regular driving warnings. She tried to protect us from him, yes, but used us to shore him up, to remind him to do right when the opportunity arose. She too was trying to keep the family together.

At Eva's urging, LaClaire and I reluctantly signed on for a trip with Daddy to visit Rusty at Staunton Military Academy in Virginia. A *long* ride. "You gots to go," Eva admonished. "Yo daddy trying he best to keep this family going. Sides, Rusty pow'ful homesick. Go on now." Did Daddy initiate the trip because he remembered his own homesickness at exactly the same age in exactly the same setting? Was he responding to a request from Mother because of Rusty's homesick letters? Whatever the reason, the trip was on.

Rusty lined up dates for LaClaire and me for the Staunton Academy's annual dance. The harrowing nine-hour drive through snowy, mountainous roads with Buster's unsteady hands at the wheel left us exhausted and running late. Rusty looked so endearing that night, hair slicked back with pomade, dimpled smile. He proudly introduced his sisters to the upperclassmen he'd chosen to be our escorts. I remember stepping into a light blue evening dress with no time to fix my hair . . . and fending off a cadet with fast hands all evening. Eva would have been proud.

A homesick puppy indeed, Rusty wrote Mother religiously, cheering her, showing his concern for her health, saying he missed her. I found two letters he wrote to her just after she was released from Pinehaven, before the end of his sixth-grade school year:

Rusty

Dear Mommie,

I sure am glad to hear you are out. Just think of the good times we can have. Do you think we will go to Wampee this summer? We can have lots of fun there.

Is Angela home yet? Do you think I have to go to summer school? If I do that will ruin my whole summer. Do you still have to take air when you are home? Do you do much at home? Have you been swimming yet? I sure am homesick. I wish I was home with you.

Tell daddy I don't won't to come back next year. If I do come back I won't get rank.

Much Love, Rusty Williams

P.S. I wish I was home with you. Will you send me a roll of stamps?

Another letter mentioned that he got in trouble. "I went to the bathroom out the window. I just didn't think about it before I did it. Please don't be mad." He ended with, "I am glad you are home and hope everything is ok with you and daddy and the business." Clara Lee's eleven-year-old son knew the two areas his mommie desperately needed to be "ok"— his daddy and the business. When God created sensitive souls, Rusty got a lion's share.

Rusty came home only on holidays. LaClaire and I rarely went home on the weekends, but when we did, we took laundry bags full of dirty clothes and hearts laden with apprehension. Eva tended to both, our hearts and our laundry. She was there when we woke and there when we went to bed. She let us sleep in, cooked our favorite foods, and washed the mountain of clothes. She listened to tales of fun in Charleston. And she gave us the lay of home base. The coast was clear in the mornings, quiet except for Eva's humming and shifting across the kitchen linoleum. "It's been a good week for your daddy," and we felt relief. Or, "Your daddy been tru a lot this week," and we laid low. Up and down. Because he was running the business without Mother's help, we hoped he'd straighten up and fly right, as Uncle Charlie encouraged him to do. And Viv Ingle too. During their haranguing conversations, it was Viv who called the disease by its true name: alcoholism.

For the first time in twelve years, Eva's primary residence was not Buster Williams's house at 114 Library Street. Because of *his* finances, *her* homeplace changed. That's when Buster built Eva a brand new house about a mile away. Probably *not* what Clara Lee had in mind when she encouraged Buster to use fiscal restraint. White clapboard with blue shutters, it had plenty of room for a flower garden in front and a vegetable garden out back. Eva pulled together furniture and other household goods to make a house a home, but she spent much of her time at her parents' house because Miss Hattie and Daddy Bill were elderly and ailing, and Miriam, Eva's foster child, as she liked to call her, was still in school.

Miriam had grown up with Eva's family since a baby. Miriam's mother, Eva's cousin, lived in Florida and couldn't provide for the child. Up to this time, the teenaged Miriam had the responsibility of taking care of the elder Edwards when Eva was with us. It was fortuitous that Eva now had more time to be with her family of origin. And for the first time in over a decade, Eva integrated into her cultural community, which she'd all but abdicated when she signed on to be a part of the Williams family.

This was in the mid 1950s when the smoldering Civil Rights Movement began to spark. Eva and her family knew precious little news beyond the border of our community, where things were quiet, at least on the surface. The social preaching that flared up in black churches around the South did not occur at her Rock Hill Baptist Church. "All the preaching was Bible preaching," Miriam told me. "Guess they figured we could handle anything if we knew our Bible." The policy was for local preachers to avoid social issues in their sermons so they wouldn't get in trouble.

But Samuel Taylor, a young black activist who lived in Berkeley County at the time and later married Miriam, had another story to tell about *his* church. At the more liberal Great Redeemer Reformed Episcopal Church, just up the road a piece in Pineville, they hosted preachers and political speakers from up north. Samuel recalls a powerful sermon advocating integration one Sunday delivered by Bishop Kerney, a white bishop from Philadelphia. Similar messages spread to other congregations through churches, the primary conduit for significant news.

Some folks visited the more liberal churches or dropped in on Parent-Teacher meetings at the black schools, which in many cases were disguised NAACP meetings. Updates on what was going on in the Civil Rights Movement and suggestions for dealing with potential trouble in biblical fashion headed the agenda. Locals also passed along information about sticky spots like Bonneau, a lake community beyond the Tail Race Canal. Blacks walking or riding buggies planned their trips to be "past Bonneau by dark, otherwise they'd end up in jail," said Samuel.

Nearby St. Stephen had a reputation too. As a boy, the black artist Dr. Leo Twiggs was a movie projectionist in Moncks Corner. He said his mom worried until he got back home safely to St. Stephen. (Interestingly, Dr. Twiggs became known for his iconic drawings of the Confederate flag.) "The irony is that Berkeley County was generally considered a 'safe place' because there's no recorded history, but not because nothing ever happened," Samuel said. People dropped out of sight, but nobody reported the incidents. Did Eva know of such disappearances? Or about George Stinney from Alcolu who was executed at fourteen—conviction overturned seventy years later? He had been helping two little girls look for maypops. And he was later accused of killing them.

Occasionally Eva brought Miriam to our house when she was little. Quiet as a kitten and bespectacled, Miriam was LaClaire's age. The two of them spent afternoons coloring at the kitchen table while Eva went about her business. They spread out all twenty-four crayons, wrapped their arms around their coloring books, and colored page after page of princes and horses and clouds. Heads down, not talking much, just coloring. Once they became teenagers, Miriam seldom came around. A tacit custom in the South was that when black children reached eleven or twelve, they didn't mix with whites, even out on the farms where boys and girls had daily worked and played together as children. "After twelve, my white girl friends became 'miss' and I became 'boy'," Samuel told me. But his parents would jerk a knot in him if he defied the guidelines they had instilled in him for his protection.

Adults suffered similar indignities. People commonly added a prefix to older black women like *Miss* Hattie. I recall whites calling elderly blacks "auntie" or "uncle" and thought nothing of it. When my friend Brantley Harvey began law practice in Beaufort, he was told to call all black clients by their first names unless they were preachers or doctors. "Then you address him *Mister* Jim," not even his last name. He defied the suggestion. Even Charleston's long-time mayor Joe Riley was reprimanded by his parents as a boy because he called a black man "sir."

In Charleston I vaguely remember the scarcity of blacks when shopping on King Street. Blacks generally didn't shop south of Calhoun Street any more than whites shopped to the north. But if either ventured into the other's terrain, one or the other made a shift. Sidewalks particularly were territorial property. Whites and blacks walked on different sides of the street. White folks crossed the street to avoid a black who happened to be on the same side of the street as far as a block away *and* vice versa. Sometimes they played a subtle form of chicken to see who would cross over first. There was even a time blacks weren't allowed to wear hats on the streets of Charleston because it obscured their identity. These and other customs, like doffing hats, calling bosses "massa," and not looking people in the eye, hung over from slavery days. In the 1950s and 1960s, young, educated blacks started getting their backs up. When John Lewis was a student at Morehouse College, the dean phoned to tell his parents of his arrest during a student sit-in. Lewis and fellow students entered the Nashville jail singing, "We Shall Overcome."

"My mother sent me a letter [she had no telephone] saying, 'Get out of that mess before you get hurt'," he recalled. He and many others bravely disobeyed the guidelines of their parents who feared for their children's safety. "Most of the activists in South Carolina were educators," Samuel told me. This gave them a safe forum for teaching the younger generation.

Eva's generation mainly continued to hold their peace. She surely knew more than she let on because she was forty years old before her world had become primarily a white world. She'd been called an Uncle Tom. Few doors closed to Eva, at least few doors that mattered in her daily doings. She was Buster Williams's Eva. And she seemed satisfied—until this year, the year she didn't work full time, the year she was gifted with a house of her own, the year her landscape broadened and she saw a wider world . . . from *her* people's view. Coincidentally, my world view expanded at the same time . . . but only a short thirty miles south, to Charleston.

The Whaley's home on Church Street became a regular refuge and a second home for LaClaire and me throughout high school. Visits there always lively with Ben Scott, a flamboyant lawyer, blaring forth tirades on the mayor's latest stupidity. Emily Whaley, or Cheeka as we all called her, was an expert gardener and talented musician, always banging out show tunes on the piano. Stir in the Whaleys' three bright, vivacious daughters and you have a captivating family. LaClaire and Miss Em were in the same class. Angie and I, a year apart. Marty only slightly younger. It was like visiting cousins. We felt at home at "58 Church," as we called it. Kat helped in the kitchen, the way Eva did on Library Street. And in Cheeka's famous garden, Cuffie Robinson pulled weeds just like Chester. Cheeka kept a watch on us as if we were her own. Anything to help her friend Clara Lee, whose life had taken a terrible tumble.

On Fridays we'd peel off our school dresses to don pedal-pushers, eager to walk over to East Bay Playground to watch tennis battles among the cutest boys in town: Sam Applegate, Beansy Frampton, Franklin Robinson, Bennie Varn and Paul Scarpa. Sometimes we'd ride bikes to the Battery to watch a regatta, hang over the wall to spot fish, or fool around on the bandstand at White Point gardens. Or we'd go to the post office to visit the basket weavers and flower ladies that Elizabeth O'Neil Verner painted, pictures that hung in all our houses. When the weather turned hot, we'd escape to the Whaley's beach house on the Isle of Palms where Cheeka required everyone to read during rest hour. Looking out the window at shrimp boats lowering their butterfly-wing nets, I'd often drift off to sleep to the lapping sound of the sea licking the shore.

Debutante balls highlighted winters in Charleston. Planning began a year in advance with mothers divvying up duties to write invitations (in calligraphy, of course), choose the caterer, reserve a ballroom, and select a band.

During Christmas break, we went to balls almost every night. And the same crowd, with little variation, attended them. Ashley Hall girls, Porter Gaud boys. Downtown Charleston was, in fact, a small place. Those who lived downtown were referred to as SOB's—they lived *South of Broad Street*—the point of the Charleston peninsula where *true* Charlestonians were born and bred. Prep school boys and girls came home from boarding schools

Mr. and Mrs. John Hampden Brooks

Mr. and Mrs. Lucius Gaston Fishburne

Mr. and Mrs. Gilmore Simms McDowell, Jr.

Mr. and Mrs. Ben Scott Whaley

request the pleasure of your company

at a dance in honor of

Miss Jane Hamer Brooks

Miss Patti Gage Fishburne

Miss Courtenay Cordes McDowell

Miss Anne Sinkler Whaley

Monday, the twenty-sixth of December

at ten o'clock

Francis Marion Hotel

R.s.v.p.
58 Church Street

like Episcopal and St. Catherine's in Virginia. Out-of-town cousins like the Fishburne girls from Walter-boro descended on the city at holiday time as well. To even out the matches, additional young men from other areas of the Charleston peninsula were invited, as long as the party hosts viewed them from good families who taught their sons how to treat a lady and how to wear a tux. Boys who breached the unwritten protocols were not invited again.

LaClaire and I opened the deb ball invitations which arrived weeks ahead eager to see our dates' names on the enclosed white cards. We agonized over what we'd wear and planned when we'd arrived at the Whaleys. Boys' mothers called to find out the color of our dresses, making sure the roses, camellias or carnations complemented our gowns. On the day of the ball, the doorbell at 58 Church rang frequently with corsage deliveries. By early evening, a gaggle of girls filled the upstairs bedrooms and baths—Miss Em, Angie, Marty, Moonie, LaClaire and me. Maybe cousins Dargan and Patty Gage from Walterboro. All scurried to tighten "merry widow" corsets, arrange hoops and hairdos, taking turns to check gowns at the long mirror and praying the first caller was someone else's date because no one was ever quite ready.

Ring! Then we appeared at the top of the stairs. The frantic fussing turned into measured motion. Head high, long skirt lifted slightly with one hand, the other hand poised on the banister. Next, the smile, the best thing you can wear, according to Eva. Then one pointed-toe shoe touched each step in a theatrical descent. The evening had begun.

The balls mirrored those in *Gone with the Wind*. Large rooms at the Hibernian or Carolina Yacht Club overflowed with flowers, food, and rose-cheeked girls in wide hooped gowns. Boys made handsome by tuxedos and puffed chests spun girls around polished floors to the beat of the band. Dance cards full, no wallflowers on the sidelines. We girls "perspired." The boys "sweated." Dancing never stopped. Between songs we nibbled crustless

tea sandwiches, benne wafers, and pecan sand-
ies. Bowls of shrimp and plates of fruit and cheese
sat on long, candelabraed tables. We quenched our
thirst with fruit punch ladled in little glass cups—
then kept on dancing until we dropped or the band
played "Ole Lang Syne." When we girls arrived back
at 58 Church about one or two in the morning, we'd
quickly undress, put on our pajamas, and raid the
refrigerator. We'd gather upstairs on the beds, reliv-
ing the evening with stories of who spiked the punch,
who spilled over her strapless gown, and who might
be our date for the next ball.

One cold winter night, Dowse Rustin waltzed
into my life at Hibernian Hall on Meeting Street. I
didn't know his name. He didn't say a word—just
threw me a wondrous sweet smile, stretched out a
hand and gently pulled me to him. Those hands, so
warm and solid. Like Eva's. Safe. I returned his
smile. We started dancing—and didn't stop for eight
wonder-filled years.

Dowse, a student
at Rivers High School in
downtown Charleston,
called for me many times
at the Whaleys. The invitation's insert card that read
"Dowse Rustin will call"
never failed to please me.
Good looking in his tux-
edo, he greeted me with a
sunny smile, his bedroom
eyes shining. Always with
a camellia wrist corsage
his mother fashioned from
her garden on the Ashley
River. One evening I wore
a strapless cherry-red, velveteen gown with a wide

Dowse Rustin

hoop skirt. The next morning Cheeka asked about
the evening, as she usually did. "When you came
down the stairs, that young man looked up at you
like he could eat you with a spoon," she said. That's

the first time I recall anyone ever thinking I was pretty.

Debutante season featured billowy ball gowns of every hue, which meant shopping. We shopped mostly in Charleston, our buying habits not yet changed to fit the shift in our family's fortune. Daddy encouraged LaClaire and me to charge whatever we wanted, and knowing no better, we did. We frequented the higher priced stores on upper King Street, where I bought shoes from Ellison's to match my Lanz dresses with their trademark rickrack trim. We bought our brown and white Oxfords for school from Condon's Department Store, where a new boxlike machine X-rayed our feet to check the fit. I could not believe I could see my toes butting up against the tip of my shoes! At Kerrisons Department Store we bought our garter belts, stockings, and leather gloves that stretched just above our elbows. For the balls, of course.

When we shopped at Porgy and Bess on church street, we sometimes stopped in the antique store next door to say hello to cousin Lawton Wiggins. For birthday presents, sweaters from Porgy were excellent for male friends, and Bess next door was popular for female gifts. The twin stores operated on Church Street where the crippled character Porgy—immortalized by the Gershwin brothers—was said to have lived on Catfish Row. When *Porgy and Bess* opened in New York in 1935, the all-black cast refused to play to a segregated audience. In 1950, while I was listening to mostly black music on the radio, Dock Street Theatre cancelled its production of *Porgy and Bess* because of segregation issues. It took until 1970 for the production to come to Charleston even though Debose and Dorothy Heyward wrote the original novel and play in the mid-1920's right on Folly Beach outside of Charleston. Long time coming. I didn't know those details when I saw the play in town many years later. It remains my favorite opera.

How could I have known that several summers down the road LaClaire would be teaching swimming lessons to pay off debts that Buster couldn't pay. Elza and David Altman were proprietors of Elza's where we bought many dresses; they knew the Williams girls well, treated us like family. Both charming, Blossom and Saul Krawcheck ran Krawcheck's that we also frequented. Only later did I learn how graciously both families treated us during our family's financial downslide.

Amazingly, during my Ashley Hall year of 1955, activities remained pretty much the same as when we lived in Moncks Corner. We attended the downtown movie houses. From the Whaleys or Ashley Hall, it was only a short walk to the Gloria and Rivera Theaters on King Street. The starry blue sky in the ceiling at the Gloria enchanted me. *Rebel Without a Cause* was a big hit that year, James Dean's death a tragedy to many teenage girls, including this one.

Charleston peninsula felt familiar, like a small town, a mere fingerling at the juxtaposition of the Ashley and Cooper rivers, which local folks claim form the Atlantic Ocean. Up and down Market Street around the corner from the Whaley house, farmers from Johns and Wadmalaw Islands sold their fresh greens and ripe tomatoes. Street vendors pushed wooden carts calling out "swimps" and "wedgetubbles" for sale, tipping their hats even to us children. Margaret Street lived around the corner from the Whaleys on Tradd Street. Bright and bubbly Margaret made double-dating with Dowse and Dan Batten lots of fun. I hoped her father would be home from work at the shipping company when I visited her. A smart, handsome man, he reminded me of my daddy at his best. I reveled in our conversations because he elicited my opinion on everything from politics to history. He listened to my answers with rapt attention, leaning forward in his chair. I thought how blessed Margaret was to have such a fine father . . . and to be his only child.

One of my most embarrassing moments happened as a guest at Lizzie Huger's house during a Saturday mid-day meal. The family and I had finished a meal of fresh flounder. After the maid removed plates from dinner, she came back from the kitchen and placed clear glass bowls of water with a lemon wedge in front of each of us. She then set a large bowl of chocolate pudding before Mrs. Huger. Since I was the guest, she asked me first if I'd like some dessert. A little befuddled, I glanced at the bowl in front of me, picked it up, and passed it to her. Her silver spoon poised to dip into the pudding, she looked at me, raising her eyebrows quizzically. She held my bowl of water in one hand, the spoon in the other.

"Just put it in there," I said. I looked around the table. Everyone was dipping fingers into their bowls.

"Why don't I just use one of these," she said as she smiled and picked up a glass bowl from a stack beside her that I'd not noticed. When I told Mother about it on my next visit to Pinehaven, she blanched and swore that I knew what a fingerbowl was.

"There're a dozen of them in the china cabinet. I can't believe you made a spectacle of yourself." Everyone at the table overlooked my fingerbowl faux pas, even my sweet friend Lizzie.

Other Ashley Hall day students became friends as well. In fact, all my Ashley Hall friends lived within walking distance of each other. Frenchie Hewitt, Sister Dotterer, and Rosalie Smithy all opened their homes for overnights, for weekends, for dancing. And dance we did. One night in Frenchie's basement, Bill Haley blasted out "Rock Around the Clock" on her 45RPM record player when I arrived. I had a crush on Hal Ravenel before I met Dowse, and when he asked me to dance to Nat King Cole's "Unforgettable," I was all aflutter. Alas, he spent the whole song bending my ear about unforgettable *Lizzie*!

The Charleston life helped to drown out Daddy's drinking, Mother's illness and Eva's absence. Dancing occupied most of our evening entertainment in the 1950s. Music being Cheeka's forte, she taught hundreds of young people in the Lowcountry to dance and organized numerous balls as each of her three daughters came of age—Mrs. Whaley's Cotillion, famous for generations on the peninsula. Parents like mine, eager to give their small-town children some city polish, engaged Cheeka and her sister Peach to teach dancing to a group of Moncks Corner and Pinopolis boys and girls. Teenagers waltzed, foxtrotted and shagged at Trinity Episcopal Church's Parish Hall in Pinopolis many Saturday afternoons—a far cry from Clara Lee's no-dancing upbringing at the Baptist Church in Estill. Eva was a Baptist too, so I tip-toed around the danc-ing subject one day. She put her hands on both hips and looked at me with mischie-vous eyes.

Trinity's Parish Hall, where Angie and friends learned to dance

"Baby, ain't you readin' your Bible? The Lawd *love* dancin'. Just be sho you keeps it cleanlike," she said with a grin. Thank goodness. Because I *loved* to dance!

Someone once said that the Baptists banned dancing because it was doing standing up what you'd normally do lying down. I didn't get the joke for a long time. It all seemed innocent until swiv-el-hipped Elvis Presley came along. Black and white pictures on a square box called a television had just come into our world. Initially the *Ed Sullivan Variety Show* refused to host Elvis. His first appearance showed only waist-up shots. On the second show, when the camera widened during "You Ain't Nothin' but a Hound Dog," his pelvic gyrations shocked everyone—except Eva.

"Do, Jesus, ain't that boy got de beat?" Eva said.

"That's vulgar," said Mother and promptly flipped off the set. I recall her snapping off the car radio too when "Baby, Let Me Bang Your Box" came on. I thought it was about banging on a piano. I didn't understand her aversion to many of my favor-ite songs like "Annie Had a Baby."

But Dowse and I kept dancing—in homes, at Folly Beach pier, at Thornley Beach on Lake Moultrie, the Anchor on East Bay Street, and the

Sands Club on Savannah Highway. Juke boxes, live bands, record players, whatever was at hand. Most dates ended with sweaty hands and perspiration dripping down our necks. Between numbers, we drank water, Coke, and ginger ale—no booze. Dowse came to know that alcohol scared me, and he never took a drink in my presence. How could I not fall in love?

When Dowse first sneaked out of Charleston in his mother's gray Cadillac on that thirty-mile night run to Moncks Corner, he met Eva. She didn't say much more than "Howdy" and then watched us playing chopsticks at the piano and cutting the fool. He made me laugh a lot. Some months later Eva gave her tentative approval. She planted her feet wide and looked him up and down. "Any boy what's good to my Baby be okay wid me." He responded with his amazing smile, just for me. And then for her. He was no fool.

A number of years later, Eva made one of her predictions: "Dere's a lid for ev'ry pot, Baby. You might done found yourn." I thought so at the time.

So in this dark winter of our family life, a passel of good friends and an extraordinary boy painted my sky bright blue. Dowse grew to love me in all my petulance and exuberance. He tapped my joy, the child-like joy that Eva and I had once known when I rode a pony "boogity-boogity" on her knee. No way to imagine the frightening year ahead for both Eva and me.

Chapter 11

The Nor'easter

You do not have to be good.
You do not have to walk on your knees for a
hundred miles through the desert, repenting.
You only have to let the soft animal of your body
Love what it loves.
          —From "Wild Geese," Mary Oliver

"Do Lawdy, if is ain't my Baby!"

We rushed to each other in the driveway. I was so glad to be home, back within arm's length of Eva's warmth. My joyful experiences the last part of my year at Ashley Hall fueled my natural optimism. I felt like a hummingbird eager to suck in the sweetness of this new season. Mother came home from the sanitarium. Rusty and I returned home to Daddy and Eva. I dared to hope a happily-ever-after story would play out.

It didn't.

LaClaire, who had blossomed at Ashley Hall, stayed in Charleston. "Angie'll be fine back home," Mother said. It was meant as a compliment, I suppose. I felt slighted just the same and ambivalent: happy to be back home, disappointed not to be chosen. Delighted to be with Eva part-time, nervous to be around Daddy full-time. But inevitably my Pollyanna spirit raised its head. "Life will be good again," I imagined. But taking no chances, I drove to our Pinopolis church, knelt at the altar rail and, with the earnestness of a new convert, prayed for God to do His magic—make Daddy give up the bottle. And it worked.

For a while.

The family landscape shifted according to my father's fluctuating state of sobriety. Buster was good at stopping for a few weeks, even a few months. Then he'd go on binges like a runaway train flying down a mountain, brakes screeching but not holding. Some mountains small like Pisgah, others steep like Everest. Some days he was the wonder-filled man who excited; more days, the demon-driven ogre who tormented. No one knew which Buster would turn up—Dr. Jekyll or Mr. Hyde.

I became afraid, and not just a little angry. I sometimes treaded a thin line of obedience. One day while I was in the kitchen stirring Hershey syrup into a glass of milk, Daddy called from the living room.

"Angie?"

"Just a minute," I replied, hurrying to get the chocolate dissolved.

In a flash, the crook of his walking cane jerked my neck backwards so hard that I couldn't breathe. His eyes blazed. And I smelled the smell.

"When I call, you come," he said. The bruise remained for over a week.

Daddy hid pints of bourbon in the toilet tank or the clothes hamper. When LaClaire came home, she moved his liquor to even more creative places. One morning Eva found a Vodka bottle in the oven! Even when Daddy wasn't actively drinking alcohol, he ingested other things like mouthwash or Paregoric. I unwittingly fed the fuel by running to the Rexall to buy his "medicine."

Bad nights escalated the year of Mother's return, Rusty's return, my return. The sounds of straps and pleadings spilled down the hallway. At night I'd feel the uncertainty of all our lives, but by morning I'd strained out the tangibles I could live on. I bounded out of bed with purpose—ace a history test, score ten points at the basketball game—leaving all my worries rumpled among the bed sheets, yet dreading having to climb back into them the next night and the next.

Audaciously, I continued to beg God to make my daddy the father of my early years, to make him sober so he'd return to the enchanter or the jester and muss my hair affectionately. Off my knees for a few days, and he was on the sauce again, the late-night sounds streaming through the heating duct. I was heartened when he pleaded for forgiveness and Mother quickly acquiesced. *This time it will be different, this time he'll keep his promise.* But the prayers for Daddy skipped like stones across the waters of our lives, then sank like lead.

My theology became convoluted. Was God wrathful like my father or loving like Eva's Jesus? Many's the time I heard, "Do Jesus, help Mista Busta get scrate" or "Please Jesus keep dis family safe." So I prayed to God-the-Son and tried to be good—to love, honor, and obey my parents—with Eva's regular reminder to "honor your daddy like the Bible say."

One night, noise from the master bedroom startled me awake. My wide eyes darted in the dark. My mind felt sluggish from sleep and the weight of worry, my body was alert but so, so heavy. It felt as if bricks were being stacked on my chest, one by one, heavier and heavier. I looked up and saw a thick, black cloud hovering between me and the canopy. I watched it sink lower and lower, felt it pressing down, down, threatening to smother me—closer and closer until I couldn't breathe. I jerked up, sucking in air by the gulpfuls.

"I'm sorry, I'm sorry!" I cried. "I will pray harder, pray without ceasing . . . just make him stop, please, please God." I fell back on my pillow and waited for my panic to subside. As my breathing became regular, I thought, *the Prince of Darkness has surely paid me a visit.* Because of my lapses in prayer, my unfaithfulness, my forgetting to thank God for my blessings, the good times, my daddy's demons would not be cast out. And then an inexplicable epiphany made my eyes run, my limbs shake: my selfishness caused Daddy's drinking. I cried myself to exhaustion and fell asleep.

In the morning I poured out my revelation to Eva. I'd had a visitation. It was a sign of my black sin. I went on and on, pouring out my anguish. Silence. I expected the usual understanding sympathy, the reassuring words, the inevitable hug. But this morning was different. Eva set down the grits spoon, turned round and looked at me under crumpled brow. With measured words she spoke. "Who you think you is? Gawd?"

I stepped back, stunned. The onions she'd diced for the salmon cakes piqued my nose. Water pooled in my eyes. How long did we stand rooted there, looking at each other, her eyes unwavering, mine shifting uneasily. She eventually reached out her arms and pulled my head to her shoulder. We were the same height now.

"Ain't none of yo' doin', Baby. You don't gots the power. Just get back to prayin'. De Lawd's the onliest one can lif' this burden." She held me back and looked me dead in the eye before delivering an Eva prophecy that gave me goose bumps. "Your daddy gonna be de ruination of dis family yet. Mark my word."

Those days, Mother and Daddy spun in their dual worlds like the twin blades of the rotary beaters on our Mixmaster—stirring, twirling—coexisting, not touching. Except when they got off kilter and careened into each other. But I never once witnessed a confrontation between my parents, no knock-down-drag outs. The clashes and crashes happened behind their bedroom door at the back of the house.

As was her way—her way of keeping peace—Clara Lee dodged questions from me and stepped like a soldier to avoid Buster's landmines. Where was Clara Lee when Buster unleashed his fury on *us*? What was she *doing*? I honestly don't know. I can't recall seeing her. She never interceded, at least not for me. She believed that parents stuck together, presented a united front, didn't undermine each other—all admirable parenting principles. But what about her children? Thinking all my angst was about Daddy, I realized I was also disappointed with *Mother* . . . for abdicating her role, for not protecting us. I now tell myself: *Her energy was depleted from struggling to be a devoted wife and helpmate, trying not to add flame to the fires Buster ignited, and working from dawn till dark to save her husband's declining business.* I never heard my mother utter a negative word about my daddy. God, how she loved that man.

And I, this genial young girl, returned from Charleston to a couple on the brink of imploding. Upon my return to Ashley Hall I fit in, felt at home in Charleston, made new friends and felt at ease with a prince of a fellow who gave me looks you could pour over a pancake. But that homecoming year, inexplicably I tied the knot of my life around the tumult of my daddy.

I went solemn-faced through classes my ninth grade year at Berkeley High School. Having been away the previous school year, I felt out of touch with boys who used to be my best buddies and girls who wore bigger bras. I felt like a bumpy blackberry in a bowl of smooth blueberries. Much of the confidence I'd gained at Ashley Hall slipped into the shadows. I gradually retreated into myself, hiding the family secret when outside the house, bolstering myself for Daddy's next binge when inside the house. I checked in with Eva mopping the side porch with a lick and a promise to ask how things were. If she answered, "'E ain't crack e teeth. Best be quiet now." I knew he was either sleeping it off or smoldering for an eruption.

I alternated between being uncharacteristically quiet to being brought home by the police. This new Angie, this stranger, felt disassociated from the original one. Mr. Mims was a family friend who lived around the corner on Main Street. His dry goods store Law & Mims just across the railroad track was where Daddy Bill bought Eva's patent leather shoes forty years ear-lier. All the coun-ty's little children, white and black, bought their shoes from his store. Me too. At Law & Mims, both white and black patrons were treated po-litely though not

Law and Mims Store
—the first Berkeley County Courthouse—

served equally. Eva was treated with deference because she was Buster Williams's Eva.

When I was in grammar school, Eva walked me across the railroad tracks in the door of Law & Mims. John O. Williams, LaClaire's godfather, measured my foot on a wooden ruler with a little bumper on the back to press my heel against. "Don' skoosh up your toes, Baby," Eva said as I'd tried on a pair of white sandals. She hooked the tiny silver buckle. I looked up to see a black woman walk in with newspaper cutouts of her children's feet—a bunch of cutouts. I asked Eva what they were.

"The mama traced her babies' feets to buy de shoes," she whispered. "Dey feet can't tech the shoe, Baby."

"Why don't I get to trace my feet like *they* do?" I whined.

"Missy, that the way things is. Don't you pay no nevermind," she said glumly. What did Eva think at such times? My innocence obscured the fact that many old Jim Crow laws implied blacks were dirty; therefore, they weren't allowed to try on new shoes that white children might wear, their mouths couldn't touch the same water fountains, or their bottoms sit on the same toilets. I felt cheated that day. That woman's children, on the other hand, had been cheated all their lives.

My friends and I had nothing personally against Mr. Mims, a large, kind man (Gracious me, he was father to my mother's close friend Zada). Behind his two-story house he tended a plot of land where he rotated crops. Rows of dark green watermelon were his pride. My friends and I were intrigued because Mr. Mims had a reputation for guarding his garden with a shotgun. This didn't deter me from leading a watermelon stealing spree.

One night we rode around in Daddy's new, white Oldsmobile station wagon. (Yes, he was still spending money like crazy.) Stopping the car beside the fence, we ran in and out of the garden in a jiffy, each lugging a melon back to the car. Triumph!

No more than an hour after the raid, the town

policeman knocked on the Williamses' front door. The white station wagon was easily visible at night. In a small town, you knew everybody's cars. Buster wasn't home. Was he on "vacation" again? Clara Lee, shocked and mortified, had a private word with the policeman and insisted he haul me down to the police station around the block for a good talking to by the Chief of Police. Scared me good. When I returned, Mother said nothing, leveling me with her hazel eyes and tightened jaw. The following morning, Eva weighed in. "Ain't no call for stealin, missy. The Lawd's done lay down de law on that. You best member who you is." She gave me her hold-too-long stare that dared me to treat the admonition lightly.

Another incident proved a bit more dangerous. Angie Whaley and I were riding horses on Saturday afternoon after watching a cowboys and Indians movie. The wild Indians on pinto ponies chased down a roaring train to rob its gold cargo. Exciting stuff. We walked from the theater on Main Street to the barn behind Williams Farm Supply where we now kept our horses. (Daddy, strapped for cash, had sold Moss Grove.) Angie and I saddled two mares and headed for the woods beside the railroad tracks.

Completely immersed in the fantasy, we reenacted the train robbery from the movie that triggered our imagination. We tied our horses under the trees and belly-crawled to the railroad. Angie and I placed two cinder blocks on the track about a quarter of a mile from the depot. We saw a speck of a person at the depot looking down the track and crept back to our horses. Waiting for the next train, time passed. No train yet. Lying stomach-down on the ground in the woods, we heard a stick crack. A policeman sneaked up behind us, pulled out his gun

Moncks Corner train depot

and escorted the two of us to the back seat of the town's lone police car.

When Clara Lee opened the door and saw the policeman with her daughter in tow *again*, she opened her mouth wide. Then closed it. She listened to his explanation of our dangerous caper, her jaw tightening with each sentence. Finally she looked at me. "Go to your room," she said through clenched teeth. She had that clinched jaw move down pat by now. I expected the worst. The wait was excruciating. The afternoon passed; the evening came and went. Once again I heard the clanging gong of Mother's silence. She didn't speak to me the next morning . . . or the next. Eva, on the other hand, held forth. "Ain't no reason on Gawd's green earth you gots to stir up trouble fo' your mama. She got burdens you don't know nothin' 'bout. You *yere* me now? You best scraten up and fly right, missy," Eva said.

I dreaded being at the house where so many things pressing—Daddy's instability, Mother's all-consuming efforts to keep the business afloat, LaClaire's reduced homecomings, Rusty's increased stuttering and sleepwalking—had gradually made me invisible. Eva too was feeling the strain. She harrumphed when Mother gave a curt directive and punched rather than folded the biscuit dough.

Eva's biscuits were famous all over town. When people had parties, they begged Mother to let Eva make the biscuits. Sadly, biscuits produced tension between Eva and Mother . . . I was eating too many biscuits for Mother's taste, too few for Eva's. The biscuit scene played out as early as I can remember and repeated itself even into the week I married:

Eva looks through the little glass square on the kitchen-to-dining room door to decide when to serve the biscuits. Daddy has sliced the roast, and we've finished our fruit salad. Eva has already passed the rice and the squash casserole and we're into the main meal. Here comes Eva pushing through the door, the silver biscuit tray held high, a white cloth cover to keep the biscuits warm. Eva wears her flat, serving-company look when passing to Mother and Daddy.

She lowers the biscuits to the left shoulder and repeats this around the table. She comes to me. Her face transforms into a closed-mouth smile; she dips both head and hands low. Mother gives me a hard look that communicates, "Angie, do you think you need a biscuit?"

I look up at Eva. Her smile frozen, her eyes steady on me. Firm feet do not move. My right hand crosses my body to lift the edge of the cloth. I take a biscuit. Mother sends me another stare. I look down at my butter plate and fiddle with the little knife.

Eva doesn't budge. I take a second biscuit. Mother then glares at Eva, who catches the look but shifts her eyes to the china cabinet. She continues around the table, pushes the door open with her backside and disappears.

Stress was evident throughout the house. I wanted OUT. LaClaire often rescued me from household drama without knowing it. She urged me to try out for the *varsity* basketball team in the ninth grade—"try" being the operative word since LaClaire received the athletic genes and everyone also knew that only tenth through twelfth graders made the varsity squad. But to please her and to get away from the house, I tried out. For the entire week of tryouts, I dashed through dribbling drills, shot fifty free throws at a clip, ran more laps than the other players, arriving home at dusk "soaked to de bone," according to Eva. Salty-faced, sticky all over, I somehow felt clean.

After a bath I flopped on the bed aching in every muscle, exhausted. In a few minutes, Eva would come in to massage my neck, my back, and finally my thighs and calves until they turned to dough. She'd rub away my weariness, kneading a deeper sorrow. Like Jesus, Eva met me wherever I was at the time—rejoicing when I rejoiced, mourning when I mourned.

Basketball tryouts felt like serious business. No friendly chatter with the coach or the girls, largely because I'd been away since seventh grade. I felt intimidated by a hulk of a coach whose sights were set on a state championship. I felt like a plug among thoroughbreds. At the end of tryouts when Coach Thrash called my name, the whole group was floored, myself most of all. In the bathroom stall afterwards, I overheard an upperclassman say that ninth graders were supposed to play junior varsity. "You know how she got it, don't you?" I paused to hear a compliment about my working so hard or shooting so well.

"She's a brownnoser," she said with an edge to her voice. (Never *did* like that girl.) I hid in the stall until everyone cleared out of the restroom then walked home.

"What's a 'brownnoser'?" I asked Eva. She looked at me quizzically.

"I ain't know, so I reckon you don't have cause to know neither. Don't study dem girls, chile. De jealous. You just show em who you is, Baby," she said. When I got the skinny from LaClaire later, I couldn't believe my ears.

So classes, basketball and other extra-curricular activities kept me busy during the day and a few evenings. Days began calmly on the surface. Mother off to the warehouse; Rusty and I off to school; Daddy sleeping in, waking to his Bloody Mary; Eva keeping the house in order, cooking and cleaning. Our ritual of sit-down dinners became rare. Even when we had them, Rusty or I was usually sent from the table before its end for not putting a napkin in the lap or chewing with an open mouth. Of course, Eva made sure to sneak food to our rooms before bedtime.

Daddy was in and out. When in, it usually wasn't pleasant. On Mother's birthday that May, Eva baked a triple-decker coconut cake and hid it in the pantry, knowing our love of sweets. Rusty found it before I did. He closed the door behind him and ran his finger all the way around the edge of the cake, scooping off icing. When Daddy discovered the misdeed, instead of the usual whipping, he forced Rusty to eat the entire cake right then and there. Eva sidled into her room and pulled the door to, her custom when Daddy caused a scene anywhere near her. All she could do was hold Rusty's head afterwards while he vomited his mother's birthday cake all over the toilet—Eva's toilet. (It never occurred to us not to use her handy bathroom whenever we were at that end of the house.) Eva adored young Rusty and he her. Their bond ran deep; this was Mista Buster's boy that she'd raised from a baby. But there's only so much saving she could do, for all of us. "Eva fixed whatever I'd done before Daddy got home, if she could. She covered for me many times, but she never lied for me. That was Eva," Rusty told me years later.

My father never touched me with his hand; the belt was his primary tool. Although the welts and bruises on my bottom and legs increased from fourth through seventh grade, the beatings miraculously stopped after I returned from Ashley Hall. The method to express his discontent changed. The drunken reprimands criticizing everything from my hair to my weight were far more damaging than the whippings.

One evening getting ready for bed, I sat in my slip at the dressing table brushing my hair. I hated my stubby bangs. In the mirror I saw an awkward girl, waist too thick and hair growing in unwanted places. Recently I'd screwed up my courage to shave one of my legs—too scared to do both. I was especially self-conscious about the scars, in my eyebrow from the joggling board incident at Wappaoola and on my chin from falling on a brick in Mother's garden—the after effects, twelve stitches on my face.

This night Daddy opened my bedroom door, leaned unsteadily against the jam. I hardly recognized his reflection in the mirror. He had practically stopped eating—except for his favorite vegetables, tomatoes and celery in a Bloody Mary. His handsome face, now gaunt. As the flesh fell off his bones, his once robust body dwindled. His full cheeks, sunken; manicured hands now veined; sharp eyes, dulled.

"What are you looking at?" he asked. Before I could answer, he threw me a bloodshot stare and yelled, "Look at you! Look in the mirror." I focused away from him to myself, my face in the mirror, the limp hair, the scars. "You think you're so pretty.

Well, you're not. You're ugly." My heart squeezed in on itself. My head bent down. "Look in the mirror!" I lifted my eyes. "You're fat and plain," he shouted. The last reproaches fell on deaf ears. "You're ugly, you're ugly" had drowned them out. He hopped on his one leg back to his room without another word. I wished he had beat me with a belt.

Weeks afterwards, I was propped up in bed reading and listening to Ray Charles' "Georgia." I heard the joy when Charles described how he felt when his hit became the official state song of Georgia,

> That was a big thing for me, man. It really touched me. Here is a state that used to lynch people like me suddenly declaring my version of a song as its state song. That is touching.

In my ignorance, I thought he was talking about lynchings *way* back, during slavery times, not in *my* lifetime. Usually I turned on the radio at night, but this evening I was christening my new 45-record player. I was a big Ray Charles fan. His show in Charleston at County Hall had been a sell-out—*whites* in the balcony, *blacks* downstairs, at Charles's request. On WPAL, the black Charleston radio station that played my favorite rock and roll music, I'd heard that the US government had used Ray Charles and Dizzy Gillespie as ambassadors to Asia and the Eastern Block in a grand experiment of cultural exchange. I smiled, thinking, "How great is that!" until the announcer closed by saying that they weren't allowed to eat at the White House when they returned.

It was late at night, and the wind was picking up the rain and hurling it against the windows. So absorbed in Ray Charles's plaintive voice, I was startled when my father's face appeared at the door beside my bed. I jerked my head around to look at him. I couldn't imagine my infraction, but I rarely could these days. His narrow face and black eyes looked sharp as a ferret. Wearing only his boxer shorts and a sleeveless undershirt, he hopped inside the room on his good leg, balancing himself with a hand on the table that held my record player. "Turn off that music," he said, touching my record player. As I moved to lift the covers off to do his bidding, in one quick move, he slammed the record player clear across the room. Plastic pieces scattered.

He picked up a stack of 45-records and threw them toward the windows. They flew like an accordion Frisbee and made staccato clicks on the panes before falling to the floor. His hand accidentally caught one record by the two-inch hole, and he twirled it around his finger. He looked down at it and then fiddled clumsily with his shorts. He found the slit in front and pulled out a flaccid piece of wrinkled flesh. My mouth gaped open. I never before had seen a man's private parts. He shoved the hole in the record over the flesh he was holding. Horror-struck, I dove into my pillow. Thereafter I locked my bedroom door.

My next recollection is waking in the morning to Eva's rubbing my back. "Time to rise 'n shine, Baby," she sang. Where was Eva during those night-time visits? Much of this year she went to her parents' house in the evenings. Did Daddy Bill and Miriam need her there because Miss Hattie had died? Did she go to her own new house that Daddy built? Did my parents send her away to shield her from the frightful nights or because they could no longer pay for her overnight lodging? I really don't know, but, if there in the evenings, Eva stayed at the other end of the house in her room, eyes wide, I'm sure.

Maybe she couldn't hear everything because the house was so long, her room on one end, ours on the far side. But Eva knew what was going on, and she knew her role: the quiet observer, the buffer, the mediator, the fount of Godly wisdom. She stayed with our family knowing her "churren" needed her— not only to feed, clothe, and love us—but also to insulate us from the family mayhem when she could, comfort us in the aftermath when she couldn't. The family seamstress for so long, she kept the threads together, darning a hole here, a tear there.

But when do things become so frayed there's no mending? The paradox was that while our family was unraveling, Eva's people were weaving a new beginning. But to rise from centuries of oppression, they were paying a deadly price all over the South. Surely Eva knew about events causing unrest, like the Ku Klux Klan that conspired to frighten blacks into submission and the stringent Jim Crow rules that kept blacks down and out. Eva carried a double-heavy heart:

> *One ever feels his twoness—an American, a Negro two souls, two thoughts, two unreconciled strivings; two warring ideals in one dark body whose dogged strength alone keeps it from being torn asunder.*
> —W. E. B. Du Bois

Eva was a member of our family but also a member of a larger family.

One night seeking her solace, I found Eva sitting on the edge of the bed in her long white nightgown, cap off, head hanging down. A gauze of misery covered her face.

That evening I ignored Eva's body language. Ever self-centered, I burst forth with a confession of anger toward both my parents and the guilt I felt for not loving them like Jesus would. How could God love me if I couldn't love *them*? Why couldn't I be kind? Be good?

"Lawd, dere ain't no bottom to this chile's needs," Eva said to her image in the dark-night's window pane. Amen to that.

She listened patiently as tirade and tears spilled on her lap where my head lay. She smelled of Tide and Clorox and starch . . . so clean. When I'd run out of words, Eva scooped her hands like lifting a heavy net laden with fish, then let them fall on my head.

"None of us be good enough, Baby. God jes slam down his grace on our head. That how we gets tru the misery," she said. That's the first I learned of God's grace. She explained that you can't *see* grace, but you can *feel* it, like warm water pouring over you, washing away fear, anger, guilt. "It all come clean," she said. And you can start over fresh. Your burden gone. My Eva taught me most of what I know about the Bible, and then some.

Life at home often brightened when LaClaire visited on the weekends. Boys in the neighborhood appeared in our yard without so much as a whistle. Outside we shot hoops. On the side porch, we played canasta and ping pong to the sounds of Fats Domino and Little Richard. The boys figured out they needed to skedaddle before Daddy got home. When they heard the crunch of his tires on the driveway, they hit the screened door and scattered like buckshot.

One night in the pitch dark, some of the boys lost their bearings when sprinting across the side lawn. Danny Read slammed into the cast iron wash pot full of pansies, splitting his knee wide open. He lay writhing soundlessly on the ground knowing his football career was over. But he stoically did not let out a sound so Buster Williams wouldn't catch him.

I was thankful that Dowse didn't live in Moncks Corner to witness Daddy's erratic behavior. Would Daddy scare him away? Fortunately, we dated mostly in Charleston, our minds far from the home scene as we slow danced to The Drifters, his warm hands pulling me to him. I lay my head on his chest, safe.

The point of no return with Daddy's self-destructive behavior came one hot summer's night. LaClaire was looking forward to going out with a star football player at Berkeley High School—a sweet, good-looking fellow who lived in Huger in the bowels of Hell Hole Swamp. Daddy was home, already two sheets to the wind.

When the doorbell rang, I'm sure LaClaire wanted to dash out. She couldn't or didn't. Mother, Daddy, LaClaire and I stood in the living room when her date came in. He looked mighty fine with his white bucks polished, his pants neatly pegged, his hair slicked back into a ducktail. Daddy started probing aggressively. Where are you going? What are you going to do? When will you be back? In a Hitchcock twist, the scene escalated as Daddy spewed venom that left us all speechless. Even in his drunkenness, I had never heard my daddy be vulgar. With bleary eyes, he grilled his older daughter as the two inched out of the door, Daddy's badgering filling the night air.

When the young pair returned from their date, the car's headlights caught an object on the rock driveway—Daddy, passed out. The two teenagers lifted his limp body and carried him inside to the master bedroom.

That night was the first time I witnessed a crack in the bond that LaClaire and Daddy had since LaClaire's birth. This was Daddy at his worst, embarrassing the daughter whose adoration and loyalty never, ever wavered. Not once. I was flabbergasted that he turned on her, of all people. I honestly didn't know what went on between the two of them, so engrossed in my own self. Two years older and much wiser than I, LaClaire never shared her experiences.

The two-page letter that Mother wrote to Daddy after that incident would break anyone's heart. LaClaire and I found it in Mother's desk. Her large, half-print, half-cursive handwriting contrasted with Daddy's small neat hand. It began, "Dear Russell," not "Buster." She wrote that she loved him and would do anything in the world to make him happy. She reviewed the escalation of the family's unrest and ended with two matter-of-fact statements:

> My love for you can endure anything. But I can no longer watch the pain you're inflicting on our children.

Period.

She hoped a separation would "shake some sense into him," but it turned into a living nightmare. In wee hours of the morning, he would "visit" Mother, Rusty, or me. I felt helpless during those nocturnal visits. One night I woke to the smoky smell of fear and his sour breath only two inches from my face. Frightening . . . and maddening. I was mad because my prayers had not worked, because God had let me down. I stared at the canopy and wished my father dead.

Life that year was like riding the waves of a northeaster that wouldn't let up. Like many Southern families in small towns, we didn't lock our house, even when on vacation. But now we locked all seven doors before going to bed. He still got in. We changed the locks. He banged furiously on the doors. Mother finally got a restraining order.

My parents' marriage chocked down in jerks and starts as my father fought his insatiable appetites. Like a fine car that surprises you when a sparkplug sputters or a tire flattens. Another day a fan belt pops or the brakes give way. All the refueling with their passion (that never died), his promises (that he couldn't keep) and her patience (that seemed interminable) could not put them back together again. Clara Lee Peeples and Buster Williams dissolved a twenty-year union that had begun on a wave of promise that ultimately crashed down on all of us.

And if it hadn't been for Eva, Lord knows how I would have survived.

Chapter 12

Ebb Tide

*If it weren't for the wind in my face, I wouldn't know
how to fly.*
                    —Arthur Ashe, Wimbledon Champion

Though the storm had passed, the skies
remained dove gray. The heavy air lifted, leaving
peepholes for the sun. I could breathe again, wake
up in anticipation of the day and seeing Eva and
fall asleep on the last word of prayers, hers or mine.
With Buster physically out of the family circle, the
skies would surely clear for good.

But our family traded one problem for another:
how to stay afloat financially. And the economic
change affected both Eva and me.

Buster had already sold much of his land, Moss
Grove Plantation and the Pooshee lake property
as well as hundreds of scattered acres throughout
Berkeley County. In their heyday, father and son
had a knack for buying up land as well as acquiring
it from Russell's Spearmant Liquidating Company,
which he owned. Buying land . . . and losing it,
and buying it back again for a song. Moss Grove
Plantation is a good example. When Daddy was a
teenager in 1924, his father bought over eight hundred acres for $10,000 for farming and hunting—
Moss Grove.

Less than ten years later in 1933, the American
Agricultural Chemical Company brought a $55,000
judgment "Levied upon a certain tract or tracts of
land formerly of J. Russell Williams and appearing
on record in the name of Spearmant Liquidating
Company of South Carolina." Liquidation records
show forty-nine properties totaling over two thousand

acres. Everything from eleven lots within Moncks Corner to land in St. James, St. Johns and Goose Creek Parishes: hundreds of acres of swamp land, half interest in Willow Grove and Kensington plantations, and all of Moss Grove. Olive signed away dower rights. The judge who signed the document was none other than John O. Edwards, my friend Butch Howard's esteemed grandfather, the same whose bushes we dove behind when running away to Eva.

But wait—almost half of the properties listed in the liquidation had "Omit" hand written beside them, one being Moss Grove. Did that mean in the final record that half of the properties were retained? Turns out, Daddy, J. Russell Williams, Jr., bought Moss Gross from the Spearmant Liquidating Company for "Five and no/100 dollars" right after I was born in 1941. Good price, I'd say. As Daddy's golden years waned, he was forced to sell the whole of Moss Grove for $30,000 in 1951. Our family's woodland paradise gone.

It's not clear how much Clara Lee knew about Buster's assets, properties and investments when the marriage ended. Certainly not everything. In the settlement, she asked for the house and Williams Farm Supply. She needed the business to provide an income for running a household and rearing three children. She also had counted on three paid-up educational insurance policies to send us to college. What a punch to the gut when she realized too late that the business was bankrupt, and Buster had long since cashed in all three of our education insurance policies. Clara Lee would have to start from scratch.

Eva ran the home front while Mother struggled with the fiscal reality of Williams Farm Supply. Three men helped—her daddy, Lawton Shuler, and Rene DeBacker. Van and Lillian Peeples rarely set foot in Moncks Corner; we had always gone to Estill. Clara Lee called her daddy for help for the first time in her forty years. Van Peeples came running across two county lines to hunker down over numbers with his eldest daughter. He floated her a loan and helped negotiate bankruptcy terms, fifty cents on the dollar. Daddy Van was a godsend. Reimbursement took considerable time.

"I paid him back every red cent," she told me.

Lawton Shuler lived up the road in the Jamestown community, where he served as magistrate and lived with his wife and six children. The lynchpin manager for the business until brother Rusty took over many years later, Lawton knew the business inside and out and related easily to white and black customers. After work he'd occasionally join Mother for a drink in our kitchen. I often heard their laughter trickle down the hall to my room. I was glad she had a friend to unwind with. No one else dawned her door during those nose-to-the-grindstone years—until Aunt Alice died and Uncle Charlie came calling.

Lawton and Clara Lee worked side by side for about a decade. A true family friend, it was Lawton who dispensed after-the-fact wisdom for me: "Don't drive a big white Oldsmobile station wagon that everyone in town recognizes if you want to steal watermelons." It was Lawton that Rusty called when he got into some devilment in Charleston and landed in the "Seabreeze Motel," a euphemism for the Charleston County Jail on the Cooper River marsh.

Another blessing was Mr. DeBacker, a striking Frenchman and a principal in one of the oldest, most reputable accounting firms in Charleston. Regular as a full moon, he'd pull his sporty convertible up to the steps of the warehouse, comb his thick hair back with his fingers, and stride to the door. Clara Lee splashed him with a wearied, dimpled smile that drew him into the back office where he wrestled the numbers and dispensed advice to the damsel in distress hell bent on saving a sinking ship. His fiscal guidance allowed the company to veer back on course, helping the business and the broken family find an even keel.

The divorce became official my tenth-grade year. Our lifestyle changed abruptly with no explanation. I was either insulated from or oblivious to the truth of our family finances. Probably a bit of both. It wasn't proper to talk about money in our family. I remember embarrassing Mother when she overheard my telling a friend how much I paid for a new pair of shoes when I'd found a bargain.

"When you receive a compliment, just say 'thank you.' Never mention cost," Mother said coolly.

I hadn't yet learned how to read Mother's taciturn nature, to translate cutting clothes budgets into sacrificing for our education, to understand that expecting me to work as a sales clerk was not punishment but helping ends meet. In retrospect, I see myself as blind . . . and stupid. Eva's occasional "Times is hard now, Baby," I took as a general statement about life's being tough. (No news to me on that score.) When Mother said, "Turn the light off behind you" when I left a room, or "turn the heat down" at bedtime, I read it as her being picky, not pinching pennies. I missed other clues, including LaClaire's living arrangement at Ashley Hall. She boarded with Mrs. Brown across the street instead of in the campus dormitory.

The worst thing of all—for me—was Mother's cutting Eva's work hours. How did Eva feel about the reduction in time on Library Street? Was she relieved to be away from the tension? She surely understood our turn in finances, but how was she going to live without the income she'd become used to? No longer living in our house full time, Mother now called Eva's room "the ironing room." I stubbornly held out.

"I'm going to Eva's room to iron my blouse," I said pointedly.

Eva was often absent, and Clara Lee stayed on her own schedule like a robot. She worked all morning, walked home two-blocks for lunch, took a thirty-minute rest prescribed by her doctor, worked all afternoon, and stayed home in the evenings, mostly reading in bed.

During ginning season, her schedule changed. She worked all day and often stayed until midnight. When I grumbled to Eva about Mother's not attending my basketball games, she looked disappointed and repeated her increasingly frequent mantra, "Your mama gots a burden, Baby. She need her rest. Be good now."

When Eva wasn't around, the glue was gone,

and it was more conspicuous that Mother, Rusty, and I lived in different spheres rarely landing at home together. Mother worked at the warehouse from dawn till dusk. Rusty went to school; he was two classes below me, so our paths seldom crossed. He practiced football in the afternoons. He and Eva must have seen lots of each other in the kitchen

Rusty, Berkeley High School football

because that boy was growing into a big, strong young man like his both his grandfathers Daddy Van and Daddy Grand. So wrapped up in my world, I didn't know my brother at all.

Eva glided to the side of my life as Mother slid to the front. I hardly noticed the subtle shift because of teenage self-absorption: studying for school, practicing piano, basketball and cheerleading, soliciting ads for the newspaper and the annual, working at the warehouse, meetings for church Y.P.S.L., and dating Dowse every chance I got (only on the weekends, no week dates allowed).

Eva's slumping shoulders or bunions bursting from her shoes barely registered. I came home long after she had trudged home. Yes, sometimes she had to walk home because no car or person was free to drive her. But when supper was waiting, the clothes freshly ironed, a corner of the bed turned down, and prayer time came, I felt Eva's presence.

I stayed on the move. I filled every waking moment, even on the weekends. In town, my friends and I went to the drive-in movie and ate ice cream at the Diary Queen afterwards. When my buddy Judy Young turned sixteen, Dowse and I danced the night away at her house on the lake in Pinopolis. Sue Roach celebrated her sixteenth birthday at The American Legion Hut down the street from my house.

The same place Terry and Kay Woodcock taught us acrobatics. The Hut was the scene of many parties for young people, the high schoolers and junior highers having separate nights. My sixteenth came and went with a blip.

When the county fair came to town in the fall, everybody showed up, sometimes more than once. A special night was designated for the black community. I liked the Ferris wheel and the funnel cakes and walking through the long building with animal and food exhibitions, where the Eva-Angie biscuits once won a blue ribbon. I was a little afraid to go inside tents that boasted a gorilla-man or a fire-eater . . . still a scaredy-cat, I suppose.

One evening my classmates and I noticed a tent that had lots of boys we knew hanging around; sometimes they went inside more than once. Unable to contain our curiosity, Martha Woods and I sneaked around back and crawled under the flap of the tent to see what was going on. Lo and behold, on the stage up front we witnessed a phenomenal feat. Three nearly naked women twirling tassels on the tips of their voluminous breasts, first in one direction, then another. Mesmerizing! No wonder the boys couldn't get enough of that fair exhibit.

In spring I watched Dowse race his moth sailboat in regattas from Capt. Lockwood's boat in the harbor with my Charleston friends. I danced until totally tuckered out. I visited the Whaleys and enjoyed debutante balls during holidays. I stayed overnight at Dowse's house on the Ashley River if we had a full weekend planned. We went deep sea fishing on his parents' yacht seldom because I got seasick half way out to the jetties on my first trip. Mr. Rustin, a soft-hearted soul, immediately turned the boat around and headed back to shore.

I wouldn't call Dowse's feisty, blue-eyed mom "soft-hearted," but I'll never forget her kindness one night when I was awakened with a painful ear ache. I struggled to stifle my crying. It really hurt. She appeared like an angel and poured warm oil in my ear that brought instant relief. I adored her from that day forward. She made me camellia wrist corsages out of her garden for our deb balls, much more practical that the big pin-on ones most girls wore.

Dowse and I double-dated lots with Margaret Street and Dan Batten. We also went on house parties to Bluffton on the May River where the Peeples and Laffittes often summered, going with Charlie and LaClaire, his parents chaperoning the group. One day we'd been water skiing and swimming off the dock all day long, looking forward to driving over to Hilton Head for supper that evening. Dowse got sick as a dog with chills and fever. My first thought? Annoyance that I'd miss the trip to Hilton Head, not sympathy for Dowse. I pouted the whole evening.

By this time Dowse was no longer secretly driving to Moncks Corner, and my boy and girl friends accepted him easily because of his open personality. However, the local boys didn't appreciate LaClaire's Charlie moving in on their territory, as evidenced by the night someone swiped the new hubcaps off his car sitting in our driveway. Dowse attended the Junior-Senior Prom with me. That night I made a huge mistake.

As junior class president, I was in charge of planning the prom for the seniors. We'd chosen *Show Boat* as the theme. I had the bright idea to transform the school lunch room into a Southern riverside garden, replete with a bridge, a water wheel and moss dripping from the ceiling. We descended on Gippy Plantation where classmate Sandra Henderson lived. Standing on back of a two-ton flatbed truck from Williams Farm Supply, a crowd of us pulled every

Gippy Plantation

stitch of moss that we could reach off the oak trees at Gippy Plantation. We hung the moss over rows and rows of string stretched across the lunchroom ceiling. The back-stretching task took longer than expected, and I barely made it home in time to dress for the prom. But it looked perfect. We had indeed created a beautiful enchanted outdoor garden.

Halfway through the dance, bare-shouldered girls started itching as microscopic chiggers descended from the mossy ceiling—a disaster. We scratched the night away! Good-natured Dowse laughed me through that evening. Afterwards he wrote me a sweet note in his neat, slanting handwriting:

Dear Angie,

Another memory has been added to our many good times together. I hope that we will have many more. The time and effort you have put into the dance sure paid off. It was wonderful and I couldn't have taken a more beautiful girl. Best wishes, luck and love always,

Dowse

Speaking of Gippy, one of the highlights in the Lowcountry in the fifties was the annual lancing tournament held there. The whole community participated in the gala event. Thanks to the generosity of Mr. and Mrs. Nicolas Roosevelt, owners of Gippy, a reenactment of a popular antebellum event first begun in 1851 in Pineville was resurrected in 1952 with the creation of a newly-formed association in Pinopolis.

Angie at Lancing Tournament - Gippy Plantation

"Charge, Sir Knight!" Thus began the costumed horsemen's competition to spear small metal rings with a lance, riding at full speed of their steeds. Thirty or so riders from throughout the state dressed in colonial costumes wearing the colors of their stables. The winner received a big silver cup and a chance to crown his queen of love and beauty. Locals participated in the pomp with gusto. I dressed as a belle in the queen's gallery one year, a costumed rider another.

But back to reality. During this transition time, our family went from owning two new Oldsmobiles to one basic Chevy. From clothes shopping at Elza's in Charleston to Barrons in Moncks Corner. From eating Harold Cabin delicacies to Piggly Wiggly products. Summer jobs took the place of the vacations at Wampee, Pawley's Island and Rockbrook.

Eva cooked more meatloaf and fewer steaks. Clara Lee cancelled Buster's standing order for cases of fish row and salmon, so Eva made oatmeal, corned beef hash, and Mepkin Abbey eggs for breakfast. Clara Lee delivered directives to Eva with that lock-jawed firmness. "Make chicken tonight" or "You're using too much Clorox in the wash," she said. Eva understood the reasoning behind Mother's anxiousness, but it must have hurt Eva not to be in charge of the cooking and cleaning, her areas of expertise. Didn't Mother know Eva was doing her best to cut corners? She didn't need constant reminders. It wasn't just food and clothes that were different. Clara Lee's ready smiles had long since disappeared. So had Eva's. But they soldiered on. Complaints to Eva that Mother was being persnickety were met with a twinge of melancholy. "It's okay, Baby. Yo' mama carryin' a heavy load," she said with lowered eyes.

And my weekends became compromised when Mother suggested that I work on Saturdays. My first job experience came at Read's Department Store on Main Street, a store that blacks crossed the railroad tracks to patronize. All the black businesses were on the eastern side of the railroad, from the barber shop to Gathers Funeral Home. But white and black knew that the Reads sold lower-priced dry goods, so they crossed the track only one block to snatch up bargains. In addition, they let folks charge or put their purchases on layaway. Agricultural communities always had lean times because of the weather. No rain, no crops; farmers suffered more than others.

My first interactions with the general black population occurred at Read's. I don't count occasional hellos to the young men who lifted the sacks in the warehouse or the farmers who dropped by the house to borrow money from Daddy. The girl who worked my shift, a lithe, cheerful girl named Shirley, outsold me every Saturday. She had a knack for chatting comfortably with the blacks and knowledge of the inventory that led her straight to the work shirts or overalls they needed. I didn't know how to "push the sale along," as Mr. and Mrs. Read often suggested to me.

As a teenager, I found myself unable to make conversation with people whose worlds differed from mine. If I hadn't been Clara Lee and Buster's daughter, the Reads would probably have fired me. It wasn't long before Mother pulled me in to help at the warehouse with bookkeeping, not customer service. I worked at odd times, weekday afternoons or evenings. It never crossed my mind that she wanted to free me up to keep my Charleston connections, to enjoy time with Dowse on the weekends. I suspect she did.

Most of the time Lawton, Mother and I worked in the same small office space. No idle chatter. All business. They handled the customers while I checked inventory, which I wasn't very good at. I prepared the monthly bills for mailing. During lulls, Mother worked the books and ordered feed, seed, and farm supplies. Lawton dispatched Tokeo Kadoma either to pick up fertilizer in the two-ton truck or to deliver feed in one of the other smaller trucks to farmers and plantations throughout the county. Tokeo was a reliable driver for our family for years. The first "foreigner" I'd ever known, Tokeo had golden skin, a short and thick body, and narrow eyes filled with mirth. He brought us cookies from his mother's kitchen. His face always lit up when our paths crossed; I mirrored his smile. No matter how big I got, Tokeo always gave me a big, welcoming hug.

During those struggling years, my contribution to the business was minimal but constant. Once I finished the bills, grading and crating eggs came next. The chickens at nearby Mepkin Plantation on the Ashley River were prolific, and the monks brought their eggs to Williams Farm Supply for grading. Cranking up the egg machine, we scrutinized each egg as it passed over a light. A red spot indicated the beginning of an embryo. Bad egg. Out. LaClaire's date one weekend found himself in front of the egg-grading machine looking for red spots! Then we'd crate and load them into the red-and-white paneled Purina truck to send them back. Everyone in the county loved Mepkin eggs. (Years later PETA forced the monastery to shift to selling mushrooms.)

Of all the monks living at Mepkin Abbey monastery, Brother Moses was my favorite. We all anticipated his come-to-town ritual. Every few weeks a dull green pick-up bobbed its way down the dirt road leading to our warehouse. Brother Moses took pride in coming in from the river plantation to load up with seed, feed and fertilizer, or to deliver eggs—a duty coveted by his fellow monks.

The two-hundred-and-fifty-pound belly struggled to get out from under the steering wheel. A mass of gray stood up, brightened only by a thick, off-white rope, which served as a belt. He sported an extra-large-egg head, devoid of hair except for a stubby auburn ring. A rust-colored beard covered half his face, and his unruly eyebrows guarded a set of delicate, vivacious blue eyes.

Rumor had it that Brother Moses was an ex-convict from the north, in hiding at Mepkin Abbey. He lived with an order that stressed silence, so his rowdy laughter always attracted customers as he bounded into the office, thrusting a hunk of freshly-baked monk bread on the counter.

"For my lady," he'd say, bowing to my mother behind the desk. After trash-canning his written list, he clapped his hairy hands together and threw his head back. Eyes leaping with freedom, he bellowed out an order for ten meal cakes, eight sacks of 4-10-10 fertilizer, and five hundred pounds of chicken pellets.

Next, Brother Moses' massive arms gathered in the newspapers and magazines lying around— old and new—and marched towards the workers' cramped bathroom, where he stayed for almost two hours. That Trappist monks are to know nothing of goings-on in the outside world inhibited him not in the least. Finally, out he strutted, talking energetically with Mother and nearby customers. He then stuffed himself under the wheel to head for the river. As the beat-up truck passed through the streets of Moncks Corner, people lifted a hand or hat to the saintly monk who lowered his eyes and respectfully nodded to the passers-by. Everybody knew Brother Moses . . . and bought Mepkin Abbey eggs.

Brother Moses could brighten the dullest of days at the warehouse. His world never changed, but ours certainly did. Eva made me cotton skirts that billowed over stiff crinolines. No more matching shoes with every outfit, penny loafers became my go-to footware. That Christmas the difference in quality between the pale blue rayon sweater I'd bought myself from Read's and the yellow cashmere sweater that Mama Lillian bought me in Savannah was obvious. The once-elegant Clara Lee stopped dressing up. Now she wore the same three or four cotton shirtwaist dresses; flat, sensible shoes; and no accessories except her diamond watch, the one Buster gave her. For church at Trinity on Sundays, she brought out her suits from earlier days; the yellow wool one caught the light in her hazel eyes and almost made them shine again.

Clara Lee Peeples Williams' metamorphosis was gradual but remarkable. Her role as devoted wife and socialite—over. She focused entirely on the business because she had three children to send to college. As a charter member of Berkeley County Historical Society, she retained her interest but stopped attending meetings. Her closest friends in the bridge club kept her spot open until she was able to take an afternoon off on occasion. Somehow she maintained her membership in both the garden club and book clubs without attending.

Mother had a particular fondness for the Pinopolis Book Club because her own mother helped found the Estill Book Club in 1913. The clubs were founded by energetic women who needed a social and intellectual outlet, who wanted to look beyond the boundaries of their own lives and exhibit their skills as hostesses. Dessert and coffee were served with fine china and silver. People dressed in hats and gloves for meetings at plantation houses along the Cooper River and homes along the Pinopolis lakeshore. Membership was by invitation, and only after someone died did a space open. Roll call by the husband's name ("Mrs. James Russell Williams, Jr.") was responded to with the name of the book the member was reading. Prominent speakers included authors as well as Mother's naturalist friend, Edward von Dingle. The ladies' Southern manners and Clara Lee's social standing kept her membership secure until time allowed her to return.

Being the first divorcee that the club, perhaps the town, had known must have caused quite a stir. I never knew anyone divorced until my parents. It just wasn't done. Perhaps in Hollywood where morals were loose. Grandmother Olive and Daddy Grand didn't get one, for goodness sakes. But they couldn't have anyway because a South Carolina divorce wasn't even available until 1949. Yes, South Carolina lagged in updating laws about marriage. For example, in 1967 the Supreme Court ruled that laws prohibiting people from marrying based on skin color or race were unconstitutional. South Carolina kept the race prohibition in its state constitution until 1998—thirty more years.

Not much time to ruminate over how the family got to the point of divorce. One move at a time, we each played the hand we were dealt. Everyone's mood lifted on the weekends LaClaire came home. She often brought Ashley Hall friends for a visit, and Eva suddenly appeared, aired all the beds, cooked up a storm, wore her best smile. Between skiing on the lake and dancing at the beach, the girls laughed and enjoyed Eva's company. It felt like old times.

When LaClaire came home alone one weekend, the two of us stretched out to sunbathe on the side yard. Eva stepped out to sweep the screened porch.

"Don't cook yoursef to burnin'," she reminded us.

LaClaire looked up from her towel and asked Eva to squeeze us a cup of lemon juice. We used it to lighten our hair. The request required Eva's aching legs to trudge all the way through the house to the kitchen. And back again. She brought the broom to a halt, lifted her head, and sent LaClaire a steely look.

"I reckon you can do that well as me," Eva said.

I was taken aback. Eva never refused us anything—ever.

Trying to break the tension between LaClaire and Eva, I piped up.

"Oh, pretty please," I said in my sweetest voice. She continued to look at us, still as a stump.

"Pretty please . . . with *sugar* on it," I whined.

Eva wiped sweat from her brow with a thick forearm.

"Yunna best not git 'bove your raisin'," she said as she turned away.

Ten minutes later Eva appeared with a cup full of fresh lemon juice, the seeds and pulp strained out. Like old times—with an edge.

Chapter 13

The Undertow

Every time you suppress some part of yourself or
allow others to play you small, you are in essence
ignoring the owner's manual your creator gave you
and destroying your design.
                                    —Oprah Winfrey

Eva's mumblings increased as did Clara Lee's sharp looks and pregnant silences, both dispensing words by the thimbleful. I was unsure why their interactions grew to be wrought with such tension. But the undertow that had been subtly churning for the last couple of years became palpable.

Their moods permeated me, and I longed to flee; yet, curiously, I felt drawn to each, hoping to ease the strain, bring a smile to one or the other. When I grabbed for either one, each seemed to slip out of my fingers like a slippery bar of soap. I couldn't hold on to either of them. So I shifted my focus to something I *could* control—my grades. They became such a passion that when Mother diagnosed me with measles one morning and told me to stay home, I crawled out of the bedroom window and went to school anyway. When Eva found me missing, she dialed 310 for the warehouse.

"Miss Clara Lee, that girl done climb out da winda," she said. Within minutes Mother was standing in the doorway of my algebra class making an announcement.

"I'm sorry Angie has been so thoughtless. She has exposed you all to the measles." Without looking at me, she turned to leave and said, "Let's go."

We rode home in silence.

Eva tucked me in bed with a rough, "Is you

plum crazy, Baby? Your mama down on *bofe* us now."

Home was no haven. The kitchen and the bed-room became temporary sanctuaries—Eva in the kitchen, books and music in the bedroom. The rest of the house was a walkthrough. No lingering on the couch or at the piano, no rocking on the porch, and no helping Rusty with homework, even when Mother asked. He gravitated to his godmother Peach to help with book reports and such. My selfishness appalls me now.

School days overflowed with writing papers on Walt Whitman, begging Logan Merritt to do our chemistry lab report so I could stay in Beta Club, and editing "Angie's Angles" for *The Stag*. Afternoons packed with basketball and cheerleading practices, Fridays busy with ballgames, Saturdays crowded with work at the warehouse. Or escapades in Charleston with my steady cohorts, Sue and Judy. (We became known as "The Big Three.") Sundays filled with church, the youth group and afterwards the Berkeley Drive-in movie, where we hid friends in the trunk to cut expenses.

In my precious little spare time, the converted Trolley Car lured me downtown for music and ice cream. I listened to Fats Domino and Little Richard on the jukebox while eating chocolate ice cream. Two big scoops. Miss Kitty never needed to ask. She let me run a tab.

"I know where to find you," she'd say. Everybody knew everybody in town.

Extra time on the weekends I'd head to Pinopolis to water ski or play tennis. Miss Busy Bee.

I ignored Eva's pained looks and Mother's rare outbursts. Sometimes they appeared out of nowhere as sharp turns on a narrow road, making me grab the seat to keep from slipping—like the day I got my driver's license. Eager to take Eva for a spin, I ran in the house, dragged her outside by the arm, and dramatically opened the front car door for her. We cut the block and headed toward Pinopolis. But we'd only reached the school when Eva spoke.

"I best get home t'reckly. Miss Clara Lee might

need me." So home we went. She scuttled inside as fast as her sixty-year-old legs would carry her. When had my Eva become old?

Mother met me at the steps, eyes hard as hickory nuts. Without a word she slapped my cheek with such force that my head spun sideways. My mouth flung open as a hand flew up to my stinging face. For the first time in my life, my mother had hit me. I had absolutely no idea why. My stunned expression forced the answer from her.

"You know better than to let her ride in the front seat. She needs to know her place."

Her "place"? What was Eva's "place"? For over a decade, most things having to do with running the household and the children had been Eva's sovereign territory—everything from deciding the meals to buying the children's underwear. Once Daddy left, a shift took place for both of them. Clara Lee needed to get her life under control, and that included a new role for her: making decisions about finances, children and household matters—no matter how terrifying and unfamiliar that role felt. With Clara Lee at the helm, Eva seemed less sure of herself, her position, her future. How devastating this must have felt, after giving her life to our family for so many years.

Eva and Mother knew something else was brewing too—that blacks were making whites uncomfortable with their changes in attitude, their lack of obsequiousness. Yes, tight finances strained the budget and the household atmosphere, but the shifting of roles of the two women in the family was more upsetting than any penny pinching we had to do. The tectonic plates underneath us were moving, and who knew where each of us would land?

Did Mother and I connect at all during those teenage years? She did call me "Baby" one evening, in an offhand, benevolent way. I should have been overjoyed. Hadn't I longed to be the focus of her attention, hoping to get even tacit approval?

"I am not a baby, not *your* baby!" I insisted. Like a spoiled child, I stomped off to my room. Was I

Mother's baby? Eva's baby? I didn't want to be anyone's baby. What did I want?

Petulant at home, I sought whatever was outside the house, sports or academics. Mrs. Wiley's
biology class engaged me particularly. She reveled in
seeing students' eyes light up when they understood
photosynthesis or mitosis or drew blobs of amoebas
and strings of paramecium with colored pencils. She
smiled at me, complimented me on my drawings,
encouraged me to stretch. Her class inspired me to
be a nurse—like Eva who had worked as a hospital
maid, nurse's aide and a midwife.

It was like pulling pinfeathers from a duck to
get Eva to talk, but when pressed, she spoke with
pride about her work at the hospital and the midwife
course she took from Miss Maude Callum, a black
nurse who worked with Doc Fishburne. Eva and I
pored over their pictures when LIFE featured their
extraordinary work in rural Berkeley County.

The interest in nursing took me and Beth Lacey
to her father's medical books, where the male anat-
omy page was dog-eared. Dr. Will Lacey had an office
at the back of the Rexall Pharmacy on Main Street.
When Eva took us to see him for checkups, she
skirted the waiting room marked "colored" and sat
right down with us inside the door labeled "white."
Maybe Eva's behavior, her confidence, her not sub-
mitting to certain rules yet remaining socially gracious protected me from seeing the discrepancies in
treatment of blacks and whites, kept me from being
aware of the tensions. Eva herself never seemed
anything but comfortable sitting besides whites in
a doctor's office. And I loved going to see Dr. Lacey.

In my mind, my classmate Beth had the perfect father—a quiet, caring man. His wife, however,
had a tongue that could clip a hedge, according to
the bridge club ladies. He drew me to his heart after
his two daughters left for Ashley Hall and I returned
home. He taught the teenage Sunday school class at
Trinity Church in Pinopolis. When those soft eyes
looked at me and he spoke barely above a whisper,
I saw Jesus talking. He was the first person I ever

heard mention the word "race." He believed that God was colorblind, that all people were the same underneath. He tucked this fledgling young woman under his wing just when she needed a positive male figure in her life. And exactly when she needed an infusion of godly wisdom to get her through her high school years.

The traits that emanated from this gentle, selfless man led me to believe that everyone in the field of medicine possessed these qualities—an assessment I subconsciously lived out for many years. I revered the doctors in my town either for their skill, like the surgeon Dr. Walsh; their fortitude, like my godfather Doc Fishburne; their humor, like Dr. Solomon; or their kindness, like Dr. Lacey.

Eva lived all these attributes. She did anything she set her mind to, persevered through every storm, and displayed a totally unselfish, cheerful spirit. And Eva's profession had been nursing. I wanted to be like Eva. I shared my nursing dream with no one except Eva.

"Baby, just you memba that Jesus do all the healin'," she said, handing me a beater to lick off the batter.

Jesus aside, Eva's role became less constant but more vital when I slowed down long enough to suck in her warmth, her strength, her wisdom. My very own balm of Gilead. Rubbing me down after cheerleading practice, she'd sing:

> Swing low, sweet cha..ri..ot,
> Comin' for to carry me home.
> Swing low, sweet cha..ri..ot.
> Comin' for to carry me home.

Many years passed before understanding the dual message that Eva's songs carried.

When Eva sang about angels carrying her "home," it seemed she was simply singing about heaven, Petty's heaven, Daddy Bill's heaven. Much later, I realized that home for her was also the land of freedom, a place free from a plethora of oppressions. Her songs rang with hope of finding the Promised Land. Hadn't Moses already led his people to freedom? Since going back to live in the black community, Eva learned a lot about blacks bravely breaking through to more freedoms during the fifties. Her ministers' interpretation of the Christian faith always saw Jesus as a liberator. Eva kept singing about freedom at church and at our home, not the home of her dreams, sadly.

The only freedom that interested me at the time was the kind that Mother seemed hell bent on taking away. The most intense discussions between us involved my wanting to quit piano lessons after ten years.

Clara Lee made all three of her children learn piano, hoping it would take for at least one. I wanted her to be proud of me, so when LaClaire and Rusty stopped taking lessons, I persevered. She hung onto the hope that I would stick with it. I tried. I really did. I even changed teachers from Mrs. Spann to Mrs. Page because it seemed the best players in town took from Mrs. Page.

The talent contest tipped the scale. The battle between my classmates, Sammy Driggers and Ceille Baird, at the high school auditorium was a thing to behold. Sammy's brown fingers glided across the keys and squeezed out the most beautiful rendition I'd ever heard of "Autumn Leaves." Then Ceille banged out a boogie woogie that had the whole audience jumping. Ceille won, but it should have been a tie. And I definitely needed to quit piano!

"I thought you would do something meaningful with your life," Mother said. I won the argument by plain stubbornness on my part and fatigue on hers. If I'd been paying attention, I'd have noticed that Mother never missed a piano recital, and they were in the evenings just like my basketball games. Had she hoped her daughter hadn't inherited her tin ear and would fulfill the dream that she lost? It seemed I constantly disappointed her.

But she insisted on typing. I resisted flippantly on general principle.

"I don't intend to be anyone's secretary." Mother—a single woman long before it was socially acceptable, sending three children to college without loans, and running a large business, unheard of for a woman in the county— wanted her daughter to be prepared to earn a living, run a household, prepared in ways that she had not been.

"Listen to yo' mama, Baby," Eva said. So I did.

Mother also insisted on home economics class. I could see why she wanted me to know the basics of cooking and sewing because she had learned neither. But I'd been at Eva's elbow watching her cook, iron, and sew for years. The course didn't teach me much. Eva beamed at my progress in the class. She knew life was no feather bed and wanted her baby to be prepared too.

Mother's strangest request came my senior year in high school. She pressed me to enter the Miss Farm Bureau Contest. I'd not even seen a beauty pageant, much less been in one. My physical appearance always fell short. Mother constantly reminded me to hold up my shoulders, brush my hair out of my eyes. She never said, "You look nice. I like your hair. Your new skirt suits you." It was Eva, not mother, who regularly reminded me that "pretty is as pretty does."

And when Eva said, "Don't be ugly, missy," it had nothing to do with my looks, you can bet on that.

"Why in tarnation does Mother want me to be in a *beauty* contest?" I griped to Eva. She kept her eyes on the succotash she was stirring.

"Come on, Baby, don't be no trouble," Eva said.

Turned out, leaders in the local Farm Bureau office pressured Mother and other parents connected to the farming community to participate in the organization's main fund raiser. Berkeley County's biggest business was agriculture, and Williams Farm Supply was the largest purveyor of feed, seed, and fertilizer for everyone from the sharecroppers to the plantation owners.

Mother convinced me that entering the contest was good for the business, which had her running late the night of the contest, so it was Eva who straightened my gown and hugged me tight.

"Memba now, de best thing to wear is yo smile," she teased. She used to tell me this when I was a little girl, given my tendency to pout. This night she shooed me out with a pat on the rear.

"Show your chocolate side now, Baby." That would be the left side of my face, the side with the one dimple mother bequeathed me.

Eva's Baby was crowned Miss Farm Bureau of Berkeley County. Eva didn't attend. By this time I knew why. No blacks allowed. They seemed clairvoyant about where and when they could appear in public places. Stores, okay. Movies, side entrance, upstairs. Doctor's offices, laundromats, side entrances. Restaurants, nope. How did they keep it all straight? I remember thinking how thrilled Eva would have been to be there. Did Mother make it? I can't remember. A hollow victory all around in the school auditorium a block from our house.

Angie, as the Berkeley County Farm Bureau Queen

The following year the high school moved from the old two-story building downtown to a new sprawling campus on the road to Pinopolis, a stark contrast to the black's Berkeley Training School. Eva had closely followed the changes in black education over the years because Miriam was her charge. Because Miriam and LaClaire were the same age, Eva was well aware of the contrast in the two girls' education.

Miriam's hand-me-down wooden desk had a white boy's initials carved in the top. She noticed LaClaire reading from new textbooks, Miriam learning from marked-up, tattered books, answers-already-filled-in workbooks. A county regulation stipulated that black schools distribute to their students used books only. The budgets for white students were ten times what they were for blacks. Miriam dressed with multiple layers of clothing in winter because the heat frequently didn't work. More often than not, the toilets didn't flush either. And Miriam took extra food because of the spare and unappetizing lunches.

But all of that changed. Eva announced proudly one day that a new school was in the works for her Miriam. When the Supreme Court reversed the separate-but-equal law in 1954 saying it was a violation of the 14th Amendment, Berkeley County, along with most of the South, dug in its heels to show that separate *could* be equal. We looked on in awe as politicians punctuated the ruling by erecting a state-of-the-arts school for the blacks, complete with a huge gymnasium that dwarfed ours. Folks seemed satisfied on both ends of town. Blacks had a brand new school, whites continued their segregated education and shortly thereafter built their own new school, the one I attended as a senior.

Eva's friend Lela Session returned home with a PhD in hand and sat right down in the thick of school integration issues. "You know Miss Lela back in town," Eva said with an air of pride one morning." Berkeley County, making every effort to keep integration issues peaceful, designated Session the teacher supervisor for the black schools from 1952 to 1959. The position was paid for by a Philadelphia Quaker, Anna T. Jeanes, a philanthropist with a keen interest in the plight of blacks in the South.

Years later Miss Lela and I talked about those times as we sat in her house not far from Kitfield Plantation where the first Monck's Corner sprang up. We talked about how I walked around like a dumb mule with blinders, looking neither right nor left. What had I missed? A lot. Session was given an office in Berkeley County's Department of Education "along with Jim Crow," she said with a wry smile. For several years she still had to drink out of a separate water fountain and was not allowed to use the white rest rooms. She elaborated in her memoir:

> *I did not allow the separate facilities issues to become a barrier in developing relationships with my white co-workers who had blue blood when it came to the issues of equality. I feel that some of my white friends were just as offended by the separate facilities as the blacks.*

"I kept my peace. Brought up our needs at meetings. Gradually our voices were heard," she told me. Many whites in the community did not agree with the old laws and went out of their way to give books and supplies to the black schools.

Eva and Lela both knew about the two sides of Buster's friend, Strom Thurmond. Session confided that she regularly tapped Thurmond for supplies for the black school, which he secured by going through a white merchant in St. Stephens, another small town in Berkeley County.

"Within twenty-four hours or so, my request would be granted," Session said. "In the public eye, Mr. Thurmond played the role as a true segregationist, but in the private world, he helped me accomplish many of my goals." Like many white men of influence, Thurmond straddled the integration fence.

These same white men straddled more than a fence to satisfy their appetites. Thurmond, for example, had fathered a child with his family's maid when he was a young buck of twenty-two. His daughter Essie Mae Washington-Williams began college the same year that I began my first year in college. Imagine that. Behind the scene he took care of her financially. Speculation ended when Thurmond showed up unannounced to visit her at South Carolina State in Orangeburg. Essie Mae told him then of her mother's death.

"He didn't cry, but tears filled his eyes." After a long pause, he said, "I truly cared for that woman. She was a wonderful person."

At that meeting, talk turned to Thurmond's politics, and his daughter did not let him off the hook when he tried to justify the States' Rights (Dixiecrats) party.

"A lot of Negroes are hurt by what you said," she told him.

"That's politics, Essie Mae. You're in the heat of a campaign, you get misquoted, taken out of context." At the end of the conversation, he handed her an envelope.

"This is for your marriage," he said. When he tried to hug her goodbye, she left him standing alone. In her dorm room she opened the envelope full of hundred-dollar bills. He continued to keep in touch with her, sending notes and gifts to her and her children—his grandchildren. Eventually, the South Carolina legislature had Essie Mae's name chiseled beside his other children on the Thurmond statue on the Statehouse grounds in Columbia.

Buster possibly knew about Essie Mae because he and Strom were close friends at the time. In those days, it wasn't uncommon for white men to sleep with black women and sire children who were never publicly recognized by their fathers. One couple in our Pinopolis church split up because the wife caught her husband red-handed with the black maid in their own home. I asked Mother about the rumor.

"We don't talk about such things. It's poor manners," she said. I had a feeling she knew more than she let on.

Regardless of laws and tradition, in the 1950s, long before the mandatory integration of the 1960s, it appeared to me that Berkeley High School was "integrated." Racial incidents? Never heard of 'em. Largely due to Jim Bradley.

On a number of fronts, Principal Jim Bradley was an excellent role model for students. He ran rigorous academic and athletic programs, had a winning personality and a commanding presence. He was so drop-dead handsome that when he taught geometry one semester, I could hardly concentrate. (This is beside the point, of course.) No one got away with anything either. It was Mr. Bradley who expelled LaClaire and her friends for shooting spitballs back at the old school, one his own daughter.

And it was Jim Bradley who had feelers longer

than a Palmetto bug. The Big Three (Judy, Sue and I) enjoyed escapades to Charleston during school hours. My two cohorts, both sharp as diamonds, were foils to each other: Sue Roach was the porcelain doll with silky-milk skin, flaxen hair and a quiet demeanor. She won the National Betty Crocker Homemaker Award one year. (Didn't cook a thing. Just aced a test!) Judy Young, a tall brunette with big brown eyes, took Spanish dancing and played castanets. She was praised by the boys for being well endowed with the four B's: beauty, brains, breeding, and breasts. Breasts we all envied. An adventuresome spirit was Judy's trademark.

Angie, Sue and Judy—Berkeley Cheerleaders

Under the guise of selling ads for the school newspaper and annual, Sue, Judy and I devised multiple ways to get out of class and go to Charleston. When I packed my bathing suit and movie money getting ready for school, Eva gave one of her predictions.

"Mista Bradley gonna catch you girls, mark my word," she said.

We even signed up to take the School Bus Drivers Course—the only girls—so we could miss a week of classes. Judy was the only one who ever drove a bus, subbing on the Pinopolis route occasionally. We also got out of classes to enter the Driving Rodeo and outshone all the boys. But Mr. Bradley found out we entertained boys in our rooms at the state newspaper association meetings in Columbia (just listening to music, no hanky-panky). He laid the hammer down, called us to the principal's office, gave us a good talking to and told us he knew what we were up to with all our escapades.

Mr. Bradley treated every student with respect and firmness, regardless of gender, grades, linage, location, or skin color. My class was diverse and multi-cultural: A scattering of Native Americans, Hispanics, Filipinos, Summerville Indians, and Brass Ankles mixed with in-town, middle-class whites, out-of-town farmers' kids, Pinopolis villagers. Every shade of skin from creamy white to warm walnut. None of these were considered "colored" or "black." And the term "African American" was unheard of.

I asked Session about the diversity I noticed among my classmates, but she first launched into a history of discrimination among blacks themselves, mulattos in particular. She explained that "mulatto" by definition refers to those with half-white and half-black heritage, though it can mean any mixture of races. She told me that as far back as the 1700s, mulatto elite in Charleston created a Brown Fellowship Society to show blacks and whites that they were "different from common Negroes." And Session herself explained that when she went to school at the Avery Institute in Charleston, she had to overcome two areas of discrimination: being poor and too dark.

Some historians have speculated that South Carolina's relatively smooth transition from segregation to integration came from a rather unusual history of light-skinned blacks who actively collaborated with the whites when the latter set about to implement segregation. This theory bears out what seemed true in Berkeley County—people of African ancestry with mixed blood were not automatically classified as "black" and therefore were accorded more status.

The Brass Ankles of Berkeley County, however, had a more specific heritage, according to Session. They were the children of black mothers and white British fathers, sailors who docked in Charleston and "seemed to have an attraction for women of color," she said. The light-skinned offspring were called "Brass Ankles" because their ankles took on a brass complexion. Another group, Summerville Indians, had a combination of black and Native American blood. So proud of their distinctiveness, they requested a separate school for themselves on the road between Moncks Corner and Summerville. When that school finally closed, those students came to our school.

It's commonly held that one drop of black blood deems one "black." In Berkeley County, the one-drop theory seemed reversed. One drop of white blood, and doors opened as if you were white. Perhaps we were ahead of our time. A number of my classmates had wavy, curly, or straight silky black hair, and skin various shades of brown from café con leche to espresso. It never crossed my mind to use these features to stereotype them. Heaven forbid. Then the tall, svelte girls could discriminate against us short, plump ones!

I never noticed overt discrimination from my classmates, teachers, or parents. On second thought, Mother did have a hissy fit over my going out one evening with a handsome, brown-skinned fellow. She wouldn't give me a reason for her objection, so I went. Years later I pressed her about her opposition. "That family has a touch of black blood," she said and walked out of the room.

She needn't have worried because in high school Dowse had my heart, and I didn't go around kissing other boys. We dated steadily but didn't officially "go steady" like lots of couples. Berkeley boys gave girlfriends their athletic jackets with a big B on the front. By junior year, when everyone received high school rings, the girls wrapped wads of tape on the backs of the boys' rings so they wouldn't fall off. And couples who went steady drove around in town smack up against each other and parked on back roads to make out—both of which Mother forbade LaClaire and me to do.

To drive her point home, Mother scared us to death with the tale of the Pamplico murders. One night a fifteen-year-old girl and her boyfriend parked on DeWitt's Bluff, a local lovers' lane. On this wintry evening, a robbery attempt went bad, and the decapitated girl and her friend were tossed down a well. And, she said, a deranged black man did the dirty deed.

"If you want to park, park in our own front yard." We did.

Dowse and I were dating as steady as we could given all the activities we were both involved in. A multitalented fellow, he wrestled, played football, and "covered the harbor like he covered the ball," the newspaper said when he won yet another regatta. He wrote me pages of poetry and reams of letters and composed a piano piece just for me.

He showed up unexpectedly at important moments. He appeared in the audience (so did Thurmond) when I gave my speech as Governor of Girls State at the Capitol in Columbia. And he kissed away my sadness riding around the farm roads after Daddy Van's funeral in Estill.

Too absorbed with our own activities and romance, we didn't think much about integration. But in the fall of 1959 after I graduated from high school, I saw on the evening news that six-year-old Ruby Bridges in Louisiana made history by being one of the first blacks to go to an all white school. Federal marshals marched her up the steps where she became the only student in a classroom for two days because white parents wouldn't let their children be in the classroom with a black. On the third day she was relegated to a second-floor classroom when the other students came back to school, again alone with one teacher. Not long after that, I saw a Norman Rockwell poster of his painting Problem We All Live With that caught the poignant image of little Ruby Bridges making her way to school. It made me sad.

"Legal" integration didn't happen at Berkeley High School while I was there. In fact, it wasn't until 1963 when I graduated from college that pretty, quiet Millicent Brown officially became the first black to enroll in a Lowcountry high school. She calmly walked in Rivers High School on Meeting Street in

Charleston, Dowse's school. I smiled when I heard.

Much of those high school days I was preoccupied with cheerleading and basketball. Mother's attending a basketball game happened so infrequently that when I saw her sitting alone at the top of the stands one night, I could barely concentrate. It wasn't my best night. She never went to an out of town game. I felt disappointed and unsympathetic to her tough work schedule and need to rest to keep her TB at bay. I just wanted somebody there, anybody to watch me who cared about me, who yelled when I scored, who hugged me when I hit my career high 26 points.

Angie's set shot

Intellectually, I understood her focus had to be on her health and on the business—for us. I just wish she'd talked to me, explained her priorities. But Mother wasn't a talker. Though on the surface I accepted her detachment, deep down I felt alone. And deep down I knew she was doing what she had to do and felt alone in her private battle too. Both determined to be strong, what a shame that we didn't have the tools to support each other.

Eva was with me in spirit, but Eva couldn't sit on those bleachers. I never questioned why; it was understood. In all the busyness of those days, Eva somehow kept up with my schedule. Though she might have already gone home, on game day my uniform would be washed, pressed, and laid out on the bed.

"Well, how de ballgame turn out, Baby?" she always asked the next day.

Some days the only time I heard Mother's voice was when I came in late from an out-of-town ballgame and stopped by her bed to tell her the score or when I'd yell down the hall while doing homework.

"What does 'inundate' mean?"

She'd call back "flood, overwhelm," and life moved on. Occasionally she'd suggest turning out my light when it was really late. She never pressed. One night I worked on a science project until the sun came up. I walked back to her bedroom to ask her a question. She wasn't awake. Watching her sleep, both hands together and tucked under one cheek, she looked like a little girl. When Mother woke, she found me coloring a poster drawing of the final stage of tuberculosis.

We had no goodnight ritual of hugs or kisses. Mother wasn't a toucher. I said my prayers aloud lying in my bed staring at the white canopy. Mother said her prayers beside the bed on her knees. Silently. What did she pray for? I don't know. I prayed her TB wouldn't come back. I prayed she'd talk to me in other than her direct, sparse way. Or hug me like Eva. Oh, how I longed to hear her say she was proud of me, that I'd done a good job at something.

In my secret place, I sensed my mother loved me, what little there was to love. But she never liked me very much. By this time, I accepted our relationship with reluctant grace.

Eva, Mother and I rode out our individual storms stoically, separately. Mother's impatience with Eva grew. Eva's discontent with Mother's treatment became more evident. Evident by a lack of joy in the daily tasks, a slowed pace when Mother called her to come. Her eyes no longer looked straight at Mother; instead they rested on a nearby wall. No more "Lemme help you, Miss Clara Lee" when Mother came home with full arms. The undertow remained, no matter how fast or slow the daily tide.

One day I heard Mother's voice escalate—a rarity. As I ran to the kitchen door, Mother pushed tight-lipped past me. Eva stood by the sink. Fat tears rolled down her cheeks.

"What's wrong?" I said

She looked at the floor. I didn't recognize the soft, weepy voice that crescendoed into a loud, guttural cry.

"She ain't got no cause to talk to me like that. Lawd knows I been good to that woman in all her trouble. I ain't got to put up wid such. My feelin's is soft and I got a bad heart. I can't take much more. I does all I can—I ain't no *dog!*" she said.

Appalled that Mother could elicit such vehemence from Eva, I stood speechless. Helpless, I watched as she lifted her apron to pat the dampness from her cheeks. Drawing sniffles up her nose, she turned and walked around the corner to her room, the ironing room, and shut the door.

I didn't speak to Mother for two days. I doubt she noticed.

Times like this, I wished for Daddy—the one from my early childhood. I shoved the thought away.

With Daddy absent, the house became quiet, even somber. I adjusted to the changes in finances and schedules. But I missed Daddy's charismatic authority, Mother's steadying presence, and Eva's omnipresent attention.

We all, Eva too, missed Daddy's convivial spirit, the lively parties, the weekend treks to Moss Grove and lazy summers at Wampee. And Eva missed his exuberance as well as his loyalty. Buster had been Eva's friend. Buster would have cajoled both Clara Lee and Eva out of their ill-temper. But he was long gone, back home in Pinopolis with Nannie. Since the divorce, Mother—ever the caretaker or, more precisely, care*giver*—supported grandmother Olive, Nannie, and by extension Daddy since he moved into the Pinopolis house. Not one of them her blood relative.

Mother insisted that Rusty and I drive out to visit Daddy regularly. I fought the edict like crazy, to no avail. Rusty sometimes rode the bus to Pinopolis so Daddy could help with his homework. When I complained to Eva about the trips, she didn't look me in the eye or stop scraping the carrot for the pot roast.

"Baby, is you got trouble wid your daddy or yo'sef? That yo' daddy. Now hush," she said. Eva meted out tough love long before it became a cliché. So I went to the apartment Nannie had sectioned off in the big Pinopolis house, and I sat in a rocker across from Daddy counting the minutes before I could leave. He always put on his wooden leg and dressed up for our visits, wore his charmed smile, and opened with a compliment.

"I like your new haircut, Angie" (I hated it!) or "Looks like you've lost some weight" (I hadn't.) Then the polite questions began, about school, basketball, Dowse. And always at the end, "And how's your mother these days?" I replied in monosyllables delivered through tight lips.

Why did I treat my father with disdain? If I'd examined my feelings, would I have found anger? Embarrassment? Disappointment? On some level, I felt sorry for his solitary life away from the handful of us he loved, books now his best friends and bedfellows. But reconciliation and forgiveness were traits I did not yet own. I simply did not know how to deal with this man before me—the man I had adored, who hung the moon—the man I came to fear, who crushed my spirit.

Nannie temporarily moved in with us because her rheumatoid arthritis had flared up so badly that she became bedridden, which meant Eva returned to our house full time to take care of Nannie. A mixed blessing for Eva.

Only then did I really notice Eva's health problems. Her own arthritic knees gave her great difficulty when walking. Tending Nannie required many extra steps through the long Williams house. The mood was glum. Eva's strained relationship with Nannie stretched back to when the young Williams family first moved into a new house the year I was born, when Eva took over running the Buster Williams family, when Nannie's habit of parking outside our house honking her car horn for Eva to fetch something or other increased. Their stubborn antagonism never slacked over seventeen years, even when Eva's knees slowed her down. It became a contest of wills. How long could Nannie honk? How slow could Eva walk? "You can ride to Estill on Eva's lip when she pouts," Mother once said during one of the showdowns.

Eva did pout quite a bit, especially during Nannie's live-in visit. Mother gave Nannie the front bedroom for convenience. She needed help going to the toilet, putting on her nightgown, brushing her hair, taking a bath. One day I walked into her bathroom to see white squares stuck all around the inside of the blue bathtub. Turns out, she had Eva wash her handkerchiefs and spread them wet on the tub so they would dry flat with no wrinkles. A strange sight. She kept Eva jumping to the tinkle of Mother's silver dinner bell by her bed. Water. Pills. Glasses. Newspapers. Meals. Tissue. In the early morning hours, a bell's relentless tinkle often summoned Eva for an alcohol rubdown so Nannie could sleep.

Sometimes when she was bone tired, Eva would call out, "I'll be there t'reckly," and take her time. Eva made more trips to that room in one day than there are bristles on a brush, without so much as a "please" or "thank you" from Nannie.

One morning after a rough night, I came upon Eva resting in the kitchen, the blustering wind cracking the sheets outside on the clothesline. Nannie insisted her linens be line-dried even though we owned a dryer. Eva's moist face not wet with tears, her dark, extravagant eyes not swollen or red, but her sorrow palpable. She wore her grief like an elegant black shawl.

"See you after school, Saint Eva," I said. I squeezed her shoulder. She mustered a half smile.

Eva and Nannie were in town at our house in Moncks Corner one sunny spring day as Rusty and I drove to see Daddy for our weekly visit. A wailing fire truck flew past us on the road to Pinopolis.

"Let's see where the fire truck's going," I said, speeding up to follow the truck. Eager for excitement, Rusty agreed. We followed the engine about a mile. It turned into Jacob's Lane—straight into Nannie's yard.

An inferno rose before my eyes! Nannie's house looked like a giant torch on stilts. The house was so far gone that the studs created a skeleton draped in a curtain of orange and red. Tall flames licked the trees around the house while frantic firemen searched for the well to pump water. I jumped out of the car and bolted toward the steep stairs collapsing like dominoes.

"Daddy's in the house!" I screamed.

Running headlong into the blaze, I felt strong arms cross my chest stopping me short. Struggling to free myself, I yelled, "Daddy's inside, Daddy's inside!" The arms held firm, even with my feet kicking and head flinging backwards. Hysterically I cried, "Daddy's inside, Daddy's inside!"

John Waddell, a Pinopolis artist who lived nearby, continued to hold me as he whispered in my ear.

"It's okay. Your daddy's okay," he said.

I fell to my knees in the dirt, covering my face with both hands—exhausted, relieved and perplexed. A flood of emotions bombarded me. Didn't I dread the visits when Daddy coaxed me out of my aloofness? Wasn't I furious that he'd torn asunder his marriage, our family? Hadn't I wished my father dead?

Still, the thought of his being caught off guard in a fire, with no one else in the house, no time to put on his wooden leg, no phone to call for help . . . the thought was unbearable.

I didn't know that he had hopped on his one leg down the tall steps, hopped all the way up the dirt road to Marie Harvey's house. Or that he had broken the door's window to get inside to call the Moncks Corner fire department.

I can't imagine what my daddy felt watching his past go up in flames.

The house of heart pine that Thomas West Williams built in 1902—Gone. The brick pillars stood alone among the grayness when the fire hose hissed on the last ember. The porch where I'd cracked ice with Jacob, Nannie's giant bed that we hid under when lightning struck, the kitchen where we ate cake for breakfast—Gone. Family silver and portraits, Daddy's books and walking canes—Gone. Playing with the parakeets, eating Sunday dinners, picking scuppernongs, feeding the goldfish—All gone. The Williams family homeplace—Ashes. Only Jacob's cabin remained unscathed. I watched the cinders fly to the sky, the boards turn to powder. An era gone up in smoke, smoke that stung my eyes to crying that I could not stop.

Once back home, my feet took me to the kitchen. Eva pulled me to her sagging breast and held me close.

"Baby, we all be ashes one day. You jes be glad your daddy okay," she said softly.

I rested there thinking, *This one place, here in Eva's arms, is the safest place I know.*

Chapter 14

Through a Glass Darkly

I do not believe that sheer suffering teaches . . . . To suffering must be added mourning, understanding, patience, love, openness and the willingness to remain vulnerable.

—Anne Morrow Lindberg, author

"Go on now, Baby. It's awright, Just memba who you is," Eva said, her eyes filling as we hugged goodbye.

When the car crossed the North Carolina line taking me to Charlotte, the girl it carried had been out of the South Carolina Lowcountry only briefly, for camp in North Carolina and family vacations in Florida and Washington, DC. The sun splashed through the oak leaves warming the old brick of Burwell Hall as I glimpsed Queens College, a small all-girls Presbyterian school in the heart of the growing city. The high-ceilinged parlor with its oriental rugs and gilded mirrors reminded me of my grandparents' house in Estill. I felt right at home.

Mother couldn't understand how her daughter could break the family legacy of attending Converse College—my grandmother, mother and sister's alma mater. She'd made it clear to LaClaire and me that we must attend an all-girls college for at least two years before transferring to a co-ed institution. Seemed strange to me because the state schools were much less expensive, but she was adamant—no male distractions until we matured somewhat. She assumed I'd choose Converse. But by the end of high school, an urge to get away from family strain and expectations drove me to disappoint my mother yet again.

This small-town girl entered college like a deer, eager yet anxious to ease into the edge of a stand of lush corn sprouts. Eager to broaden my world and start fresh where no one knew me or the family. Anxious that Mother couldn't afford to keep up two college payments, even with our scholarships, plus Rusty's starting school the next year—three in college at the same time. Anxious about competing academically with smart girls from all over the South from bigger and better schools. And anxious that Eva would not be close by.

"Don't pull no long face," Eva said as we hugged goodbye. "When you scared, Baby, jes sing 'this little light o' mine, I gonna let it shine.' Memba now."

Turns out, most of my fears were allayed, and miraculously my light didn't stay under a bushel. My monthly twenty-five-dollar allowance covered my needs for toiletries and stockings. Mother wrote weekly Sunday letters, phone calls not in the budget. I wrote Eva. (So there!)

I gulped the fresh air, feasted on the invigorating classes, and savored the professor's erudition and wisdom. My weeks were jammed with studying and working in the dining hall and admissions office. I didn't go out for sorority Rush because I was afraid it would take too much time away from studies and would cost too much.

Davidson College, an all-male school, was located just up the road from Charlotte. Early freshman year, an eclectic bunch of boys spilled off busses for a dance in the Queens gym. Weekends became a blur of fraternity parties, symphony concerts, ice hockey games, and riveting sermons on Sundays from the legendary Carlyle Marney at the Baptist Church across the street. (I could sleep in for thirty minutes more if I didn't go to the Episcopal church up the street.)

I treasured visits from Dowse when he could get away from The Citadel, which was seldom. He wrote dear letters and mentioned the ruckus over the band's playing "Dixie" at football games. He sent pictures of himself in uniform standing in front of his barracks, which I wedged in my dresser mirror. When he came to visit for quick overnights, we stayed with his sister's family not far from Queens. We went for walks outside her house at night so we could catch up with each other, hold each other tight. He never asked whether I dated Davidson boys. (I did.) He never asked whether I kissed them. (I didn't.) We understood that he'd chosen a confining environment that would limit our seeing each other, and I'd chosen a broadening experience with no tether.

During vacations, we made up for lost time by hitting the party scene in Charleston and going to the Bonneau lake house that his parents owned . . . just down the sandy road from the Pooshee property our family had to sell. Oh, how I looked forward to those times. Mother's only guidance about boys came one day as Dowse and I planned to go to the lake house—without his parents being there. She didn't forbid me to go but encouraged me not to put myself in an environment that might lead to something I'd regret. She trusted both Dowse and me and appealed to our good judgment. I heeded her good advice and cut down on the lake visits because the holy temple was being sorely tested. Southern gentleman that he was, Dowse always respected the boundaries.

Romance wasn't on the forefront of my mind at Queens. I focused on my classes, all of them challenging and interesting. But my nursing dreams vanished in Miss Noey's biology class. The antithesis of Mrs. Wiley's relaxed, engaging teaching style, Miss Noey's formidable demeanor frightened me—an old-as-Methusalah Amazon of a woman with a nest of gray plaits on her head, like Nannie but without the perpetual smile.

Mrs. Chalmers, however, proved to be the antithesis of Miss Noey. Her warm, worn face looked at you directly through thick rimless glasses. She donned soft bulky sweaters in soothing earth tones. At ease with herself and her students, her voice deep and gentle. Like Eva's. Roberta Swartz Chalmers came to Queens in 1959, my freshman year, with an impressive academic history: BA, magna cum laude at Mt. Holyoke, MA from Radcliff, and a B Lit. from Oxford. She taught English at Mt. Holyoke and Kenyon College where her husband served as President. She published two books of poetry.

I knew none of this background before I fell in love with this serene woman who happened to be my freshman English teacher, a teacher who guided more than graded our writings. She encouraged creativity but didn't let sloppy writing slide. One day she wrote "spicket" and "licker" on the board. "Does anyone know what these words mean?" Silence. *Of course I did. Hadn't I used them in the last paper I'd turned in talking about Eva's scrubbing sweet potatoes at the "spicket" and straining the pot "licker" off the butterbeans?* After bursting forth with my answer, how odd it felt to learn the phonetic spellings of words I'd grown up hearing were not correct. But no Victoria Crawford she, no rapping of the knuckles. Mrs. Chalmers turned it into a teachable moment by moving on to a tangential lesson on vernacular speech to help me save face. What a teacher!

Another professor also picked up on my provincialism. The striking, theatrical Dr. Charles Hadley headed the drama department and was voice coach for the likes of Charlton Heston, Nick Nolte and John Travolta. At a meet-the-faculty social in Burwell Hall, he and I were talking when he stopped in mid sentence, rested his long fingers on my shoulder and spoke to me in a slight falcetto voice.

"Daah . . . lin', you *must* take ma speech cose." I had no idea he was mocking my dropped consonants until he went on to say that "year" is not "yeah" and "ear" is not "air." People in the Lowcountry had been talking like this for "yeahs"! I signed up immediately. Dr. Hadley's speech course taught me how truly Southern my speech was.

A voracious reading habit held me in good stead in literature and history. But I'd never encountered philosophers, theologians and poets the likes of Kierkegaard and Hegel, Buddha and Tillich, Plath and Cummings. All made me ponder how their wisdom played into my own life. On religion, Eva and Trinity had made sure I knew plenty about the Bible and Jesus, but I dreaded required Bible courses.

I kept my mouth shut, however, after a classmate turned me into the administration because of an after-lights conversation. It seems I questioned the virginity of Jesus' mother and the validity of his resurrection. Not a happy meeting with Dean Gephardt the next day.

With an eye to the future, I used college summers to explore two areas that had captured my interest—helping people in a medical setting and serving folks through church work.

The first summer I worked at Berkeley County Hospital where we three Williams children were born and where the doctors I idolized practiced. It was also the hospital that refused to let Dr. Walter Evans, the first black physician in the county, practice medicine. When his patients became so sick that they needed hospital care, he was forced to refer them to the white doctors like Dr. Lacey, Dr. Walsh or Dr. Solomon who were allowed treat them in the hospital. You'd think a college student would have noticed that both white and black patients filled beds in the hospital yet no black doctors graced the door. I discovered this many years later when I drove out to Mepkin Abbey one day and noticed a sign: Dr. Evans Road. I asked who he was. The road sign small tribute to Dr. Evans's many years of healing service to those in rural Berkeley County.

I still wore blinders back then. I remember talking to my friend Jack Kilpatrick, syndicated columnist and former editor of the *Richmond News Leader* about the ignored injustices.

"We grew up to believe that segregation was the natural order of mankind. It was no more to be challenged than the morning tide," he reminded me.

Segregated as it was, the hospital where I worked that summer was also Eva's hospital. She was thrilled her Baby was walking the same halls where she used to work and so happy that I was staying in Moncks Corner for the summer. I typed X-ray reports that radiologists dictated. I also covered the front desk. *Nothing* like Eva's stories of cooling fevered brows and feeding crying babies.

Between the speed and brogues of the Charleston doctors who read the X-rays, I *lived* in the medical dictionary and practically wore out the back-up peddle on the Dictaphone.

I functioned no better at the main desk. One day a large woman with a flushed face barged through the front door and marched up to the counter. Her brown hair disheveled, bubbles of sweat dotted her forehead. Two heavy hands slapped the counter with a smack. Looking me hard in the eye, a tight burst of words came out.

"My water's blue," she said.

I paused. "Excuse me?" I said.

"My water's blue," she said again with more vigor.

"I beg your pardon?" I said one more time.

"My water's blue!" she shouted. Obviously something was wrong with the water at her house. It had turned blue.

"Oh, I think you have the wrong office. You need to take a sample of your water to the health department on Gulledge Street near the dairy. They can tell you why it turned blue," I said, relieved to have figured out her problem.

As an exasperated look crossed her face, nurse Grooms scurried over to the woman.

"I think your water's broke. Come with me and let's get that baby out," she said.

When I told Eva about my gaffe, she said that in her midwife course years ago she learned that "water breakin' is step one to birthin', but you ain't know, Baby. It awright. Come on 'n eat your supper now."

I thought of Eva and the glowing letter of recommendation she received as a teenager when she first left Berkeley County Hospital to head "north" over fifty years earlier. No accolade forthcoming for me, I feared.

The following summer I didn't go home, I left the country. And Dowse was hurt. He wrote a heart-wrenching letter that challenged my decision to be away for three months. We had so little time together as it was. Did I not care about our relationship? *Of*

course I cared. He thought, not enough. Soon thereafter, he gave me a tiny orange booklet entitled "What
Men Know About Women." On the Outside he wrote
a note:

> This is a little more than I know about you.
> Love, Dowse

The inside was blank.

But I itched to follow up on an idea that had
been incubating for a couple of years. My senior year
in high school, Brailsford Lacey, Dr. Lacey's older
daughter, enthralled our congregation at Trinity
with a talk about her mission work in Puerto Rico.
She described a small team of girls working out of
an Episcopal convent in a house for underprivileged
little boys. It sounded fascinating, exciting. So I
worked toward the prerequisites—two years of college Spanish and involvement in church work. I didn't
share my dream with anyone for fear I wouldn't be
accepted because of the stiff competition. So while
Dowse saw a summer of our togetherness, I imagined hugs from needy little brown boys.

That summer shook me awake when I didn't
even know I was asleep. The experience stretched
this little WASP's narrow world to almost bursting.
The setting was Ponce, a town proud of its Hispanic
heritage and resolute in not speaking English; they
viewed the city of San Juan as too Americanized.
I'd never seen a Puerto Rican except in *West Side
Story*, and Natalie Wood wasn't even Puerto Rican!
I had peered at nuns walking in twos down the
narrow sidewalks of Charleston. All I knew about
pious, penguin-faced nuns was that they never married, couldn't wear lipstick, and prayed a lot—which
seemed like the perfect solution to my chaotic life
years before.

I saw Sister Esther first. She dispelled my mis-
conception of nuns within minutes of my arriving on
the grounds of the nunnery. A deeply tanned Native
American was playing shortstop with about ten little
boys—habit pulled to her bent knees revealing thick,
patched stocking and mannish black shoes dulled by

a thin coat of yellow-green dust from the ball field. The only full-blooded Indians I'd ever seen were dancing around a campfire wearing feather headdresses and moccasins entertaining tourists in Cherokee, North Carolina. A far cry from Sister Esther.

With a stiff white cloth folded around her head, she appeared neckless and androgynous. Springing for a grounder, she yelled directions to the batter, first and second basemen. This leadership ability covered activities other than ballgames, I learned. She was the primary speaker inside the convent, and her gravelly voice and stern demeanor did not invite conversation. As director of the small convent, Sister Esther ruled with rigor.

Her antithesis, Sister Althea, the principal of the convent school, gave me a jolt. A beautiful woman with well-proportioned features—and skin as black and polished as the stones on the shores of Martha's Vineyard. Her mellifluous voice was never raised, yet when she spoke, everyone gave full attention, students and nuns alike. The composed, articulate, intelligent woman with a passion for teaching completely captivated me.

I, who grew up in a county with more blacks than whites, had never met a formally educated black person, man or woman. I'd glimpsed Lela Session at the library when a tot and heard about her from Eva, but we'd not yet crossed paths. Sister Althea touched something deep within me—her professionalism as well as her tenderness with the boys who stretched their hands skyward for her attention. And I thought of Eva, Eva who recognized me without ever having to strain. I couldn't wait to tell her about Sister Althea.

The gaggle of brown-eyed boys ranged from preschool to high school. All summer long, one boy or another stayed wrapped around my legs or wriggling in my lap. I loved it! Most of them wore no shoes, some no shirts. On the playground their little privates showed through torn shorts, underwear an unknown luxury. Their exuberance and affection melted my heart.

I also grew close to Julio, one of the older boys,

who helped me as I stumbled through my poor
Spanish. A couple of summers later he joined the
U.S. Army and was stationed at Fort Jackson in
Columbia. When he made a trip to see me in Moncks
Corner, I recall the awkwardness of the visit. All I
know is that something compelled me to end the
visit before Mother came home, and I felt ashamed.
Why? Was Julio too dark for the setting?

Four girls worked in the Episcopal convent
that summer, each representing a region of the
United States. I represented the Southeast and drew
the lucky card for my roommate. Shannon, from
California, was tall, beautiful, intelligent, fluent in
Spanish with skin the color of a toasted fall leaf. She
was the brightest and most effective student worker
among us. I encountered my first experience of inferi-
ority with a peer, feeling "less than" on all fronts. An
enlightening occurrence. Gutless, I never mentioned
my roommate Shannon's ethnicity to my mother.

Until that summer in the early 1960s, this sheltered Southern girl had never engaged in an intellectual conversation with a black. The two of us
connected immediately. Peppered with questions,
Shannon talked long into the nights about the racial
unrest in Los Angeles, about regional prejudices,
about discriminating social systems. I grew elephant
ears that summer.

I returned stateside full of energy and enthusiasm, tasting a little humble pie, and eager to see Eva.
First thing, I drove out to her house in the Purina egg
truck, which I could use when the warehouse was
closed. It was a hot-as-Hades August Sunday. I spotted her through the screened door. She looked tired,
more rings on her neck than a giant oak. Brambles
of gray covered her capless head. She sat sewing a
new uniform to wear for LaClaire's wedding. She
looked up, dropped her stitching and cried out.

"Sweet Jesus, it my Baby!"

She pressed herself out of the chair, and we
fell into each other's arms and stayed a while. I sat
down as she eased herself into the upholstered chair
and fingered a crocheted doilie on the arm. A fan

swiveled through the muggy air. Her eyes seemed cloudier, her ankles thicker. Her face shone from the heat as she readied herself to listen.

My words flowed in torrents. She dispensed hers in teacups, benign comments like "Ain't that nice," after my description of the precious boys.

"Don't you worry none bout talking foreign," she advised after complaints about my awful Spanish. Her eyes brightened when I told her that Sister Althea was the best teacher I'd ever seen in my life. And she pressed her hands together when I talked about my roommate Shannon.

"Change be happenin', Baby," Eva said. And by now, Eva knew about the undulations and eruptions in the country, in the South, in her county, in her town.

We talked until dusk, until we sipped the last drop of sweet tea. We walked to the door and hugged.

"Take care yo'self now," she called as the truck pulled away. Waving from the window, I thought what a comfort to talk about my widening world and have no sweeping shifts in our relationship though so much was shifting in our minds and in our worlds. What mattered to both of us was being together, holding on to each other.

I went back to Queens impatient. Shannon and Sister Althea lit a fire in me that alternately simmered and smoldered. I returned eager to entertain teaching as a profession and to learn about black history and current discord in the very states where I lived and went to college. Embarrassed by my ignorance, I read antislavery fiction like *Uncle Tom's Cabin*. When someone called Eva an "Uncle Tom," I hadn't known what that meant. And I didn't ask. Now I could understand how Eva's immersion in our white world could have been misconstrued as abdicating her own. When I studied Mark Twain, I realized Huck Finn and Tom Sawyer drove home the cunning writer's views on discrimination.

I read black poetry. And guess who came to campus? Maya Angelou! And when I heard her read from *I Know Why the Caged Bird Sings*, I wondered, "Does Eva feel like a caged bird?" I was struck not

only by the poignancy of the poetry but by something she said in her talk afterwards.

"I've learned that people will forget what you
said, people will forget what you *did*, but people will
never forget how you *made them feel*."

I also glimpsed how Eva and her people felt
when I read "We Wear the Mask" by Paul Dunbar.

> *We wear the mask that grins and lies,*
> *It hides our cheeks and shades our eyes—*
> *This debt we pay to human guile;*
> *With torn and bleeding hearts we smile*
> *And mouth with myriad subtleties.*
>
> *Why should the world be over-wise,*
> *In counting all our tears and sighs?*
> *Nay, let them only see us, while*
> >   *We wear the mask.*
>
> *We smile, but, O great Christ, our cries*
> *To thee from tortured souls arise.*
> *We sing, but oh the clay is vile*
> *Beneath our feet, and long the mile,*
> *But let the world dream otherwise,*
> >   *We wear the mask!*

Reading those lines made me wince.

One evening expecting to enjoy a relaxing evening with friends at the Manor Theater up the street
from Queens, I watched Sidney Poitier deal with
social struggles in *Raisin in the Sun.* Was he acting?
Or had he actually suffered like Walter, felt the barriers to living and functioning in a white world, a
minority in business, the theater business?

Most of what I learned about Civil Rights activities before the Puerto Rican summer had come hap-
hazardly. College weekends teemed with music, yet
I was unaware of musicians' impact on the progress
of integration. It was all the rage for college boys to
play the guitar and gather people round to sing "Tom
Dooley" and "Where Have All the Flowers Gone?"
Before my giant-eared summer, I'd sung folk songs
along with the Kingston Trio and Peter, Paul and
Mary, oblivious to the lyrics. And I sang along with

Joan Baez and the Weavers—not realizing I was singing "protest songs."

Woody Guthrie sang "The Blinding of Isaac Woodard" one night for more than 36,000 people. "I got the loudest applause I've ever got in my whole life," he said. I had never heard of Woodard! I had no idea that Pete Seeger had gotten arrested for singing the non-standard verse of "Blowing in the Wind." After my return, I started paying attention.

One song grabbed my attention. "We Shall Overcome" I recognized as a tune that Eva hummed (never sang) from time to time. Where had she heard it? I learned the song was launched in Charleston! The year was 1945, when I was just three years old and Eva was wrapping my blonde hair around her brown finger to make the ringlets that LaClaire envied.

Seeger appeared on television one night talking about the history of that song. Members of the Food and Tobacco Workers Union, mostly African-American females (young women again), initiated a five-month strike against the American Tobacco Company. This affected the cigar factory on East Bay Street. To keep spirits up, Lucille Simmons sang "We'll overcome, I'll Be All Right" in a slow long-meter style version of a gospel hymn written in 1901. Seeger said that Septima Clark, director of Highland Folk School's Adult Literacy programs at the time, changed "We Will Over-come" to "We *Shall* Overcome." Who was Septima Clark? I probed.

This was the same Septima Clark and Charleston native who stood fast when the South Carolina legislature passed a law banning city or state employees from being involved with Civil Rights organizations.

"I have a great belief that whenever there is chaos, it creates wonderful thinking. I consider chaos a gift," Clark said.

Well, plenty of chaos in those days. But I didn't hear of Clark back then. Old clippings brought to light that the famous educator, activist and friend of Martin Luther King, Jr., refused to relinquish her position as vice-president of the Charleston NAACP branch. Consequently, in 1956 she was fired from her teaching job in Columbia.

More and more blacks just didn't seem to know their place, it seemed. And this was when Berkeley County brought Session to help ease the segregation tension. A dichotomy, to say the least.

Stuffing down the clichés that fit me for so long—green-as-a-gourd, head-in-the-sand, babe-in-the-woods—I probed, prodded, and pieced together snippets I'd seen and heard, creating a collage. I realized that long before our politicians got around to writing and enforcing laws against discrimination that brave musicians, athletes and teachers had been stepping out with drive, dignity and no little discomfort. I'd seen Althea Gibson in her white tennis outfit on a news clip when she received the Wimbledon trophy from the Queen; I watched Arthur Ashe made his mark on tennis and social issues as well. The long-legged sprinter Jessie Owens looked like a gazelle in pictures on the newsstand. He and Jackie Robinson broke barriers on the track and on the field but couldn't eat or bunk with their teammates. I'd seen them all yet not seen them at all.

Sports Illustrated reported that Robinson, the first Negro to break into professional baseball, was the target of "racial epithets and flying cleats, of hate letters and death threats, of pitchers throwing at his head and catchers spitting on his shoes."

I once lived in the South Carolina community that spawned an educator from way back who impacted the movement toward racial equality—Benjamin Mays. Former Atlanta mayor and UN ambassador Andrew Young said of the Greenwood County native:

> It all started in a log cabin and a cotton patch. If it hadn't been for Benjamin Mays, there probably wouldn't have been a Martin Luther King . . . In fact, the legacy that came out of this little area, forgive me, I don't mean any heresy—but it is like Jesus coming out of the little town of Bethlehem.

Mays became President of Morehouse College where

King graduated. King called Mays his intellectual father and credited Mays with leading him into the ministry.

Across the nation in the 1950s, most blacks were saying, "I'm grateful to be here." But by the 1960s, still catching hell, they were fed up with the system.

In Berkeley County black churches now heard people like Roy Wilkins, head of the NAACP, and Walter White, editor of *The Crisis* magazine. The black community embraced the messages, but they chose not to upset the applecart with activism. They looked to locals like Dr. Lela Session working in the schools and Judge Matthew Perry maneuvering in the courts to work within the system. The biggest changes were slow in coming, but amidst the outrageous acts of violence, some known and many not, there were signs of progress.

And a few brave South Carolina souls *did* upset the cart early on. The year after Eva came to live with us and I blew out one little birthday candle on a cupcake in 1942, The Reverend Joseph A. DeLaine asked the Clarendon County Board to provide a school bus for the black students. They said no. That request would prove monumental in history. This seemingly insignificant incident in the back woods of South Carolina triggered what culminated in the United States Supreme Court's decision in 1954 to integrate schools over twenty years later.

Did the decision in 1954 have anything to do with LaClaire's being sent to Ashley Hall that very year? I wonder.

The mid-1950s were turbulent times—chaotic at home and in our country. Daddy's disintegration affected our family tremendously; our country's integration affected everyone. I unburied my head from *Moll Flanders* to catch the headline on May 17, 1954. In response to the *Brown vs. Board of Education* landmark decision to end segregation, *The News and Courier* ran a front page editorial. Perhaps I glimpsed the headline because we subscribed to "the newsless courier," as we called it. But it didn't seem to have anything to do with me as a young seventh-grader. Part of the editorial read,

> We receive the decision with distaste and apprehension. But it is too late to secede and start another War Between the States. Other means must be sought to live within the laws of our country.

South Carolina immediately employed "other means."

The legislature formed the Gressette Committee, which was charged to preserve states' rights. Thus began the creation of all-white Citizens Councils, largely an outlet for white rage. These councils cropped up in communities all over the South. Charleston boasted six such councils. A Lowcountry boy from James Island, Fred Moore, who was the student body president of South Carolina State College, an all-black school in Orangeburg an hour up the highway, was expelled from school two weeks before his graduation. He led a boycott of white Citizens Council's businesses in Orangeburg. A year later, in 1955, the court ruled that schools be desegregated "with all deliberate speed."

Young blacks took up the mantel to move the establishment, and *they* did it with deliberate speed.

History unfolded only a few blocks from Queens while I studied for exams. One day newspapers screamed that students from Johnson C. Smith, a local college for blacks, staged a sit-in at Woolworth's in downtown Charlotte. This triggered a wave of lunch counter strikes across the South. At one counter a white waitress said to a young black student, "We don't serve niggers." The student responded, "We don't eat em either."

Dowse sent me word about Charleston's first sit-in happening at S. H. Kress, a store

Sit-in at Kress Department Store
Charleston, SC

we stopped in for a Coke when shopping on King Street. It was led by several members of the NAACP Youth Chapter. Woolworth's was targeted too, first by Harvey Gantt, a Charleston boy and Burke High School student. He became the first black to enter Clemson University and later mayor of Charlotte.

"Good for them," I said to myself.

The older John Lewis, who was fumigated in a Krystal hamburger stand as a youth, drew up some "do's and don'ts for the sit-ins." Things like wearing Sunday clothes, being prepared to sit quietly and be denied service. Students took books and papers, did homework at the lunch counters. Some ideas, he said, came from the bus boycotts. Don't talk back. Sit straight up. Don't laugh. Don't curse. At the end of the rules, "Remember the teachings of Jesus, Gandhi, Martin Luther King. God bless you all."

Unbending segregationist Kilpatrick was so impressed with the decorum of the early sit-inners that he wrote in Richmond's *News Leader:*

> Here were the colored students, in coats, white shirts, ties, and one of them was reading Goethe and one was taking notes from a biology text. And here, on the sidewalk outside, was a gang of white boys come to heckle, a ragtail rabble, slack-jawed, black-jacketed, grinning fit to kill, and some of them . . . waving the proud and honored flag of the Southern States in the last war fought by gentlemen. Eheu! It gives one pause.

The younger generation of blacks took the action that their parents could not have borne.

By this time we'd all heard of Matthew Perry, a black lawyer from South Carolina, and chief counsel for the NAACP and US District Court Judge. In the news often, he defended the youths who were jailed. Perry represented over seven thousand people fighting to integrate restaurants, beaches, parks, hospitals, and public schools. Harvey Gantt was one he defended.

My Queens years were so full that I rarely sat down to watch the news on the one television set in my dormitory lounge. But it was impossible to miss the flurry of activity going on, and a few students talked about the uprisings. Following the sit-ins in fifty-four cities came the Freedom Riders, targeting both Greyhound and Trailways buses.

I do remember tears coming to my eyes when I heard about Emmett Till. I could just *see* that cotton gin fan. I knew exactly what it looked like: a huge metal square structure embedded high in the wall at the far end of our gin, Harry kept it running all the time to suck the hot air and flying cotton particles out of the air so the machines wouldn't catch on fire. The news said a fourteen-year-old black boy was visiting relatives in Mississippi. He suffered from infantile paralysis and spoke unclearly, sometimes with a whistling sound. He was killed for "whistling" at a white clerk. A youngster found the boy's mutilated body at the bottom of the Tallahatchie River weighted down with a cotton gin fan. I couldn't get that image out of my mind for weeks.

Cotton Gin Fan

Does his wandering soul know that he and Anne Franke share co-billing in the play "Anne and Emmett" written by Janet Cohen, the African-American wife of former Secretary of Defense William Cohen? I hope so.

I asked Eva if she'd heard about Emmett Till. She looked up from her ironing and looked down again. Never said a word. To this day I don't know what she knew. I never could flush out Eva's feelings the way she flushed out mine.

South Carolina, of course, wasn't immune. Friends from Edisto Island told me about Freddie Robinson, the twelve-year-old black boy from Edisto who liked to dance with young white girls on the pier. He mysteriously drowned while fishing, his string of fish found on the riverbank. I thought at the time how gutsy the white girls were who danced with a black boy, regardless of how good he could dance. My mother would have smacked me good for that one. I gave the young boy barely a thought.

It was primarily the North—not the South—that heard, watched, read and reacted to the news of Southern agitation and atrocities.

Jack Kilpatrick, an intellectual bulldog and prolific writer, along with South Carolina's Senator Strom Thurmond, held out to the end. Thurmond's last gasp was his twenty-four hour and twenty-eight minute talk to block the 1957 Civil Rights Bill—the longest filibuster in U.S. Senate history.

But with patience and prodding, progress was possible. Who would dream that some fifty years after his scathing writings, Kilpatrick and I would become friends. When his first wife became ill, she wanted to move to Charleston, so they bought on South Battery. I'd read his columns on writing religiously. A random visit to The Citadel where I directed a Writing Center began a long, rich relationship. After he moved back to DC, for the first time we talked politics, not writing, in his Washington apartment. He admitted that eventually "terrible evils came into focus." He gave me a copy of the article which detailed his coming to his senses.

Thurmond ultimately came around too. Time heals, times change, and time led him to truth. And he had plenty of time to shift, living to over 100! He gradually modified his views and toward the end publicly acknowledged his black daughter.

Civil Rights leaders, black and white, fought hard to make evils clear, with two vital weapons—technology and the press. Civil Rights issues became hot news with the advent of television in the 1950s and the doggedness of many Northern journalists. In the early part of the movement, about 50 percent of the public got news from television, but Southerners were only 5 percent of the national audience. *The New York Times* was the only national newspaper providing regular coverage of race story in the South.

But gradually Southerners like me came to listen to announcers like Edward R. Murrow, who humanized the white perception of blacks by show-casing black soldiers, musicians and athletes who were making history in their own right.

Up until my senior year in college, I'd never been north of the Mason-Dixon Line, that line originally drawn in the 1800s over a border dispute between British colonies in Colonial America, which later came to symbolize a cultural boundary between the Northern and Southern United States. Deciding to venture out of Dixie, a group of college friends took a road trip "up north" to New York City.

Beth Rivers was one of the group. This petite,

Beth Curry at Queens College

quiet girl grew up in a large family on her father's peach farm in Chesterfield, South Carolina. On her application to Queens College, her father wrote that his eldest daughter would not necessarily be a leader but she'd make an excellent follower. One of the brightest students at Queens and President of the Student Body, we all laughed at his prediction. He graciously let us use his station wagon to drive to the Big Apple.

Fresh out of our fathers' fields, we walked around the city with mouths open and faces unbuttoned. We gawked at skyscrapers and gaped as multi-racial couples pushed their way to work or walked hand in hand in Central Park. This was a city where blacks like James Earl Jones won Emmys on stage and Marion Anderson sang Puccini at the Metropolitan Opera House.

Mrs. Chalmers arranged for her two sons to take Beth and me out on the town during our stay. Polished, bright young men, they engaged us with interesting conversation. After dinner they asked if they could join us in our hotel room for some Drambui. We glanced at each other nervously. Young ladies never allowed boys in their rooms at home, much less in a hotel room with no chaperone. And we had absolutely no idea what Drambui was. Was it a card game? Hanky-panky? Not wanting to seem like bumpkins, we acquiesced with trepidation. Turns out the boys were perfect gentlemen, and we innocent Southern girls were initiated into the world of alcohol as we sipped a heather, honey and golden scotch liqueur called "Drambui."

That reminds me of young Gladys Nettles who was crowned Miss SC Tobacco Queen back in the 30s. Senator Olin D. Johnston invited the young Lake City girl to a party in DC. She was thrilled to attend.

> *"Would you like a cocktail?" he asked.*
> *"I'd love one," she replied.*
> *"What kind?" he asked.*
> *"Fruit cocktail will be fine," she answered.*

Beth and I were small-town girls, but not quite *that* naive.

Back to the New York trip . . . I saw how things could be. Strangely, I felt free, liberated in that city. But once back down South, the human landscape shifted again to black and white and to the only avenue I knew to deal with the ambiguity.

Mrs. Chalmers and my writing class became that fixed mark upon which my compass swung. Her steadfast support allowed questions to rise regularly, emotions to flow unabated. I admitted being embarrassed by my ignorance of issues that were going on under my nose, right in my own house (the house of Eva too), my small town (the town with black/white water fountains), my "smiling faces and beautiful places" state (the state of Strom Thurmond), and my free country (the country of segregated schools and restaurants). It was a time of sorrow, fear, anger, and . . . growth. For my country, for me. And I returned again and again to my source of strength and comfort, to Eva and the God she leaned on.

I met all of myself in the writing group that gathered regularly at Mrs. Chalmers's house. Students critiqued each other's writings with candor and care. "Truth without embellishment" was Mrs. Chalmers's motto.

"Write what you know," she said. Eva stayed the subject. Eating my sweet fish at Wampee, teaching me to make biscuits and spit watermelon seeds, brushing my hair. Her smell of Clorox and baby powder, the warmth of her hand on my head, her soft tone when she said, "Hush now, Baby." Writing became a refuge and a catharsis. It helped me hold onto something constant and safe. Some measure of peace came, knowing that our love transcended race, that we'd already found our way.

When I came home for the holidays, she was always at our house. With Eva and me, everything except "us" slipped way. During these visits her first words usually were something like, "My, you growd nice 'n plump, Baby." Eek. Mother wasn't going to be happy about *that*.

"How're things going?" I'd say.

"Tol'rable," she'd mutter. Or "fair to mid'lin'." Getting information out of Eva could be like frisking a catfish.

One evening it became clear how things were going at home. It was dinner time. Eva had just left the room after passing the biscuits. Mother pierced a tomato with her salad fork so hard that is screeched across the plate. I looked up.

"Sometimes she forgets whose house this is," she whispered.

I buttered my biscuit. How often did Eva have to be careful of her ways or words, deflect Mother's slights or sighs? Over time, osmosis damages the psyche. What multitude of daily surrenders did Eva make to keep the equilibrium? Was she preparing for the worst and hoping for the best, doing her small part to take the hypocrisy out of democracy? What emotional pockets had lain dormant that now seeped to the fore?

Back in the kitchen, Eva's swollen feet shuffled like sandpaper blocks across the floor. Her head hung down, her voice barely audible. Her body slumped as if the starch had vanished, not just from her clothes but from her bones.

Had my house become a microcosm of the country?

As powerful white bigots fought to defend their turf, integrationists responded with non-violent protests. Some, however, ended violently, whites having the upper hand. Eva and I happened to be together in the television room the day Governor Wallace of Alabama appeared on the screen vowing to keep schools segregated. Eva was vacuuming. People like Wallace believed that blacks were genetically inferior to whites. He was adamant that the races "not mix—in schools, in public arenas, in the political process, and particularly in marriage." Eva snapped off the vacuum just in time to hear him bellow to the nation.

"I say segregation now, segregation tomorrow, segregation forever!" We both stared at the screen, stunned. Eva looked at me. I felt her eyes on my face before I turned to her.

"Is that man plum *crazy*?" she asked.

"Yes," I answered as my arm circled her drooping shoulders.

Fortunately, in South Carolina more battles were fought in the courts than in the streets. Education was the arena that seemed most vulnerable and most visible. Everyone in the Lowcountry knew the Waring family in Charleston. People read *The News and Courier* daily. Its editor, Thomas Waring, Jr. became as forceful a spokesman for segregation as there was in the South. On the integration issue, he was in direct opposition to his uncle, Judge Waites Waring. Family against family. Charleston elite gossiped about Judge Waring and his wife "from off." The couple had newfangled ideas about blacks being equal to whites. People threw bricks in their windows. It wasn't long before the judge lost his prominence in Charleston society largely because he forced the SC Democratic party to open voting rolls to all, and he wrote a dissent that formed the basis of *Brown v. Board of Education*.

His conscience and sensibleness encouraged Judge Thurgood Marshall to go for *desegregation* instead of *equalization* in Clarendon County's *Briggs v. Elliott* case. The very case that started in South Carolina that led to the end of school segregation in the United States . . . on paper. I didn't know all the details back then, but what I have learned since has made me proud. Proud of South Carolina's part in shaping the social fabric of our nation.

I didn't get home much, but when I did, I caught up on the local happenings, and I could see that local leaders did a lot of relationship building to make the transition to integration smoother than it might have been. Berkeley County was fortunate to have Superintendent W. H. Bonner as an advocate for both black and white children for over fifty years; his son Henry followed in his footsteps. Well before integration, Bonner attended ballgames at black and white schools and allowed the black baseball team to use the white facilities. He and his wife tutored black students in their front parlor and thought nothing of it. I remember them fondly as gentle, generous people, their silver hair glinting in the sun as they crossed the street from their house to my school where she taught grammar school. The Bonners served on interracial committees that helped the races have problem-solving conversations.

South Carolina was a part of the South yet in its own world. Both blacks and whites kept the Southern tradition of treating others with respect. Historians admit that South Carolina was far more flexible than some other states. The state was small and most of its towns were as well. The powerful and the humble knew each other by name; they were mutually dependent upon each other for their livelihood and their positions. So in this time of unrest, people tried to work together in this largely agricultural state. Both blacks and whites wanted to work peacefully within the system; they didn't want their towns, their communities destroyed for a principle. A principle they both were willing to wait for—the whites politely and grudgingly, the blacks, politely and persistently.

Admittedly, South Carolina's governors had been hemmed in by the mindset of the day. I remember hearing Governor Fritz Hollings boldly declaring the NAACP subversive. When a U.S. Senator, he later admitted to *The New York Times* that he "knew it was wrong, but there wasn't anything you could do about it, coming along politically."

Hollings's final speech to the South Carolina General Assembly in 1963 was heartening:

> *South Carolina is running out of courts . . . . We must realize the lesson of one hundred years ago and move on for the good of South Carolina and our United States. This should be done with dignity. It must be done with law and order.*

Latching onto the word "dignity," I thought of Eva. And Martin Luther King said it best: "All labor that uplifts humanity has dignity and importance."

Turns out, an old friend of my daddy, a Lowcountry boy, Governor Robert McNair, paved the way for blacks to enter Clemson and the University of South Carolina peaceably. Unlike James Meredith's tumultuous entrance to college in Mississippi, Harvey Gantt's entrance to Clemson University caused not a ripple.

"If you can't appeal to the morals of a South Carolinian, you can appeal to his manners," Gant said.

That was the year 1963, the year that everything started coming together . . . and blew up. The old Septima Clark chaos theory.

Chapter 15

Scales Fall Off

Life for me ain't been no crystal stair.
—Langston Hughes, poet

Eva's life took another turn by the time Rusty left for college. Frugal Clara Lee now had three children in college and money was tighter than ever. Eva worked only on special occasions like our visits home and garden or bridge club days. Both Miss Hattie and Daddy Bill had by this time gone home to Jesus, and Miriam had moved to New Jersey to find a job after high school.

Eva had depended upon Miriam more and more as her legs gave out and her spirits waned. Miriam did all the work around Eva's house and helped out with Miss Hattie and Daddy Bill as they aged because Eva was doing for us. When they died, Miriam became Eva's mainstay.

Eva couldn't brag enough about her foster daughter. "That gal's a reg'lar work horse. I sho couldn't do widout her, now that the trut." Eva rarely talked more than when she was carrying on about her Miriam. Miriam who sang in the choir, Miriam who studied so hard, Miriam who rubbed her knees.

But Miriam was gone, gone up North.

"De chile gots to get a job. She'll send me some money now 'n again. Lawd knows she been a help to me—she a good chile. She be coming on back shortly, soon is she make a little bit," Eva explained.

Two years passed. Miriam wrote. I read. Eva listened. Miriam sent gifts—a scarf, an apron. Eva oohed over them and wore them proudly. "That chile sho preshates all I done for her. She'll be getting on home now," she reassured herself.

"Yeah, won't be long," I'd answer brightly, wondering. Eva wasn't getting any younger and had been running two houses single-handed since Miriam left. Her feet were dragging, her laughs less spontaneous. Now a surprise slap on the behind from me elicited a negative response.

"Ya ain't got no feelings. Ya knows my heart can't stand sech," she said. It didn't used to be that way.

One weekend when Dowse was visiting, he sneaked up behind her while she was Electroluxing and popped a hand firecracker. She drew a short breath, clutched her bosom and collapsed on the sofa. Scared us to death! A stiff dose of ammonia fixed her right up. After that, when Eva insisted, "I can't take it like I usta," we knew it was the gospel truth.

The telegraph office called one day to say Eva had a message. She asked me to go pick it up. A wide-eyed Eva met me at the front door. She turned the yellow envelope over in her lined palm and handed it back to me to read aloud:

MAMA EVA, SAM AND ME GOT MARRIED. DIDN'T WANT IT TO BE NO TROUBLE ON YOU. RECKON I'LL BE UP HERE A WHILE NOW. YOUR MIRIAM.

She dropped her hands and lifted her eyes to mine with a blank gaze. She sucked in a hunk of air and stretched her lips into a tight smile, eyes still fixed. Silence. I rushed to fill the space.

"Well, she's got good taste. She went to New Jersey and found her a good ol' Lowcountry boy— Samuel Taylor," I said, trying to cheer her.

Then she started talking—about how she saw me born, how Daddy charmed her into leaving the hospital and coming to work for us that very day.

"Seems just yestiddy I was brushin tangles out-cha purty head—and memba dem weeks it be just me one wid yenna churren? You sho 'nuf had a goin mama and daddy back then," she said. My mind wandered with her.

Remembering Eva's sneaking me a peanut-butter-and-jelly sandwich and a round glass full of milk when Daddy sent me to bed without supper, her teaching me to fold crisp hospital corners, to iron the collars and cuffs first, to cut biscuits by spinning the juice glass. Remembering rushing to Eva during storms, inside and out.

Two arms suddenly enfolded me. A heavy head hung over my shoulder, and without a sound Eva cried. Her chin bobbed.

"You still my baby, ain't ya?" Without waiting for an answer, she continued.

"Course you is—I raised you—it's for sho you won't leave me—that's one thing I knows."

Eva had lost to the world a child she'd taken in and loved as her own. A child like me, I thought. As I held my breath and squeezed my eyes to hold back tears, her anguish became mine. Eva's life had been no crystal stair, but she always gave me the full measure of her love.

Fortune provided Eva with something to brighten her days for a time. She was in her glory when LaClaire married Charlie Laffitte the same day he graduated from The Citadel as a Gold Star private! LaClaire and Charlie's wedding at The Citadel Chapel went off without a hitch. The weather was ideal for the outdoor reception at the Berkeley Country Club.

Eva at Charlie and LaClaire's wedding

That same day Eva greeted Strom Thurmond with grace.

"Mr. Strum, we glad you come!" a smiling Eva said and offered him a drink.

Eva never heard about my later encounter with Thurmond on an airplane. Thank goodness. If she had, I think she and Daddy too might have risen from their graves.

Newly married and teaching in Charleston, I headed home from an educational conference in DC. Thurmond was leaving Washington after a congressional session. Our plane seats happened to be next to each other, his beside the window, mine on the aisle. What a pleasant surprise! We chatted a bit. I asked about his new wife Nancy; he asked about Daddy, then Mother.

"I'll bet she's pretty as ever," he said. I agreed.

When the plane leveled off, he pulled out small nail scissors from his coat pocket and began clipping articles out of a bundle of magazines and paper. I asked what he was doing, and he explained he liked to keep up with anything that mentioned his name. I pushed my seat back and closed my eyes to catch a nap.

The next thing I recall is feeling a large hand resting on my thigh. Was I dreaming? My mind raced, my eyes clamped tighter. My gracious! Is Senator Strom Thurmond really trying to feel me up?

Of course I'd heard the rumors about his being a lady's man, but for heaven's sake, this was Daddy's old buddy. I was the toddler he teased when he stayed in our home.

The hand moved imperceptibly. My heart pounded. Surely he could hear it! What should I do?

Make a decision, I said to myself. *What are my choices? Turn around and slap the tar out of him? My first inclination. Start a conversation to distract him? Or say, "Get your cotton-picking paws off me!"?* How many minutes elapsed, I don't know. I do know that it seemed a millenium.

A stillness eventually came over me. I envisioned

Eva's looking down through the clouds in dismay. *What would she do?* I remembered her calmness in the face of disconcerting situations. I remembered her treating people with respect, even if they didn't treat her the same. Finally I breathed. Had I been holding my breath the whole time? My eyelids unkinked but stayed shut.

Gently but deliberately I covered Strom's hand with mine. I squeezed, lifted the hand and placed it on his own thigh. I slid my hand back to my leg and never moved again until the wheels touched the ground. We said pleasant goodbyes at the terminal. Eva would have been proud.

Back to the subject at hand. LaClaire and Charlie's wedding at the Citadel Chapel was sweet, and the sun shone during the outdoor reception. Just before the ceremony Eva dispensed her wisdom when the couple had a disagreement about stopping at Kerrison's to buy stockings. LaClaire's unhappiness spilled over to Eva, who responded with an analogy.

"When you gets married, it like throwin a rope over a house. One on one side, one on de other. Can't pull de rope too hard on one side, gots to keep a balance," she advised LaClaire. Neither the bride nor the groom pulled too tightly, and we all enjoyed the festivities, no one more than Eva.

Although marriage was the last thing on my mind that summer, my love life took an abrupt turn my final year at Queens. I met a tall, blue-eyed Davidson boy who literally swept me off my feet. I'm not kidding . . . knocked me over. He sang me songs on the guitar, used double-entendres like "pregnant pauses." He read me poems like "How Hard it is to Keep from Being King When it's in You and in the Situation" by Robert Frost. We wrote daily letters though only twenty minutes apart. That boy could lock eyes on mine so hard that I couldn't look away. And . . . he planned to be a doctor.

I wore a perpetual smile in his presence. His

little brother asked me when he visited one weekend, "Why do you smile all the time?"

"I can't help it," I smiled. It was true—I couldn't help it. I couldn't help when I saw his handwriting on an envelope, my heart bumped.

I couldn't help that Dowse slid to the back of my mind as he immersed himself in his first year of medical school in Charleston. Yes, Dowse too decided to become a doctor. For years I'd assumed that Dowse and I would marry, although we never spoke the word. I pictured our little boy, a miniature of him, a spunky bundle with chubby cheeks and dancing eyes. My best friend for eight years, Dowse brought me nothing but pleasure—and dynamite kisses. What more could I ask?

I told Eva about feeling guilty for being attracted to someone other than Dowse, seeing it as a sign I shouldn't marry him. She put her hands on her widening hips and sent me a scathing look.

"Is you taken leave of yo' senses, Baby?" she said. She had grown to love Dowse too. She cooked for him, he laughed with her. The three of us hugged a lot. Dowse and I broke up, long distance. I sat on the floor of the dorm talking to him on the phone for hours. I cried in my pillow all night long, the night I took leave of my senses.

My infatuation with the knight-in-shiny-armor lasted less than a year. It was some consolation that we'd never used the magic word "love," a good indication that it wasn't—certainly not *unconditional* love. I'd not measured up to his expectations. The week before May Day, the bloom fell off the rose.

May Day. The last memory of Queens College. Eva's Baby was crowned Queen of the May in the cool, green dell—without Eva or mother, sister or brother. Earlier that morning, Mrs. Chalmers slipped a note under my door. On the envelope she'd written, "Queen Angela." At the top she'd drawn a little crown with her pen. I wished Eva could be there too. Mrs. Chalmers watched the procession and the crowning of a heartbroken queen. She hugged me afterwards. "You could have smiled," she said pensively. That evening I did smile, thanks to Henry Laffitte who dashed up from the University of South Carolina to be my last-minute date for the May Day dance. What a friend and an excellent dancer to boot!

> May 5, 1963
>
> Dearest Angela,
>
> It's about six o'clock now, and I can already see what a day it's going to be — the wall is covered with rainbows from my prisms! How I wish Eva could be here! I hope, dear Angela, everything will be happy for you: inside as well as outside.
>
> Your loving teacher,
> Roberta Chalmers

That's the spring, spring of 1963, things got crazy in the country.

May: By then I regularly watched the evening news on television. I first saw Martin Luther King, an activist in Birmingham, get locked up for leading boycotts. On the television he seemed okay to me . . .

dressed well and spoke correct English. I thought he might look a little better without a mustache. That's about all I recall from my first glimpse of him as they carried him off to jail.

A short few weeks after that, I came home for the summer. Still intrigued with the medical world, I worked at Dr. Bob Solomon's office as a receptionist. But I never missed the evening news. Things were heating up everywhere. I watched in revulsion as police let loose with hoses, billy clubs and dogs on an unarmed crowd. "Bull" Connor, the Birmingham Police Commissioner, provided the Ku Klux Klan fifteen uninterrupted minutes to attack the Freedom Riders. Later that evening King's motel was bombed and blacks rioted till dawn.

June: Birmingham violence prompted President Kennedy to deliver an impassioned televised speech. Eva and I watched it together. He called racial discrimination in the United States "a moral crisis . . . as old as the scriptures and as clear as the American Constitution" and introduced the Civil Rights Act. Neither of us spoke during or afterwards. Someone had finally named the cancer within our country.

The very next day in Jackson, Mississippi, NAACP Field Secretary Medgar Evers, just thirty-seven years old, was gunned down in his own front yard. His children looking on.

August: Before I headed to graduate school, I watched thousands in the March on Washington and heard King's "I Have a Dream" speech at the Lincoln Memorial.

Three weeks later, four little black girls were bombed to smithereens. They were in a Birmingham church preparing their parts for Youth Sunday.

A summer to remember, 1963.

And this young Southern girl rushed to the ivory tower of Duke University for graduate school—away from the clamor. I had refused to take education courses at Queens, again not heeding Mother's advice. I found myself about to graduate with a Literature and Communication major and had not yet thought about finding a job. Many classmates were already planning their weddings or had job interviews lined up.

Providential timing put a representative on campus soliciting for a pilot program sponsored by the Ford Foundation. Duke was selected to host the new venture for students who wanted master-level courses in their major field plus a few relevant education classes that certified them to teach. It would be first the Master's of Arts in Teaching program in the United States. The scholarship paid all expenses.

Sounded perfect. I was delightfully petrified when the acceptance letter came. Duke University? Could I measure up?

The first paper I wrote traced light in three of Charles Dickens's novels. I thought it brilliant. Only one mark on the paper when it was returned—a big red F. At the bottom the professor wrote: "And you think you want to *teach* writing!" For the next six months I did nothing but attend classes, read ravenously, and write voluminously. I blocked out everything—news, boys, home and Eva. I had to keep my Ford Foundation scholarship. At the end of the term, a rumor circulated that the professor gave all his students an F on first papers. Argh!

A few months later, a boulder crashed through the façade of my myopic world, ending one of the most violent years in our country's history.

When practice teaching started, I kept my head down—taught full time during day, went to classes as night. Rarely dated. I had moved off campus with two Duke classmates, Frannie Bailey and Barbara Tew, to St. Mary's Street in Raleigh. All three of us did our practice teaching at Needham Broughton High School. I had no car. Barbara drove us back to the Duke campus for evening classes.

November: One fall morning, I walked up the hill to the sound of leaves crunching under my shoes. My mind wandered to an upcoming weekend with a long-time Darlington friend, a boy who flirted with me at Camp St. Christopher and covered my ears at Sewanee dances when the Hot Nuts sang raunchy lyrics, now a NYU law student. The same boy that prompted me to buy a red hat on my New York trip. I had to dress properly to catch a plane to be his date for the Carolina Cup horse races in Camden, South Carolina. (Few spectators see horses at this annual outdoor party.)

I greeted my students that morning with a smile. The first two classes rolled by. When I took attendance for third period, one desk was empty. I sent a student to the gym to fetch Pete Maravitch. It had become a daily ritual to lure the skinny basketball player off the basketball court and into the classroom. Pete slumped in his seat with a quick "Sorry, Miss Williams." Not two minutes later, a wide-eyed student burst through the doorway.

"President Kennedy's been shot!" he shouted.

A pall covered the school for days. My students and I watched the funeral on television. As the announcer solemnly described the procession and ceremony, I jotted unfamiliar words like "cortege" and "caisson" on the board. For days afterwards we wrote—I along with the students. We wrote impressionistic paragraphs and free-verse poems to assuage our anger, our grief, and our guilt. We, the youth of the nation, had viewed Kennedy as our savior, unifier, and healer. Together we mourned the loss of optimism and hope for our nation's domestic struggles.

I called home frequently, hoping to catch Eva because she had no phone at her house. Finally I reached her.

"Lawd, if dey ain't shooting black and white. A day o' rec'ning comin, Baby, mark my word." She ended the conversation indicating she missed me.

"Hurry on home, now. Time to be comin' home. Be sweet."

I hadn't heard "Be sweet" from Eva since grammar school when she hollered out, "Be sweet!" when I left for school. That covered all the expectations—mind my manners, say "yes, ma'am" and "yes, sir," be kind to everyone one, don't get too dirty. I missed her and that Southern custom reminder to "be sweet."

The Kennedy assassination devastated those who had been fighting in the trenches to make things right. To those like me on the sideline, praying for peaceful resolutions to age-old ills, the bullet pierced our hearts as well. Yet millions, black and white, continued doing what they'd been doing for years, trying to make things better. Not me.

I'm not proud to report that my first personal involvement with Civil Rights issues came by accident. After graduate school, I tossed around options of where to live. The world was my oyster. The Peace Corps that President Kennedy initiated appealed to me. The New York publishing world sounded exciting, and my dark, handsome NYU law school friend was there.

But my mind kept going to Fred, a blue-eyed Furman University boy, the one I'd met at Beth's wedding the previous summer, the one who wrote flowery letters, the one who hugged his daddy and took the seeds out of the lemon before squeezing it in my tea. The one who hitchhiked to North Carolina for a first date and presented me with a tomato plant. He'd just begun medical school in Charleston. Maybe I'd go there to get to know him a little better. Besides, Eva needed me nearby. I was worried about her. That tipped the scale. So back to the Lowcountry and plough mud.

I snagged a job teaching English at St. Andrews High School just across the Ashley River in Charleston. I could smell the marsh from my apartment on Elliott Street off East Bay. I roomed with Fred's sister, lanky Marguerite, and Pam Nolan, a Duke friend who also landed a job teaching at St. Andrews. Pam had a car, so transportation across town wasn't a problem. Our principal, Bernard Hester, lived across the street from us. One of my favorite colleagues was a lively history teacher named Peatsy. She loved to talk politics and later married Senator Fritz Hollings.

"Can you believe that it's 1964 and there's not one black student in this school?" Peatsy ranted. A feisty gal, that Peatsy.

The advanced English class that I taught contained several bright students. Mendel Rivers, whose father had been Daddy's friend, wrote an illuminating research paper on the women in Shakespeare's plays. And Dewey Nettles, his father prominent in the publishing business, wrote beautifully but was so shy that he rarely spoke. He left me notes when he'd have to miss class for basketball games. I looked forward to this class.

One day I asked my students whether they knew anything about the Swedish scientist Alfred Nobel. No? I gave a little background. Next I asked if they knew who had received the latest Nobel Peace Prize that very week. No.

"Martin Luther King, Jr." I announced, delighted to enlighten.

A boy burst out of his seat in the back of the room, his face burning with fury.

"How can that black nigger get a prize for peace? He's nothing but trouble!" he shouted. His rage was so real, so righteously delivered that I felt how deeply the roots of hatred and prejudice permeated our society—and into the next generation.

My explanation about King's view of Gandhi's principles of non-violence could not calm him. He remained adamant in his anger. Didn't he know about the years of black and white water fountains, about the kids who couldn't buy a burger at Woolworths, about the KKK burning crosses, beating people, bombing churches, killing little girls? Where has he been? Another question arose, a question for me—where had *I* been? On the sideline, watching. Seeing up close the struggle within my household, watching from afar the turmoil in my country. In both cases, doing nothing.

When the boy simmered down a bit, an idea came to mind. I asked him to stay after class. I charged him to interview and write a short biography of three prominent, local black men. One a politician, another a lawyer, the last a doctor. He balked,

"I've never talked to a nigger," he said.

"Well, it's about time," I replied. I supplied him with the names, plus a mini-lesson on inappropriate use of the vernacular.

When he handed in his assignment two weeks

later, he said that talking to the men was the hardest thing he'd ever done. His admiration for the three men permeated the reports, in spite of his narrow upbringing. From that day forward, I vowed to create assignments that forced students to look at their prejudices, praying their insight would lead to less discrimination—one person at a time.

About the same time back downtown on the Charleston peninsula, Ruby Pendergrass Cornwell, was getting decked out in a white silk dress, hat and gloves. She led a group of black people to the Fort Sumter Hotel on the high Battery for lunch. When I saw the news photograph, she could have been Eva on her way to church. As Cornwell walked up the steps, a policeman arrested her for civil disobedience. Why? A Charleston law said blacks were not allowed on the Battery unless they were tending a white child. "The arresting officer was most apologetic," according to the report. Still a long way to go.

But the power of one not lost, around the corner at East Bay Playground where the Whaley girls and I played, a white, ten-year-old boy was teaching his friend a lesson. His playmate, who was shooting basketball *and* shooting off his mouth about federal intrusion in school decisions, spiced up his tirade with ugly racial terms. According to Frank Wooten, the reporter, who wrote the story:

> His buddy, also ten, endured all of the harangue he could bear before cutting it short with: "But what if you were colored?"

This question caused his friend to stammer considerably. "But I'm not," he said. The criticism stopped, however, and in time the boy's racial views improved, with a simple "What if?" from a friend.

I personally resonated with a story Jane Trotter told about these changing times. She was a very pregnant young mother traveling from Michigan to the South riding on a packed Trailways bus with her two-year-old daughter. Because they were at the back of the white line when getting on, they ended up taking the last two "white seats" before the long seat at back of the bus. Four black women took those seats. That left an elderly black woman and a young black man standing in the aisle. The elderly lady kept having trouble with her balance along the rough road, so Trotter picked up her daughter and offered the lady a seat beside her, which she took with some hesitation. On down the highway, feeling cramped, Trotter asked if her daughter might sit in the woman's lap a while. They smiled and exchanged the child.

The driver immediately pulled off on the shoulder, stormed down the aisle, and lambasted the black woman for sitting beside a white woman and holding her child. His rant continued until Trotter heard these words calmly come out of her mouth.

"Sir, this is my mother," she said.

How glorious it would have been to say those words to Eva. But I never did.

Still immersed in my own world the first year back in the Lowcountry and the first year teaching four classes of English, my days overflowed with lesson plans and grading papers . . . and more papers. I enjoyed being in downtown Charleston with old and new friends, and occasionally saw Fred when he could spare a couple of hours from medical school demands. We mainly walked the narrow streets, didn't talk much.

And on Valentine's Day of that year, that quiet country boy and I went for a stroll on the Battery. We had gone out regularly all fall, and I opened my heart again. We were leaning over the rail looking at Ft. Sumter when he brought out a diamond ring and asked if I'd be the mother of his children and grow old with him. How could I say "no" to such a proposal?

Some weekends we'd ride over to see his father in the little town of Springfield and come back laden with leftover beef, macaroni and cake from Sunday dinner. I went to Moncks Corner most weekends while he was on call. One Sunday in early March I was designing wedding invitations and choosing China patterns when Bloody Sunday at the Edmund

Pettus Bridge in Alabama was a blip on the news.

Two weeks later, I watched twenty-five thousand people respond by marching from Selma to Montgomery where King made his "How Long, Not Long" speech from the Capitol steps. It broke my heart to see so many people begging for what should have been their natural right—to be treated like human beings.

By summer Eva and I were both back home arranging my wedding presents on linen draped tables in the living room. Eva was at our house every day that June, feeding me butterbeans and biscuits, displaying gifts like Diana Drexel's candlesticks from Tiffany's, ironing my honeymoon clothes. Mother was working, and Eva and I appreciated the the time to visit alone. I shared reservations about camping out across the country on my honeymoon, living far away in Oregon, writing thank-you notes in the prescribed time, and leaving her behind.

"Baby, it's gona be awright. Don't worry your head none. It'll be awright," she said with a smile and a pat on my behind, which I was trying to keep in check so I could squeeze into my going-away dress.

When Fred came to the house the day before the wedding, she thought she was entrusting me to him for the rest of my life, so she had her say. To the point.

"Mista Fred, you do right by my Baby now," she said.

I anticipated that Eva would be full of sadness and regret, but she seemed especially buoyant the week of the wedding, a spring in her step and a lilt in her voice I'd not heard for years. And she kept smiling, gums gleaming.

My smiles, however, hid a heavy heart. Who would look out for her? Surely she was sad too. Was she putting on a good front not to dampen my joy? She was stepping around fairly easily. *Well, her Baby was getting married*, I thought, and Eva always did like a party.

And what a wedding!

Rusty and I laughing our way down the aisle of the Pinopolis Episcopal church, wedding party grinning to beat the band. My uncontrolled laughter. And when I finally tilted my head to follow LaClaire's smile and Mother's glare, I saw a gum-grinning Eva marching behind me, clearly not seated in her assigned chair. She held my train in outstretched arms—shoulder high—so high that my blue garter winked at the congregation as we walked to the altar.

Then she gently lowered my train, smoothing it flat with her swollen fingers. She stepped to the first pew, nudged Mother over with her hip, and sat high-rumped on the cushioned seat for the entire ceremony. Eva Aiken plunked down by a woman she'd worked for over twenty years yet had never sat beside. The first sit-in in Berkeley County.

Her Baby was getting married. Eva wasn't about to miss this moment sitting by the back door. Head high, bold and confident, it was her day too. Beaming proudly, she watched the baby girl she had birthed from her heart into this troubled world. Eva took her rightful place . . . front row . . . aisle seat . . . mother to the bride.

Epilogue

It's never too late to honor the dead.
—Toni Morrison, author and poet

During the reception Eva stuck to my side like a cocklebur. Looking back, I see it's Eva who is prominent in the wedding photographs—with me, with the bridesmaids, with the couple cutting the cake, with the groom. A ready smile for the camera, her joy contagious. A coming-out party took place that day for my Eva.

When the festivities wound down and the sun hid behind the oaks, Eva and I climbed the steep steps into the Fishburne's house. Her puffy fingers struggled to undo the tiny satin buttons on my wedding gown and helped me into my blue, linen going-away dress. She clasped my hands between her warm ones and looked me in the eye. No hint of a tear, she squeezed ours hands together.

"You be good now. Memba who you is," she said.

Pulling her close, tears pooled in my eyes. How could I forget? I knew I'd always be Eva's Baby.

What I didn't know was that the very next day, as I was headed west in an old stick-shift Ford, Eva was headed north on a Greyhound bus. Sixty-six-year-old Eva lumbered up the steps with her arthritic knees, settled herself in the front seat, and road twelve hours north to Rahway, New Jersey, to live with Miriam and Sam. No notice. No explanation. Usually unflappable Mother was flabbergasted.

Eva finally had broken free. But she had waited . . . waited for her Baby. Just as we both had begun together twenty-five years earlier, we started our new journeys at the same time—Eva 'n me.

Eva lived for the next twenty-one years with Sam and Miriam Taylor and became an integral part of their three children's lives—Queen Esther, David, and Mark. After ten years up north, the Taylor family and Eva moved to Albany, Georgia. Eva died at eighty-seven . . . back in the South. Back home.

Eva's grandchildren talk today about her gift of wisdom, how gospel music picked her up when she was down. They named her favorite hymns: "I'll Fly Away," "Blessed Assurance," and "Must Jesus Bear the Cross Alone." They showed me the usher badge she'd saved from her Moncks Corner church days where she was a prayer warrior who sat on the mourners' bench up front. On her dresser she kept see-no-evil, hear-no-evil, speak-no-evil monkeys. There she also kept a picture of the three Williams children—and a separate one of me, her Baby.

When Eva visited Moncks Corner relatives, she stopped by Williams Farm Supply to talk to Mother and Rusty. She and I wrote and spoke on the phone. And when I moved back to South Carolina from California, she visited me and my growing family.

During her late sixties and into her eighties, "Mother Eva," as everyone called her, was active in the Sunday school, Baptist Training Union and missionary circles of her Baptist churches up north and down south. The shocker for me came as I read her obituary—Eva had been a long-time member of the NAACP.

In January of 1986, people poured in for Eva's funeral at Rock Hill Baptist Church in Moncks Corner, everyone decked out in white dresses, robes, shirts and hats. In African American tradition, white is the color of mourning and "going home." Mother, LaClaire, Rusty and I were escorted to the front row. The minister asked Mother to say a few words, but it was the hymns that resonated. Some she had asked me to play on the piano many years before: "Nearer My God to Thee" and "On Jordan's Stormy Bank I Stand." "What a Friend" is the only song I can still play on the piano from memory because Eva wanted to hear it over and over.

Mother remained an independent, strong woman until the end. Over the years, she turned Williams Farm Supply around and became respected as a prominent, successful business woman. She initiated the county's Business and Professional Women's Association, and when South Carolina Tuberculosis Association asked her to serve on the state board, she readily agreed.

Clara Lee at her garden gate

She continued working at the family warehouse until macular degeneration prevented her from seeing numbers clearly. She enjoyed playing duplicate bridge with her friends, and she never stopped digging in her garden. She turned down marriage proposals from two wonderful men—men who could have freed her from a grueling work schedule and shaky finances. Men who could have given her back the lifestyle she'd once enjoyed.

"I wanted to do this on my own, send you three to school and make the business successful," she said. And she did.

Glimpses of her earlier joy were few. The dimpled smile came back when Uncle Charlie Gold brought Mother, Mama Lillian and cousin Stevie to Los Angeles to visit. We listened to Ella Fitzgerald for Mother and danced to Lawrence Welk for Mama Lillian. Another time I remember her dressing for a party with Dr. Walsh, and she smiled that old smile into the mirror as she put on the gold loop earrings Daddy had given her. Years later she told me another reason she didn't remarry.

"Once you've experienced the magic I had with your daddy, it's hard to settle for less," she said.

She remained in the house we'd all been reared in on Library Street in Moncks Corner, the house Buster built for her. She became close to Mabel Gray, the gentle black woman who helped her after Eva left. When all the children and grandchildren piled in the Moncks Corner house for the traditional "Granny's Christmas" weekend, it was Mabel who stirred around in the kitchen and kept the grandchildren in line during meals. Adults ate in the dining room, of course. We all loved Mabel, and *her* biscuits.

As Mother became less able to be alone, Mabel became her mainstay. She even called Mabel her "best friend." She and Mabel ate meals together at our kitchen table. Until then, I'd never seen my mother eat with a black person.

Daddy moved in with his mother Olive after Nannie's Pinopolis house burned. He eventually stopped drinking and worked as the dispatcher for the Berkeley County Sheriff's Department. He read constantly and shared his interest in stamp collecting with Rusty's two boys. He continued to marvel people with his breadth of knowledge and fascinating conversation.

When he became ill, LaClaire took him under her warm wing. I kept a comfortable distance. He died from a stroke in his early sixties. Sadly, I was forty years old before I forgave my daddy for not being the father of my dreams . . . and myself for not being the daughter I might have been.

When Mother died, there was no room left in the fenced Williams family plot at Spring Hill Cemetery. Surprisingly, the conservative Baptist-turned-Episcopalian had given firm instructions that she wanted to be cremated . . . so she could be buried at Buster's feet.

My brother Rusty became Mother's partner in the business after he married, keeping Williams Farm Supply going for a third generation. He has two boys, Brett and Todd. Todd, the younger son, lives in our Library Street home and makes Mother's famous cheese wafers for annual family gatherings. Brett built a house next door to Mother and named his son after her. Little Lee and "Granny" adored each other.

"He's the only man whose eyes light up when I walk in the room," she said of her great-grandson. She blessed him with her radiant smile and spontaneous hugs few of us felt. Sandra, my sister-in-law, lovingly tends the garden in Mother's name at Trinity Episcopal Church in Pinopolis.

LaClaire and her husband and children now host Granny's Christmas in Hampton or out on farmland near Estill, a weekend of frolic for our children and grands, plus delicious Southern food. In spring, we enjoy our traditional Mother's Day festivities in the Lowcountry, which includes macaroni and cheese, ham, and . . . biscuits, the nearest to Eva's that we can come up with.

When I turned forty, I was forced to take a hard look at my marriage, my own little family where tension progressively had increased, where love could no longer breathe. Wanting to do what was best for my husband, for me, and for our two children, and to respect the woman Eva had taught me to be, I made the hardest decision of my life. I severed a union of twenty years, repeating the pattern of my mother. I had two budding teenagers, no home and no job. I left in desperation—and faith. When hurt, we reach back to the womb, so I set out for the Lowcountry, to the familiar.

The following years I was buoyed by God, family, friends, and Citadel colleagues . . . and particularly my two children. LaClaire, Erick and I created a safe haven, a place to hug with ferocity and fight with fairness. And we not only survived, we overcame. I called on the wisdom and the witness of the strong women who had gone before me and had suffered far more than I: Mama Lillian's dignity, Nannie's hospitality, grandmother Olive's passion, Mrs. Chalmers's encouragement, Mother's perseverance. And, most of all, Eva's unconditional love.

Much of the Eva story was birthed on my porch overlooking Sullivan's Island, South Carolina, where countless slaves entered our country centuries ago. Eva's relatives were among those millions. Today there's a bench near that beach that Toni Morrison gave to honor those brave men and women.

Fifteen years after Eva's death I finally began to mourn losing the woman who introduced me to her best friend Jesus. One Sunday at a small Episcopal church on Amelia Island, Georgia, a woman the color of chocolate milk officiated. Triggered by her powerful presence, images of Eva seeped in . . . her smell, her touch, her voice. Ah, her voice. I recognized the warm, mellifluous, full sound that Eva used to soothe me. I felt Eva's arms embrace me right there in that wooden pew, hugging this hurting adult child. Tears welled as I tongued the wafer out of my palm at the communion rail . . . and I thought of Eva and all the Christ-like qualities that permeated our household, our selves.

For the first time, I cried the tears for the Eva that I'd lost. That afternoon my dear friend Rick Straub presented me with a small journal. "It's time to write your Eva story."

Acknowledgements

Labor was far too long for *Hush Now, Baby*, and it wouldn't have happened except for extraordinary circumstance and individuals. Fifteen years ago, my friend Dr. Rick Straub, a professor at Florida State University, surprised me with a journal "for making your Eva notes," he said. Though his tragic death put this work on hold for a time, I know he's smiling as I write these thanks to him.

I am grateful to another writing professor, Roberta Chalmers of Queens University of Charlotte, North Carolina, who saw potential in the flowery language of a fledgling writer. She gave me the courage to write about hard subjects, free of embellishment. She recognized my need to write about Eva and the healing it would bring. I learned so much from *all* my teachers—and subsequently, my students too.

In the process of unraveling both my early life and times Eva and I lived in, I came to a devastating realization: I'd never *really known* the person I loved the most, the one who loved me the most. I thank Eva's family, Miriam and Samuel Taylor, and their children Queen Esther, Mark, and David, as well as Marie Motte and Lela Session for sharing the life and times of Eva. I know I've only gleaned a thimbleful of her cup that overflowed.

For ten years I buried myself in memoirs, the histories of African Americans, the Civil Rights Movement, and my parents' families—everything from oral transcripts to academic theses, Civil War diaries to modern histories, from movies and television documentaries, to formal and informal interviews. A great appreciation for *Historic Ramblin's of Berkeley* by Russell Cross and *The Race Beat* by Gene Roberts and Hank Klibanoff. Sometimes I was so overwhelmed by my naiveté that I wept. The

Pinopolis ladies, Anne Fishburne's writings and Bea Plyler's stories, took me back in time. I'm so grateful to the multitudes who opened my eyes to the joys *and* the terrible truths about those times . . . and myself.

The challenges of writing this story would never have reached fruition without the support and encouragement of writers and editors like John Burbage, Adrienne Rosado, Ken Burger, Susan Kammeraad-Campbell, Michel Stone, Jeanie Heath, Rosa Shand, Marcus Cox, Sandra King and Pat Conroy. Nor without the prodding questions, meticulous editing, ruthless cutting, and constant encouragement of Mary B. Johnston, writing coach extraordinaire, who believed in my story and tenaciously refused to let it die. Blessings galore, to each of you.

I'm indebted to John Harley for restoring family pictures which help bring this book to life. You worked magic, John. Thanks too to Laura Haynie of Revel Images and to photographer Brandon Coffey as well as the Associated Press, Santee Cooper, *The Post and Courier*, and Queens University for permission to use photos. And to Van, Brett, Lynn, Pard, Judy and Sue, thanks for your photos. Miriam and Sam, the last bundle of family pictures you sent are a treasure. Also, much appreciation to the artists who sketched plantations in *Trinity Treats* cookbook.

A *huge* hug to Elaine Craft. You brought tears when you played "In the Heart of Dixie." What a gift. Thank you too, Tricia Walker, for letting me share your song with my readers.

Those friends who opened their homes to me as writing retreats, thank you: Bob and Margaret Jones and Nancy Bourne at Pawley's Island; Rella Allred and Frenchie and Robert Richards in the mountains; and David King at Kiawah. You each provided a writer's haven, sorely needed.

To my long-time friends, I thank you. Judy Ash for being on the New Orleans and New York ride as I schlepped my wares and for vigorously promoting the book once it found a publishing home. To Sue Brake, for the BIG trips and margarita breaks when I needed to put writing aside—You rocked as the organizer for the Lowcountry Launch! To Richard Porcher, Pard Walsh, Cece Guerry and Lynn Haltiwanger for your excellent research. To Butch Howard, Freddie Sullivan, Dewey Nettles, Leslie and Roger Stevenson for your niggling question: "Are you finished yet?" To Lin Laffitte and Ceille and Jim Welch, whose enthusiasm and cogent advice buoyed me toward the finish line.

Much appreciation to "the girls"—Sara Swann Watson, Eva Pratt, and Beryl Middleton—for hearing the first snippet of my Eva story, for the fun trips, and especially the supportive calls and emails. A special salute to the legion of Angela's Angels—you know who your are—for the energy you put into promoting the Eva story—especially Sally Regenbogen who gave me confidence that the story deserved a wide audience and Eva Pratt who got the ball rolling. To *all* my tennis buddies, you'll never know how much I needed those times . . . to refuel, refocus, and return to my task refreshed, and to my Greenwood friends. Beth Curry and Fran Walker, you walked with me from inception to completion, regularly encouraging and uplifting me. Thank you all, dear friends.

If it weren't for my friend Dr. Patricia Williams in Texas, this book might never have been delivered. She connected me to her colleague Dr. Paul Ruffin at Texas Review Press. She insisted I send *Hush Now, Baby* to him, standing over me while I typed an initial query. "Send it. He'll love it." I did. And he did. In short order I signed a contract. Eva found her home. It's been a great fit. Thank you, Paul, for believing in the project and handling me so deftly that I thought I was in charge! That our visions meshed is a downright miracle. I thank Kim Davis, who with patience and perfection pushed us through the last editing phase. Nancy Parsons showed her creative flair with the cover design.

I attribute the final get-it-to-the-press stage to my friend and organizational guru Steve Ferber. You relentlessly, but oh so gently, prompted me to meet deadlines, agonized with me over priorities, and shored me when I lost focus or when my spirit flagged . . . or my computer crashed (as it did far too many times). Steve, my appreciation knows no bounds. Roe, thank *you* for the open kitchen that sustained us during long sessions.

Blessings galore to David Cran for his friendship, emotional support and technical expertise. He and Kate Kelly were responsible for everything about this story that made it into anyone's e-mail inbox or onto the Internet—no mean feat! Abbe Aronson of Abbe Does It deserves special mention for her marketing acumen.

What can I say about my family? I am still discovering ways that Clara Lee and Buster Williams enriched my life. Sister LaClaire Laffitte and brother Rusty, I admire both of you so much for persevering through things I don't know but can imagine. I treasure our pleasant memories. Rusty, I appreciate the effort you've put into managing Williams Farm Supply for yet a third generation. LaClaire, I admire the energy you put into keeping our family connected so we can add to our good times. And for always being there for me. You are my touchstone.

Finally, I thank my children, LaClaire Stewart and Erick Williams. Your support and love have been unwavering, especially during these last few years when my time seems to have been swallowed up by Eva. The miracle is not that you have grown with my love but that you have survived my mistakes. Thank you, LC and E, for loving me, trusting me, knowing me . . . and making fun of my quirks. I am so proud of the strong, sensitive adults you have become, under sometimes uneasy circumstances. Erick, you and the Stewart family—Bobby, LaClaire and my precious grandsons Josh and Gray—are the joy of my life. May *Hush Now, Baby* be a catalyst for us all to learn from the past and to embrace the future—with Eva's dignity and grace. And a surprise now and again.